Bird at the Buzzer

:05

:04

:03

:02

:01

Bird at the Buzzer

UConn, Notre Dame, and a Women's Basketball Classic

Jeff Goldberg · Foreword by Doris Burke

University of Nebraska Press · Lincoln and London

Library of Congress Cataloging-in-
Publication Data
Goldberg, Jeff.
Bird at the buzzer: Uconn, Notre
Dame, and a women's basketball
classic / Jeff Goldberg; foreword by
Doris Burke.
p. cm.
ISBN 978-0-8032-2411-7 (cloth: alk.
paper)
1. University of Connecticut—Basket-
ball. 2. Connecticut Huskies (Bas-
ketball team). 3. University of Notre
Dame—Basketball. 4. Notre Dame
Fighting Irish (Basketball team)
5. Basketball for women—United
States. 6. College sports—United
States. 7. National Collegiate Athletic
Association. I. Title.
GV885.43.U44G65 2011
796.323'630973—dc22
[B]
2010035061

Set in ITC New Baskerville.

For Susan, who always believed in me,
especially when I didn't.

Contents

Foreword

Watching the game of women's basketball continue to grow and gain respect in the American sports landscape has been one of the most enjoyable parts of my job as a color analyst, calling games for ESPN. Along the way, inevitably, certain moments in time have stood out, not only because of the quality of a particular game, but because they have been defining moments in the sport's history.

There have been many cases over the years where a women's basketball matchup has garnered its fair share of the media spotlight *prior* to the game. In that spotlight, the sport has not always lived up to its potential. But in the pages that follow, Jeff Goldberg, longtime UConn women's beat writer for the *Hartford Courant*, captures a night that delivered in a big way. With the exception of the members of the UConn program, no one had a better seat or was more familiar with the team than Goldberg, who not only understands the nuances of this particular season and this particular edition of the team, but also has a thorough knowledge of the program as a whole.

The electricity inside Gampel Pavilion that night was palpable. Even almost three hours before tip time, people sensed that it was going to be a special night. The media was milling about. Everyone seemed to be wondering, could the Irish, who had already beaten the mighty Huskies in a matchup in South Bend earlier in the year, deliver the ultimate insult and beat UConn on its home floor?

Certainly, on paper, UConn was the more talented team. But, before the night was over, they would endure the heartbreaking loss of Shea Ralph, a player whose heart and guts could drive a team.

But just as the UConn program has marched on steadily since the arrival of Coach Geno Auriemma, so, too, the Huskies marched on that night. The game ended as it should, with a game-winner at the buzzer. I will leave the explanation of how things got to that point in the very capable hands of Mr. Goldberg. On this night, Sue Bird and women's basketball delivered.

Doris Burke

Acknowledgments

I would like to offer my deepest appreciation and thanks to Rob Taylor at the University of Nebraska Press for believing in this topic and guiding me on my first-ever book project. His advice and counsel along the way proved invaluable, as did the cooperation of UNP's Courtney Ochsner, Sara Springsteen, and copy editor Beth Ina.

I met Barbara Collins Rosenberg in the summer of 2008, at a book-signing party for her clients Mike Lowell and Rob Bradford. Lowell, the Red Sox third baseman and 2007 World Series MVP, and Bradford, an accomplished baseball author and good friend of mine from the Red Sox beat, had just collaborated on Lowell's autobiography, *Deep Drive*.

Barbara gave me her card and told me to call if I ever had a book project of my own. In March 2009, I took her up on the offer, and *Bird at the Buzzer* was born. Not bad, Barbara, for a Yankees fan.

Once the project became official, it was time to track down the players and coaches who made the 2001 Big East final the greatest women's game ever played. That meant weeks and months of coordination with UConn, Notre Dame, and the WNBA to line up interviews. So a special thank you goes to Notre Dame Assistant Sports Information Director Chris Masters and Senior Staff Assistant Carol Copley, as well as their counterparts at UConn: Associate Director of Athletics/Communications Mike Enright, Assistant Director Randy Press, and Program Aide Sarah Darras.

In the WNBA, thanks go out to Connecticut Sun Media Relations Manager Bill Tavares and Phoenix Mercury Communications Manager Eric Barkyoumb.

Of course, if not for the insight and memories of the participants, this project would have gone nowhere. The players and coaches who offered their time and patience are owed an enormous debt of gratitude: at UConn, Geno Auriemma, Sue Bird, Diana Taurasi, Shea Ralph, and trainer Rosemary Ragle; at Notre Dame, Muffet McGraw and Ruth Riley. A special thank you goes to Niele Ivey, who was particularly generous with her time.

Also generous, particularly given her hectic travel schedule, was ESPN's Doris Burke, who called the 2001 Big East final along with Robin Roberts and graciously accepted my request to provide the book's foreword.

Although I covered the 2001 Big East final for the *Chicago Tribune*, it was my twenty-three years at the *Hartford Courant* that enabled me to conceive and complete this project. From 2001–6, I was the UConn women's beat writer, after having spent the previous four seasons as the *Courant*'s online UConn columnist; with these positions came the access to the women's program that ultimately served as the foundation for this book. I am forever grateful to my mentors at the *Courant*: Sports Editor Jeff Otterbein, Assistant Editors Jeff Smith and Scott Powers, Web Editors Chris Morrill and Gary Duchane, and fellow UConn writers Lori Riley and John Altavilla.

Not everything in this book is the product of the written word. The illustrations are largely the work of *Hartford Courant* photographers Michael McAndrews and Jay L. Clendenin, and a thank you goes to *Courant* Photo Editor John Scanlan, Archivist Rosa Ciccio, and Permissions Administrator Lynne Maston for providing the visual elements.

But the *Courant* colleague who meant—and means—the most to me is my best friend and former UConn men's and women's beat writer Matt Eagan, who provided keen insights about the 2001 season and was a source of support and advice throughout the writing process.

Following my five years on the UConn beat, I moved to covering the Boston Red Sox in 2007 and 2008. I've formed numerous friendships on the Sox beat, but two friends stand out the most, in part because their own book projects made them invaluable sources of advice as I made my way through the process. A big thank you goes to the aforementioned Rob Bradford of WEEI.com and MLB.com's Ian Browne.

A special thank you goes to my parents, Bob and Carole, for providing guidance—and occasional lodging in Connecticut—during the process.

But ultimately, none of this would have been possible

without the love and support of Susan Dellio, who inspired me to take an idea that had been kicking around in my head for eight years and finally make it a reality, encouraging me every step of the way. No wonder I decided to marry her.

Introduction

The giant red bus sat parked across the street from Gampel Pavilion, the ten-thousand-seat domed stadium and home of the University of Connecticut Huskies basketball teams. Sporting the larger-than-life-sized faces of studio hosts on its side, the ESPN *GameDay* bus stood sentry for the historic show taking place inside the concrete edifice on this chilly Saturday night.

Although classes at UConn were not yet back in session, the student section of the arena was filled to capacity, the students chanting and bouncing up and down in unison, nonstop, as the game went on in front of them, exhorting their Huskies to victory.

At center court, flanked on both ends by a vast media contingent—carefully crafting words of description for this extraordinary night of basketball—were ESPN's top broadcast crew of Dan Shulman, Doris Burke, and the iconic college hoops carnival barker Dick Vitale.

It was a scene normally reserved for the men's games at UConn. But after a decade of dominance by Geno Auriemma and his top-ranked women's program, ESPN chose this night, a contest against third-ranked Notre Dame, on which to make basketball history.

For the first time ever, ESPN *GameDay*, the network's franchise Saturday college road show, was setting up shop for a women's game, kicking off its 2010 schedule in Storrs. Vitale, the manic, Hall of Fame voice of the men's game, would be calling a women's contest for the first time in his thirty-year broadcast career. Even the regulars in the student section, normally full only for the men's games, put on their Saturday best, not only filling the seats but doing so in white T-shirts adorned with a caricature of Auriemma on the front.

And UConn, in the midst of shattering its own Division I women's record of seventy consecutive victories, set between 2001 and 2003, did not disappoint the sellout crowd, taking the heart out of Notre Dame in the game's opening minutes, sprinting to an early 17–2 lead and never looking back in the course of a 70–46 victory.

As is so often the case in the women's game—and especially when one of the combatants is the overdog Huskies—the game itself did not live up to the hype that preceded it. But nearly a decade earlier, on a snowy March night in 2001, UConn and Notre Dame met inside this very arena with even more hype and more at stake. And when Sue Bird ended a thrilling and heart-wrenching game with a full-court dash and basket at the buzzer—giving UConn a 78–76 victory and the Big East Tournament title—ESPN made basketball history yet again, replaying the contest five nights later as the first-ever women's "Instant Classic."

And what a classic it was, a battle between No. 1 and

No. 2, featuring five future Olympians and eight WNBA first-round picks, the middle game of a three-round heavy-weight fight that helped decide the 2001 NCAA women's national champion.

For Connecticut, the triumph would be backlit by tragedy. For Notre Dame, the defeat would point the team toward ultimate victory. For women's basketball, these forty minutes would show the world a sport at its highest level.

I covered the 2001 Big East women's final for the *Chicago Tribune*, the sister paper of my employer from 1985 to 2008, the *Hartford Courant*. The game was an intense roller coaster of emotion and great plays by the best players on the two best teams in the nation.

Epic games of this magnitude almost never happened on the women's side, so much so that I said to my *Courant* colleague and friend Matt Eagan in the parking lot outside Gampel Pavilion, just three hours after the game had ended, "I think we just witnessed the greatest women's game ever played."

Ten years later, the pronouncement still holds up.

The sport of women's basketball has continued to grow and evolve since 2001, with UConn starting a new decade with the first repeat undefeated seasons in the sport's history, going 39-0 in 2010 to capture a second consecutive title, the seventh in Auriemma's UConn career. By the time the tenth anniversary of the 2001 Big East Tournament final is played, the Huskies will most likely have broken the UCLA men's eighty-eight-game winning streak to claim the greatest run in the history of college basketball.

But for all the advances that would later come to the sport, the game played on the night of March 6, 2001, remains a singular, shining moment. If women's basketball lacks anything in 2010, it is a sense of its own mythology. So determined are the passionate and loyal caretakers of the sport to further advance it into the future that there has been precious little focus placed on its glorious past.

While all the other major American sports wax poetic about their respective Greatest Games—from the 1958 NFL Championship to Game 6 of the 1975 World Series to the 1992 Duke–Kentucky men's regional final—women's basketball has not yet afforded itself the time to reflect on the legacies left in its wake as it moves toward national acceptance.

This book seeks to shed light on the past, to acknowledge and expand on a seminal moment in the game's proud progression. The 2001 Big East final was a harmonic convergence of talent, circumstance, drama, and interest the likes of which the women's game had not seen before and has not discovered since.

Coming four months before a historic TV contract renewal with ESPN and a season before the start of the first UConn dynasty of the decade, the game was a right-time, right-place moment for women's basketball. This is the story of that time and place.

Bird at the Buzzer

:05

:04

:03

:02

:01

1

Tip-Off

Storrs, March 6, 2001

Sue Bird awoke this snowy Tuesday morning after a night unlike any other in her three years at the University of Connecticut. During the night, while a powerful snow-storm blanketed the state of Connecticut, Bird had lain under her blankets hooked up to a portable stimulus machine, electronic impulses coursing into her balky lower back in an attempt to prevent it from going into spasm any further.

The reigning Division I point guard of the year, Bird had not played the previous night, Monday, when her second-ranked teammates obliterated Rutgers 94–66 in the Big East Tournament semifinals at Gampel Pavilion, setting up a rematch with No. 1 Notre Dame in Tuesday's tournament final.

It was to be up to this point the most-anticipated game of the 2000–2001 women's college basketball season. Back in January, Notre Dame had handed the defending national champion Huskies the first of their only two defeats all season, blowing out UConn. The game, played before the first home sellout crowd for a women's game in Notre Dame's history, also marked the first time the Irish had beaten UConn in twelve tries since joining the Big East in 1996.

Now, UConn looked to return the favor, seeking to hand the Irish only their second loss of 2001, as both teams jockeyed for position heading into NCAA Tournament Selection Sunday, less than a week away.

Bird had injured her back on Sunday night, in the Big East quarterfinals against Boston College, and played just fifteen minutes, none in the second half. Bird's pain resided in her lower back, but the source of the discomfort was in her nervous system.

The consummate team player, Bird had two days earlier been named First Team Big East at the annual conference awards banquet. Bird's teammate and fellow junior classmate, the elegant and energetic forward Swin Cash, was a more worthy first-team candidate in Bird's mind, but Cash had been named to the second team.

The perceived slight to her teammate stuck in Bird's craw all weekend, her inner turmoil manifesting itself physically when she twisted her back painfully when turning to make a pass in the first half against the Eagles.

"I was stressed that whole weekend because personally, I didn't think I had a good year that whole junior year," Bird said. "It really was difficult for me to accept being Big East first team. I had a hard time with it. I was really

2

stressed, and there's no other reason for why my back would have done that. I just think stress got to me."

Bird, like the rest of her teammates, had endured a considerably more tumultuous season than anyone had anticipated. After having blown away Tennessee by nineteen points in the 2000 NCAA championship game in Philadelphia and ending the season with a 36-1 record, virtually the entire Huskies roster returned to play another year. Further supplemented by the arrival of Diana Taurasi, the most heralded freshman in the history of the game, the Huskies were touted not just as prohibitive favorites to repeat as champions, but as the greatest collection of talent Geno Auriemma had ever coached in his sixteen seasons at UConn.

And that was saying something, considering Auriemma had already won two national championships and had been to four Final Fours in the preceding decade. Even Auriemma, the sharp-dressed, sharp-witted son of Italian immigrants, could not resist heaping serious advance praise upon his newly minted champions.

Having just led his team to a second title—in his hometown of Philadelphia, no less—Auriemma capped the victory parade through the jubilant streets of Hartford by standing at the podium outside the state capitol building and pulling a Joe Namath. Or, for the basketball purist, a Pat Riley.

"I know what we needed to do to win the first one and the second one," Auriemma told his chilly yet captivated audience, awash in Husky blue and white. "I think

3

I know what it will take to win a third one, and I am telling you right now, in front of all these players, we are going to be back here next year with a third one. I promise you that."

Nearly eleven months later, Auriemma had discovered that the feat of repeating as national champions is more easily promised than done. Auriemma and the Huskies had exploded onto the national scene in 1995, capitalizing on the talents of national player of the year Rebecca Lobo, the fiery point guard Jennifer Rizzotti, and the explosive freshman Nykesha Sales—a Bloomfield, Connecticut, native—to ride to a perfect 35-0 season. In the title game in Minneapolis, UConn knocked off Pat Summitt's vaunted Tennessee Lady Vols 70–64, earning women's basketball the greatest share it had enjoyed, to date, of the national spotlight.

The Huskies returned to the Final Four the following season, this time losing to Tennessee in an overtime thriller in the national semifinals. While Tennessee would go on to three-peat behind Chamique Holdsclaw—who had preceded Bird as a player at New York's famous Christ the King High School—the Huskies would enter a star-crossed period in their history.

For three straight seasons, the Huskies would assemble enough talent to win the national championship, only to see those title hopes dashed by crippling injuries to key players, often occurring during, or just prior to, the six-game NCAA Tournament.

In 1997 the Huskies ended the regular season with a 30-0 record and were poised to become Auriemma's second undefeated champions in three years. But in an NCAA first-round game against Lehigh at Gampel, their freshman star, Shea Ralph, tore the anterior cruciate ligament (ACL) in her right knee and was lost for the remainder of the tournament. The Huskies never recovered from the loss of their spark plug, and fell to Tennessee in the regional finals.

Before the start of the 1997–98 season, Ralph retore the ligament in her right knee and was lost for another year. In February of that season, Sales, now a senior, was closing in on UConn's all-time scoring record, trailing Kerry Bascom's mark of 2,177 by one point during the penultimate regular-season game against Notre Dame at Gampel.

But as Sales started a thrust to the basket with a chance to set the record, she ruptured the Achilles tendon in her right foot, ending her career on the brink of the NCAA Tournament.

Sales's injury is best remembered for the controversial way Auriemma—along with friend and Villanova coach Harry Perretta—conspired to get Sales the record-setting basket in the regular-season finale.

The "gift" basket, in which Sales, on crutches, was allowed to score at one end to start the game and set the record—with UConn then allowing an uncontested Villanova basket to tie the score before the real game continued—ignited a fierce national debate about sportsmanship and the integrity of records that dwarfed any publicity the women's game had ever received.

But lost in the din was the fact that another championship-caliber season for the Huskies was imperiled, and when the freshman sensation Svetlana Abrosimova, from St. Petersburg, Russia, was injured in the NCAA regional final against N.C. State, UConn's Final Four hopes came to another abrupt end.

In 1999 the Huskies were eliminated in the Sweet Sixteen for the only time in the decade between 1994 and 2004. That season, UConn was decimated by injuries to its superlative freshman class, led by Bird, Cash, Tamika Williams, and Asjha Jones. Bird's injury was the most serious: a torn ACL in her left knee in mid-December.

So, by the time UConn survived the 2000 season injury-free and captured the national championship, the Huskies were left to wonder how many more titles might have been theirs if they'd had a little more good fortune.

"It's easy to look back at the seasons and say, 'If this, if that,'" Auriemma said. "The only time we lost full-strength in the Final Four was 1996. And then in 1997 we had the best team in the country, by far. By far. And then Shea goes down and we didn't handle it well. Then in 1998, Kesha goes down. Then 1999, Sue goes down . . ."

In 2001 the injury curse struck again, as Abrosimova, a senior and a strong national player of the year candidate, tore the ligaments in her left foot during a 92–88 loss to Tennessee in Knoxville in early February, ending her UConn career. Only the embarrassment of riches on UConn's roster—six of the remaining twelve active players on the 2001 roster would be taken in first rounds of the WNBA draft—kept UConn a legitimate national championship contender.

But now, on the morning of the Big East Tournament final, Bird's back was the latest injury scare. But Bird, who would, for the only time in her career, wear a heating pad under her jersey for a game, had no concerns.

"[Trainer Rosemary Ragle] had me on anti-inflammatories," Bird said. "I was sleeping with the machine on, doing the round-the-clock stuff. And once I got loose, I was okay. I remember the shootaround, having to warm up a lot to get moving. It's one of those things that once it gets warm, you're good."

Sue Bird was born and raised in Syosset, New York, a suburb of Long Island, as the younger of two daughters. From the beginning, she displayed an abnormally acute competitive streak. On one occasion, a teammate of Bird's in a school relay race botched the baton exchange, which caused the team to lose. Disgusted by the failure, Bird threw the baton down. She was six.

"Whether it was board games or doing things with my sister or teams that I played on, I definitely had that sore loser mentality back then," Bird said. "I just didn't like losing. It was always something that I hated, and it made me competitive. I remember that story. I threw the baton because my teammates were a little slow."

Some of Bird's intensity could be traced to her early relationship with her sister, Jen, five years Sue's senior. As a little girl, Sue often wanted to hang out and play with her older sister, but the age gap between them was too much to overcome. This would drive Sue to work even harder to gain attention.

"I think the role that it plays is unique to the typical younger-sister syndrome, because my sister was five years older and she made me competitive because she didn't care what I was doing," Bird said. "I'd be trying to play with her, and she never had time for me. It made me want to do that even more."

Sports provided an outlet. Bird excelled at both soccer and basketball, but basketball eventually won out, and she developed into one of the top players on the Amateur Athletic Union (AAU) circuit, the pipeline to Division I scholarships for the nation's top prep stars.

As her game developed, so did Bird's sense of independence. Auriemma would later joke to the media, after Bird's twenty-five-point breakout performance against Tennessee in Knoxville as a sophomore in January 2000, that her New York street cred was highly suspect.

"People ask me, what about your New York point guard?" Auriemma cracked. "Yeah, she grew up on the mean streets of Syosset. I think the last thing somebody stole was a newspaper off someone's porch. I tell her the toughest thing she ever had to do was decide what sale to go to at the mall: Neiman-Marcus or no Neiman-Marcus?"

But the joke belied a simple truth. After her sophomore year at Syosset High School, Bird's life dramatically altered. Her parents, Nancy and Herschel, were in the process of getting divorced, with Herschel moving into an apartment in Queens. At the same time, Sue was on the move as well, transferring to Christ the King High School in Queens.

"I was very fortunate growing up," Bird said. "I never had to worry about the food being on the table or the clothes on my back. I was very well taken care of. My parents gave me a great upbringing. But my situation, regardless of whether it was hard or easy compared to other people, it definitely made me self-reliant. My parents were splitting up, so there was one parent one week, the next parent the other week in this little apartment in Queens.

"And at the time, I didn't have a license, the first year that I was there, my junior year. And they had to work, so I was by myself a lot. So you have to make do, find out where I was going to eat that day. I had to ride the buses everywhere. You kind of have to figure it out. I had to fend for myself and I was in a new school, and that's never easy."

Christ the King was the preeminent girls' basketball program in New York City. When Bird arrived as a junior in 1996, its most famous graduate, Holdsclaw, had moved on to play college ball at Tennessee, where she would win three straight national championships during Bird's high school years.

9

Bird, too, would excel at CTK, but the transition from life in bucolic Syosset to the gritty streets of Queens was challenging.

"I had never been the new kid before," Bird said. "I'd been in the same school system my whole life and that was what I knew. And to pick up and go to this new school, and on top of that, [adjust to] a total cultural difference, in terms of Syosset versus Queens, that was unique.

"Looking back on it, it's almost like an out-of-body experience, like, did I really do that? But I'm thankful for it. I was forced to grow up a lot. I was 16–17 years old and I was on my own in a lot of ways, and I think my maturity level skyrocketed from those two years."

The level of Bird's play continued the rapid upward climb. In her senior season of 1997–98, she averaged 16.3 points and 7.3 assists, leading Christ the King to state and national championships. Bird was named both New York City and State player of the year.

By the time the 1998 season had ended, Bird had already chosen to attend UConn, over Vanderbilt and Stanford. UConn had always been the favorite, but Bird began having second thoughts the previous summer, after UConn received commitments from two other point guards, Keirsten Walters and Brianne Stepherson.

"I was like, what should I do?" Bird said. "This is the place I want to go to, but maybe there's no room for me. That played a role."

Stepherson made the decision a bit easier for Bird, backing out of her commitment in August and choosing instead to attend Boston College. By November, Bird's heart finally overruled her head.

"It came down to it and you just know," Bird said. "When you know you feel right and feel comfortable with the people, you just know. I remember I had a conversation with Coach Auriemma and [associate head coach Chris] Dailey and they're like, where do you stand? This is us—that's their spiel—we're not going to change. Do you like it?

"That happened in the summer and we revisited that conversation about a week before the signing period, and the last thing coach Auriemma said to me was, 'Follow your heart,' and that was that."

Bird brought to Storrs the independent streak she developed in high school, a trait that served her well at her position of point guard.

"I think it helped," she said. "When I got to college I found out you have to have two personalities anyways. For me, I'm not always the most vocal in social settings, I can come across as shy. Obviously, that changes with age. But I was definitely more reserved, and when I got to college, I realized you can't be that way if you're the point guard. I think it helped me take on those challenges better."

Memphis, Tennessee, March 25, 2000

While UConn was winning its second national championship in Philadelphia in early April, making for the most triumphant of homecomings for Geno Auriemma, another branch on the sturdy Philly coaching tree, Muffet McGraw, was suffering.

McGraw, who completed her college career at St. Joseph's University in 1977—just a year before Auriemma himself was hired there as an assistant to the new coach and women's basketball wizard Jim Foster—had just seen her Notre Dame Fighting Irish complete a devastating collapse in the NCAA Tournament's round of sixteen.

Against Texas Tech in the regional semifinals at The Pyramid, Notre Dame, led by juniors Ruth Riley and Niele Ivey and seniors Julie Henderson and Danielle Green, took a 17–0 lead, only to see the Red Raiders pull a stunning reversal and score the game's next seventeen points.

Then, in the second half, Texas Tech was able to get Riley, Notre Dame's talented, 6-foot-5 center, into foul trouble, erasing an eight-point deficit to send the Irish home with a 69–65 defeat. The loss completed a late-season fade by Notre Dame, who finished the season 3-3 after winning twenty straight games into late February, climbing as high as fifth in the national rankings.

While the season officially ended in Memphis, the beginning of the end came in Hartford, against UConn on February 26. Riding their twenty-game streak, the Irish arrived at the Hartford Civic Center determined to accomplish two historic program firsts: win the Big East regular-season title and, for once, beat UConn.

Since joining the Big East Conference before the

1995–96 season, Notre Dame had faced UConn ten times, and lost every game.

McGraw would always try to deflect the pressure that the blue-and-white albatross placed on her players. Only she had all ten losses next to her name, McGraw would tell the media. Her players, at any one time, might only have lost to UConn twice, maybe three times.

But that was of no solace to Ivey. The junior point guard, who, like UConn's Ralph, had entered college in 1996 and had endured two catastrophic knee injuries, had been a part of eight of the ten losses before arriving in Hartford for the 2000 regular-season showdown.

"I personally always hated UConn, from my freshman year," Ivey said. "I had complete respect for them, but they were the enemy and you have to hate your enemy. I hated them, every year. I didn't want to see Huskies, white and blue.

"I was angry because it seemed like every time we played them, we didn't have everybody on board. Maybe I played bad and everybody else played well. It can't be like that. It has to be everybody playing well in order to beat UConn. They had people on the bench that could start for every other team. They were eight-deep with starters."

Her anger only deepened by the end of the game. Riley had emerged in 2000 as a major post presence, earning a place on the Big East's first team for the second year in a row. But against the Huskies and their aggressive double-teams, Riley played tentative and confused. She had more turnovers (6) than points (4) or rebounds (5) and fouled out after just twenty-two minutes. UConn won easily, 77–59, leaving McGraw in tears after the game.

"That game, Geno went in and he had a plan," said Matt Eagan, who covered UConn for the *Hartford Courant* from 1999–2001. "They doubled [Riley] all the time in that game and Notre Dame never figured out any kind of adjustment for it. They got on them early and it was never a game. It was just never a game.

"They came into that Notre Dame game and they knew exactly what they wanted to do, and they did it. And Notre Dame never adjusted and never had any answers. It was like, 'This is our trick and we're going to keep doing it until you figure out how to make us not do it,' and Notre Dame never figured out how to not make them do it."

Three weeks later came Texas Tech, and a summer of discontent in South Bend, Indiana.

"That [UConn] game was the beginning of the end for us," McGraw said. "That was the first red flag, then losing in the NCAA Tournament with a team I thought could go to the Elite Eight—maybe not win a championship, but a little further than where we lost. We don't get upset too often, and that was one of them. That would have been one of those signature wins for that team. They'd had a lot of them coming in as freshman, when Ruth went to the Sweet Sixteen. Then we were back in the Sweet Sixteen and we felt like we're really building this thing up.

"And I think Connecticut was one of those teams where you look at it and say, we were maybe intimidated. We'd just never beaten them and we had that little bit of fear going into the game. So that was another disappointment. Here we have this great team and we could have won that game and we didn't do what we needed to do. And it is disappointing when you think you're a little bit better and you have high expectations and you don't reach them. I think that's the most frustrating and stressful thing in sports, when you don't meet your own expectations."

McGraw and her players vowed that summer never again to repeat the sins of the past. With Riley, forward Kelley Siemon, and Ivey entering their senior seasons, there would be no more time for what-might-have-beens.

For Ivey, who had been awarded a fifth season of eligibility after her first knee injury as a freshman, the loss to Texas Tech was especially painful. Henderson, Ivey's roommate and best friend, saw her career end at the Pyramid. Ivey had played especially poorly in the Texas Tech loss, shooting 1-for-9 from the field and collecting one more turnover than assists. As the team's point guard and vocal leader, Ivey vowed redemption.

"Seeing my best friend's reaction, I knew I didn't want to go out like that my senior year," Ivey said. "That summer, we had a meeting with the coaches, an end-of-the-year meeting, 'What are you going to work on,' etc. And after that, I said, 'There's not going to be any more meetings. I'm not accepting that. This is what the culture of this team is going to be.'

"And they all agreed with me. We're not going to go through anything like that again, ever. Weight room, workouts, pickup games, if you're not out here preparing to win a national championship, then I'm going to send you home. The coaches didn't need to do that. I took it upon myself. I was damn near thirty years old by then. I'm old enough to take over that leadership role."

Niele Ivey was actually only twenty-three in the fall of 2000, but it had seemed like a lifetime for the point guard from the inner city in St. Louis. The youngest of five children, and the only daughter of the bunch, Ivey learned the game of basketball through her older brothers. As a fourth grader, Ivey would attend their high school games, but invariably, the littlest Ivey commanded the most attention.

"At halftime, the little boys and me would go out there and shoot threes," Ivey said. "And I would increase my range. I thrived on that, being out in the spotlight. I did that every game. I didn't miss any of their games. That's where I started my love of basketball, watching my brothers."

By sixth grade, Ivey's shooting range had increased significantly, and so had her reputation among high school coaches looking for the next shooting star.

"I used to come down to half-court and I wouldn't run any offense, I would just chuck it from half-court," Ivey said. "Of course, the courts were a lot smaller in grade school, but I got good at it. And that became the joke: she's the girl who makes them from half-court.

"I felt like I came into my own when I played sports. I played everything: softball, soccer, track. But basketball is where I felt I stood out. That was my niche. I was a tomboy, a gym rat, and I grew to love it more than the other sports. And I recognized that it was my ticket to college. I was really big about getting into high school and playing and getting into college. That was my big thing. In my family, I was the first to get into college, even with my four older brothers."

Ivey's accuracy from long range was no joke to Gary Glasscock. The girls' basketball coach at Cor Jesu Academy, Glasscock had heard the tales of Ivey's long-range bombing. Glasscock also ran a basketball program at the St. Louis Boys and Girls Club, about five minutes from where Ivey lived, and soon the middle-schooler was a participant in the program. A bond developed between player and coach.

"He was very instrumental in the inner-city life of kids, making sure they were on teams and keeping them off the streets," Ivey said. "I felt like he really cared about the kids, and he did a great job of running things."

That Glasscock coached at a Catholic high school only deepened the connection. Ivey had grown up in a Catholic household and had attended Catholic grade schools, right down to the uniform and the pigtails. So when the time came to choose a high school, Ivey naturally gravitated to Cor Jesu.

"I already wanted to make a name for myself somewhere different," Ivey said. "And this had the complete package: a great coach, a small, intimate Catholic high school. It was far from where I lived, but it had the values I wanted in a high school, and he was such an awesome person and an awesome coach, I knew he was going to teach me more things than dribbling on a court. He completely developed my game, my work ethic, everything. He saw something special in me and we'll always have that bond."

That connection produced a dream season in her junior year of 1994–95. Led by Ivey's 18.1 points, 6.9 rebounds, and 5 steals per game, the Chargers went 31-0 and captured the first Class 4A state championship in school history. In the title game at the University of Missouri, Ivey made thirteen consecutive free throws in the final minutes to secure the title.

"That season was very special," Ivey said. "Everyone was on the same page. We were a young and small team. We ran and pressed a lot, because we didn't have a lot of height. It was an amazing ride to the end. It was the first time the school had ever gone to the state finals. Being in that arena, on that stage, I usually rose to the occasion. I remember being in the big arena at the University of Missouri and everyone was there to see me, and

I took my game to another level. It was everything that I played for, and I was ready to get there."

Ivey was also anxious to get to college and had originally hoped to attend North Carolina, which had beaten UConn in 1994 on the way to a national championship won on Charlotte Smith's buzzer-beater in the title game. But Ivey found out the hard way that her love for Carolina blue was unrequited.

"I was in love with Michael Jordan and I paid my own way to go to North Carolina's camp," Ivey said. "That was the place I wanted to look at. I remember going to camp and being mad because [head coach] Sylvia Hatchell came to the first day to introduce herself, then she left and didn't come back until the end. So I felt like she didn't get a chance to watch me, so she could recruit me, and that really ticked me off. I came back really mad and Coach Glasscock said, 'Don't worry, you're going to go somewhere where they'll recognize your talent.'"

Recognizing that talent was something Muffet McGraw had already done. The Notre Dame coach had begun tracking Ivey during the 4A playoffs, as Ivey's Chargers were completing their undefeated season.

"The thing that really drew me to her was her attitude and demeanor on the court," McGraw told the *Notre Dame Observer* in 2001. "She's such a great leader. She was inspirational to her team. She was always talking and getting them together. She was highly motivated, worked extremely hard. She was much more defense-oriented in high school than she was a shooter. I just really was looking for somebody that could lead our team in that kind of way, and she fit it perfectly."

So determined was McGraw to land the junior point guard, she spent the following summer watching Ivey play pickup games at the YMCA in St. Louis. NCAA rules prohibited McGraw and assistant coach Carol Owens from actually speaking to Ivey directly, but their presence at the Y spoke volumes. Ivey committed to Notre Dame later that year, while on her official visit to South Bend.

"I saw them watching me," Ivey said. "I was like, Wow. When she did that, I appreciated that. That was really cool that she came to the Y. That was huge for me. It made me realize they're serious and they're really looking at me. No coach did that, and that was huge for me.

"It was an easy call. This was where I could see myself, and I called [McGraw to commit] before I came home. When you know, you know. I felt like it was a continuation of high school: being a Catholic school, it was exactly like life at home, only on the college scale."

Hartford, Connecticut, November 12, 2000

Svetlana Abrosimova had just spent the summer of 2000 surrounded, quite literally, by the best basketball players the world had to offer. Playing for Russia in the Summer Olympics in Sydney, Australia, Abrosimova and her team finished sixth, a far cry from the success she had enjoyed six months earlier as part of UConn's national championship team.

When Abrosimova arrived back in Storrs for her senior year, it was clear that nothing would ever be the same for her, or for her sport. She had already made a dramatic change that summer, one that sent shockwaves across the globe, from Down Under to downtown Hartford. Gone was the pixie haircut that had become her trademark—and a fan favorite among the senior set that followed the Huskies as if they were their own granddaughters. Instead, Sveta, as she was fondly called, had literally let her hair down, allowing it to grow long.

So dramatic was the change that the state's largest newspaper, the *Hartford Courant*, dispatched its Olympics writer in Sydney, Tommy Hine, to devote a full-length story to the full-length 'do.

But Sveta's new look wasn't nearly as striking as the new kid on campus with the bun. Neither was Abrosimova's game. Sveta was the smoothest point producer on the team, a graceful offensive player threatening to become the school's all-time leading scorer in her senior season.

But as Abrosimova returned to the court that October for informal pickup games, it was clear to her, and to her teammates, that the best player on the team now was the one who had yet to play in an official college game.

"I've never seen a player like her," Abrosimova told the *Courant* in 2001. "We played five-on-five and she was just taking the ball, shooting three-pointers from far away. I thought I was the only one who could shoot from far away. Here was a freshman doing the same things."

Diana Taurasi's arrival in Storrs ushered in a new era, not just for UConn, but for the sport of women's basketball. The 6-foot guard from Chino, California, grew up admiring Magic Johnson but shot the ball with the deadly accuracy, unlimited range, and coolness in the clutch of Larry Bird. She played the game in a way no women's player had ever quite played it before.

As Auriemma would so often put it, in a phrase meant as a genuine compliment, Taurasi played like a guy. She shot the ball from long range with the classic snap of the wrists, not with the push of the arms, as was commonplace in the women's game. Her court vision and passing ability had no equal. Her bravado had none, either. A trash-talker who could back it up, Taurasi brought a swagger to the game that only added to the legend that preceded her.

By the time Auriemma had lured her out of California, the phenom from Chino was being hailed as the next superstar in the women's game.

Diana Taurasi and Geno Auriemma had much in common, even beyond a shared love of basketball. Like Auriemma, Taurasi was the child of immigrant parents who spoke little English. The player and coach also shared the same wit and ability to charm. Taurasi has never met a person she didn't like. She'd never met a shot she didn't like, either.

Taurasi's ability to shoot the basketball was revolutionary. The mechanics were simple. Taurasi was blessed with large, strong hands that allowed her to control the women's ball—a fraction smaller in circumference than a regulation men's ball—with little effort. This, in turn, allowed her to shoot from long distances without having to throw her weight behind the loft, giving her even greater body control to shoot off a dribble or make a one-handed pass in traffic.

"I think it comes from shooting the basketball and getting a good feel for it, shooting all day, even when you're really tired," Taurasi said. "And you have to have the confidence to shoot it. Even when I was younger, I would always shoot from really far out. It was second nature to shoot threes. I was probably shooting threes before I was taking layups when I was in third and fourth grade. I was the only one shooting them that far, even the boys."

It also didn't hurt that she grew up near Los Angeles in the 1980s, which provided a larger-than-life basketball role model to emulate. Taurasi would spend hours upon hours watching Magic Johnson run the Lakers' "Showtime" fast break on KCAL9. And as Michael Jordan and the Bulls usurped the Lakers' throne in the early 1990s, Taurasi had them to track as well on the Superstation WGN from Chicago.

"Magic was my man," Taurasi said. "And I fell in love with MJ when they beat us in 1991. It would be 115 degrees in California and my dad would turn off all the lights, turn on the air conditioning, and we'd watch the games. I remember the commentators, Doug Collins.

I have vivid memories of watching the games. And for some reason, WGN in Chicago was a channel that we always had. I don't know why. So growing up, I'd watch Cubs games at noon, and then the Bulls at night.

"I loved watching it. I would watch it all day. If I wasn't playing it, I was inside watching it. I'd be inside with the ball, banging it against the wall. I always had a ball in my hands, thinking about the game. There's something about basketball, there's nothing close to it. It's so much fun when five people are really playing together on the court. It's graceful, it's powerful, it's got all these great elements to it."

By seventh grade, as Taurasi began playing on the AAU circuit, it was abundantly clear that she possessed a skill set unlike that of any female player of her generation. She drew interest from national powers Connecticut and Tennessee, as well as from the local favorite UCLA.

But unlike the parents of some child prodigies, Taurasi's mother and father were not overbearing, never forcing Diana toward the game.

"They were too busy working, putting food on the table," Taurasi said. "'You like to play? We'll let you play as much as you want.' I had some friends who had the parents who wanted them to be the best in the world, and it just doesn't happen, because they pushed them too much and they end up not liking it for themselves.

"In my case, my parents were like, 'Boy, you're pretty good. If you want to go play, go.' There wasn't one night where my mother said, 'You should go outside and shoot.'

She was like, 'Come inside! There's not enough light!' That was every night."

The only time Lily Taurasi became heavily involved in Diana's basketball future was during the college recruiting process. Lily wanted Diana to choose UCLA, which was less than an hour from Chino. She was heartbroken at the prospect of Diana moving three thousand miles away to play for Auriemma at UConn.

But Taurasi had already made up her mind that UConn was the place for her, after making an official visit in 1999. A few choice words from Auriemma didn't hurt either. He told her that at UConn, Taurasi would play before a crowd of more than ten thousand every night at home (and most nights on the road). At UCLA, she would see maybe five hundred.

You're going to do great things in college, Auriemma famously told her. It would be a shame if nobody saw them.

With Taurasi joining forces with Abrosimova, Shea Ralph, and Sue Bird on the wings, and Swin Cash, Asjha Jones, Tamika Williams, and Kelly Schumacher in the paint, the Huskies appeared, on paper, even more formidable than the team that had blown Tennessee away in the NCAA title game the previous April.

And if they looked good on paper, there was simply no way to describe their on-court performance in the season opener against No. 3 Georgia at the Civic Center on November 12.

The game was called the Tip-Off Classic, and as it progressed, the rest of the women's basketball universe was tipped off as to how good these Huskies could be. Georgia, led by All-American twins Kelly and Coco Miller, was considered a legitimate Final Four contender in the preseason. However, the legitimate Final Four contenders trailed 54–25 with 1:42 left in the first half. Final score: UConn 99–70.

"When you wake up, it'll be we won Florida overwhelmingly," Auriemma said after the game, the 2000 presidential election still without resolution. "We'll be the biggest story in America as far as sports. You know what? There's nothing we can do about it. The only way we can change that is lose or play lousy."

From the outside looking in, that hardly seemed likely, and even Auriemma deadpanned to the media that all the joy of coaching had been taken from him because his players no longer seemed to make any mistakes.

Even when one did early in the game, causing Auriemma to turn away from the court to rant to his assistants on the bench, Taurasi commanded his attention, burying a deep three-pointer on the first shot she attempted as a collegian, causing the sellout crowd of 16,294 to erupt.

But privately, Auriemma wondered if his Huskies were already too good for their own good.

"You know, you win a national championship in 2000 and everybody's back and the player you're adding is arguably the best player on the team," Auriemma said in 2009. "So you go to practice and you see things, and you go, 'We have a chance to be pretty good. I hope we just continue to get better and better.'

"Then you go out in that first game, and they've got five or six pros on their team—Deanna Nolan, the Miller sisters—lots of really good players, they're preseason number three and we're up thirty at halftime. I remember when the game ended, I said to myself, 'I don't know how we can sustain this.'"

Madison, Wisconsin, November 22–24, 2000

While UConn's victory over Georgia captured the attention of the women's basketball world, Notre Dame did the same thing two weeks later. But no one outside of South Bend likely noticed when the fifth-ranked Irish knocked off the newly sixth-ranked Bulldogs, 75–73, in the Coaches vs. Cancer Challenge on Wisconsin's campus.

Two nights earlier, Notre Dame had crushed the host team by twenty-seven points. Only four games into the 2001 season, already there was a sense inside the Irish locker room that something special was happening to this senior-laden team so eager to climb the championship mountain once and for all.

"We beat Wisconsin pretty easily, then we beat Georgia in a very close game, and I think it was in that moment, just four games into the season, that I sat back and went, Whoa, we could be pretty good," McGraw said.

"And that's when it started to really take shape, and I think the whole team had that sense.

"It was a really interesting team, because none of them were really highly recruited. [Sophomore guard] Alicia Ratay was the highest-ranked player we had. She was in the top twenty. That was it. We didn't have any McDonald's All-Americans. So they were all the kind of player that never got too high about anything. They were so even-keeled. We won that [tournament], and everybody, without saying it, kind of looked at each other and went, Hey, how about this?"

The team had kept the promise it made to itself over the summer, taking Ivey's challenge to heart, making a clean break from the disappointing finish of the previous March. A week after beating Georgia, the Irish destroyed North Carolina at the Honda Elite 4 Classic in Florida, then handled sixth-ranked Purdue at home to reach 8-0 on the season and climb to No. 3 in the polls, trailing only behind undefeated UConn and Tennessee.

By the time the Irish prepared to host top-ranked UConn on January 15, they were 16-0 and clicking on all cylinders.

"I felt like our summer was the best summer ever," Ivey said. "Every pickup game, we were killing each other. That was as strong as I've ever been in my life. We were on it, everyone came in shape, everyone did what they needed to do in the offseason. We were gelling. Ruth was playing well, Alicia was shooting lights out. We weren't very deep and everyone understood their roles. We're going six or seven deep. Everybody was on the same page. Those first couple games, we had it going.

"We played Wisconsin, then Georgia, and we played so well. Sometimes when you hear about everyone else, when you beat those players, Kodak All-Americans, we're beating the best, so we must be the best. That's how we felt."

The transformation from also-ran to national championship contender had been personified by one player. With each passing game, it was clear that no one in the country could "handle the Ruth."

When Notre Dame played UConn at the end of the 2000 regular season, Ruth Riley had already begun the process of establishing herself among the top post players in the country. The 6-foot-5 Riley had averaged 16.2 points and 7.3 rebounds as a junior and was named first team All-American, as well as first team Academic All-American.

"She came in as a freshman and she struggled with the pace of the game," McGraw said. "She would be in foul trouble, consistently, in minutes. She could play six minutes and have four fouls, the first seven or eight games of her freshman year. It just took a while. I remember sitting down with her and saying, 'Ruth, you're the one. We're going with you. This is what I need you to do and how we're going to do it.' And start of the Big East season that year, she had like four double-doubles in a row. And then she started to come into her own."

Before Riley's freshman season was over, she would establish her career high with forty-one points against Providence. With each season, Riley's stature grew, and she earned Big East Conference first-team honors in each of her final three seasons.

But whenever Riley and the Irish faced UConn, the big center melted. Up against fellow 6-foot-5 center Kelly Schumacher, and swarmed by perfectly timed double-teams from the UConn guards, Riley committed turnover after turnover and foul after foul, turning herself into a nonfactor in the 77–59 loss at the end of the 2000 season.

"She still had a ways to go," McGraw said. "Each year, she was the type of kid, you couldn't wait for her to come back from the summer, because she got so much better every year. She had an incredible work ethic and just wanted to be so good. She would come back and [assistant coach] Carol Owens did a magnificent job with her. But I think coming into her senior year was that— what you hope all seniors have—is a little bit of a sense of urgency: that this is it, I've got to do it this year. I always wanted her to have a swagger, which I'm not sure she could ever get, because she's too darn humble. But she definitely had the confidence, and you could feel it coming into that season."

Ruth Riley's favorite movie is *Hoosiers*, and it's not hard to understand why. Riley grew up in the tiny Indiana town of Macy: population, 250. She eventually played for

North Miami High School, not the fabled Hickory High of movie fame, but her upbringing fit the script.

"When you drive through the farmlands, every house would have a hoop attached to something, whether a pole or a barn, whatever it might be," Riley said. "I think the sport is definitely ingrained in the culture of Indiana. Macy was no different. I was the last class to graduate from high school in the one-class [tournament] system. *Hoosiers* was our dream, being such a small school. Growing up, that's what we aspired to achieve."

In a community as small as Macy, it was very easy for the fast-growing Riley to stand out: she grew to six feet at the age of twelve, much to her dismay, and was teased for her uncommon height. Where Riley found refuge was in sports, particularly—and naturally, for a Hoosier—on the basketball court.

"I've always been tall, and being a tall, uncoordinated girl was not always desirable at times," Riley said. "But sports really gave me confidence as I grew older. I started playing the game because I enjoyed it, not because I was good or especially talented at it.

"I think most people assumed that I was good because I was so tall, so I had a lot of expectations to live up to. I think that drove me to become a better player, because even though I wasn't very good, people saw a lot of potential in me. And that made me realize that maybe there was something there."

By the time her career at North Miami High was over, Riley had amassed 1,372 points, 1,011 rebounds, and

427 blocks. As a senior, while earning *USA Today* All-America honorable mention in 1996–97, Riley averaged 26.0 points, 14.7 rebounds, and 5.2 blocks, good enough to have her jersey number (25) retired by North Miami in 2000.

"It wasn't until high school that I really started to progress as a basketball player," Riley said. "I started playing AAU in the summer. I had some extra coaching and the opportunity to play in front of college scouts. That's where I first felt I could play on the college level."

There was no question in Riley's mind where that college career would take place. Notre Dame, a ninety-minute drive from Macy, was so much the front-runner, Riley declined to make any other official visits. The only difficulty Riley experienced in the recruiting process was dealing with the endless stream of interested coaches from other colleges, none of which ever stood a chance against the lure of the Irish.

"I was recruited by almost everyone, so it wasn't a comfortable process for me, talking to college coaches every week," Riley said. "That wasn't my personality. It probably made the process more difficult. Notre Dame had everything that I was looking for. Coach McGraw and I got along well. I would go up there, because I lived so close. I wanted to go somewhere that had both the athletic and academic base and a competitive program, so I could grow and get a good education."

Notre Dame also allowed Riley to blossom as a person. No longer in a tiny town, no longer the only tall, athletic woman in her school, Riley began to emerge from her shell by the end of her freshman season, joining Ivey as an emerging leader on the team.

"When Ruth first came here, she was always very quiet," Ivey said. "I was the vocal one with the bubbly personality and she was the one with the work ethic. You just followed what she did. Those two things played off each other. I was the one who got in your face and challenged you, and she didn't have to talk. She let her game speak for itself. And when she got mad and said something, you took a step back and listened, because she didn't talk all the time.

"I always respected Ruth's game, how hard she worked. She got her body completely ready and she was always a very caring teammate. I always respected that about her. Very smart. She set the bar high, academically, in every way. She really was the All-American kid, from Macy, Indiana, your typical Notre Dame student, and she was an awesome person. And when you respect someone the way I did with Ruth, it made being on the court with her that much easier."

Syracuse, New York, January 9, 2001

The Huskies didn't face their first stern challenge until late December, when their good friends from Knoxville showed up at the Hartford Civic Center. It was No. 1 UConn versus No. 2 Tennessee in the twelfth edition of the biggest rivalry in women's basketball before a national TV audience on CBS, but the game was played in an arena that, for any other fan base, would have been nearly empty.

In a foreshadowing weather event, a massive snowstorm struck southern New England the morning of December 30, dumping nearly a foot of snow on Hartford by midafternoon, when the game was set to tip off.

Twenty years earlier, the Hartford Civic Center roof had collapsed under the weight of a similar snowfall. This time, what nearly blew the lid off Veterans' Coliseum was the clutch shooting of Diana Taurasi, thrilling the estimated crowd of 15,000 (out of 16,294) who had braved the conditions to witness the latest installment in the game's fiercest rivalry.

Taurasi's late three-pointer helped UConn escape with an 81–76 victory and raised UConn's record to 9-0. But already, there were storm clouds forming over the Huskies. Svetlana Abrosimova played just eleven minutes and scored only four points, all on free throws, having injured her back while playing a pickup game in Miami during Christmas break.

But the Huskies' biggest problem entering January was not physical. Since beating Georgia to a pulp in the season opener, the Huskies had slowly seen an erosion of their mental edge. At the beginning of January, the Huskies made one of the most miserable two-game road trips imaginable, having to go to tiny Ruston, Louisiana, to face a difficult Louisiana Tech team, then schlep all the way north to take on a lousy Syracuse team at dilapidated Manley Field House two nights later.

UConn's play reflected the dreary conditions. The Huskies beat the eighth-ranked Lady Techsters 71–55, then struggled to put away lowly Syracuse 76–63, leading by just ten points at halftime.

The sixteen- and thirteen-point margins of victory were UConn's narrowest of the season, outside the Tennessee game. With a week to go before their showdown with No. 3 Notre Dame in South Bend, the Huskies were a Ferrari operating on bald tires.

"That was the famous game where they were up like thirty-three in the second half and they took their foot off the gas pedal and Syracuse cut it to thirteen," the *Courant*'s Eagan said. "[Syracuse coach] Marianna Freeman was like, 'I cried.' But that's how it was. They were so much better that they didn't lose. They were like, 'Yeah, okay, we won.' The year before wasn't a problem, because they hadn't won in so long. None of them had ever been to a Final Four. I remember a game against Georgetown [in 2000] where they just killed them. It wasn't a game, but they were still playing at the end of that game.

"But if your coach comes out in the summer and says, 'We're going to win the national championship,' then by definition your season becomes all about March. It doesn't become about the meaningful game in January. So that team was really trying to figure out how to make the games that they were playing matter as much to them as they did to the other team."

Just as Ruth Riley personified Notre Dame's rise to

prominence, Shea Ralph had come to define the Huskies' malaise. The year before, Ralph enjoyed the finest season of her career, driving the Huskies with her sheer force of will—and 14.3 points per game—to a national championship, earning national player of the year honors, and being named the MVP of the Final Four.

It was the ultimate tale of redemption. Ralph had, not once but twice, torn the ACL in her right knee, both times in 1997, only to regain her form and become a dominant player once again.

"There were moments during the [2000 championship] game, I was thinking, This is why I worked so hard," Ralph said. "When we won, it was just complete elation. Just to see everyone's reaction was really cool. To see my coaches and teammates so happy, especially Coach Auriemma, because he was the reason I was able to achieve and get back [to playing]. He stuck with me and pushed me.

"And as time went on during the summer, it started sinking in, and I thought about how far I had come. And being back on the court after we won, practicing again, I was thinking, It's possible we can do this again, we know what has to be done."

But it soon became clear that for Ralph, there would be no repeat of 2000. From the start, she struggled with her game, going into a shooting slump early and remaining in a funk well into the winter.

"I think [2001, for Ralph,] was like, 'I have to do exactly what I did last year, and I have to do it better,'" Au-

riemma said. "And the pressure she put on herself . . .
you can't repeat it. You can't duplicate it. You just have
to let it run its course and say, 'Okay, I'll just play and
we'll see what happens.'

"But Shea, being so competitive, being so driven, it
was like, 'Wait until you see what I'm going to do this
year.' The strain of having to do it day in and day out,
that's why it's so hard to repeat. Shea didn't feel exter-
nal pressure. She just put that on herself, and there's
no way to prevent that."

Shea Ralph was raised in Fayetteville, North Carolina, the
daughter of Marsha Lake, herself an accomplished basketball player at the University of North Carolina. Marsha's competitive spirit was transferred intact to Shea's
DNA.

"I think I had that look in my eye when I was two,"
Ralph said. "My family, it would get to the point where
they wouldn't want to play cards with me, or checkers.
I didn't know how to just have fun and be okay with losing and say, 'Oh good game, but I lost.' That was never
me. I would be mad for two days. I don't know where it
came from. Some of it came from my mom. She was a
fighter, real competitive. Even to this day, if I'm messing
around on the court, it has to be serious."

Ralph channeled her fierce competitive drive into basketball and became the national high school player of
the year in 1995–96 at Terry Sanford High School, averaging nearly a triple-double with 33.8 points, 9.3 as-

sists, and 8.5 rebounds, all the while maintaining a 4.2 grade point average on a 4.0 scale.

Ralph became the first high-profile recruit caught in the emerging war between UConn and Tennessee, eventually choosing the Huskies and having an immediate effect in 1996–97 as a freshman, helping them to a 30-0 regular-season record.

But in the first round of the NCAA Tournament at Gampel Pavilion against Lehigh, Ralph violently blew out her right knee and was lost for the remainder of the tournament. Then, during the rehab process shortly before the start of the 1997–98 season, Ralph tore the same ACL a second time, causing her to miss the season entirely. Once again, Ralph would undergo surgery and a lengthy rehab. Now, the same mental toughness and tenacity that allowed her to succeed on the court would serve her well in working her way back to it.

"It's a cliché, but I'm a big believer that things happen for a reason and you're never given anything that you can't handle," Ralph said. "I do think that I'm lucky in that sense, because I do have a strong personality and I have a little bit of fight inside of me, and it comes out in all kinds of ways. I'm glad that if it had to happen to anyone on the team, I would take that hit, because in my mind, I knew I could come back from it.

"My approach is what allowed me to be successful. I just was not listening to anyone tell me that I wasn't going to play at a high level. There was no telling me I can't do this. Sure, some days I was sick of doing rehab, and

I would be tired of not being on the court, and those would be my worst days. I would feel like I wasn't able to be a team member because I was always on the sidelines. But never in a million years did it cross my mind that I wouldn't be out on the court playing and doing well."

Ralph finally returned in 1998–99 and played in thirty games as a redshirt sophomore, averaging 16.8 points and reaffirming her reputation as a fierce competitor not shy about diving to the floor or mixing it up with opposing players, even despite her devastating injuries. Her toughness, work ethic, and drive earned her the nickname "Shea-Dog" and the undying respect of her teammates, coaches, and fans.

"She was the epitome of UConn basketball," Sue Bird said. "She was everything that was UConn: the hard work, taking charges, diving on loose balls . . . and that's in pickup games. She was just relentless, not going to be denied. That's the way she played and that's the way she lived. And she led our team, and we took on her personality in a lot of ways."

But the circumstance that made her such a heroic figure in the public's mind also presented Ralph with a unique opportunity. Her second knee injury had afforded her, like Notre Dame's Niele Ivey, a fifth year of eligibility. Ralph had already graduated after the 2000 season, and coming off her All-American performance, she was certain to be a first-round pick in the upcoming WNBA draft. But Ralph chose to retain her eligibility and return for a fifth season.

"She was sitting in my office and I said, 'Look, if you come back, that's fine with me,'" Auriemma said. "'And if you don't come back, that's fine with me, too. Whatever you want to do, I'm good with it.'

"I think mentally, winning that national championship in 2000 and being the MVP of the Final Four and how hard she'd worked to put herself in that situation—and how much she had changed from freshman season to then, and after all she'd gone through—she was like, 'I have one more year and I want to come back.'"

Ralph had actually made up her mind the previous fall. When Taurasi came for her official visit before the 2000 season, Ralph made her the promise that she would stay for Taurasi's freshman season. Taurasi would later say that message factored greatly in her decision to commit to the Huskies.

"There really wasn't much of a decision," Ralph said in 2010. "I was pretty much committed. I don't think, in my mind, there was much of a thought that I was going to go anywhere and forgo a year that I could be [in Storrs]. I loved it here, still love it here, and I wanted to play here as much as I could. I remember telling Diana Taurasi on her recruiting visit that I would be back. In the back of my mind, I always knew I was coming back. I had a year and I wasn't going to give it up."

But just as the team followed Ralph's lead in good times, so it did in the bad. As Ralph entered her dark period in January 2001, the team hit the proverbial wall.

Complicating matters was a strange dynamic that was skewing the team's chemistry. Ralph and Abrosimova were seniors, and ostensibly still the team leaders. But the junior class of Bird, Swin Cash, Tamika Williams, and Asjha Jones were emerging as leaders in their own right. The shift in the balance of power did not disrupt the team, but it threw them off-stride.

"This was the tough year, because you still had Shea and Sveta as the leaders, and [Kelly Schumacher]," Taurasi said. "So you're in the position [of the juniors] where you are a leader but you don't want to step on anyone's toes because they've been there for so long. In a season like this, you recognize the talent you do have, and that's why the next year we were so successful (39-0 in 2002). But it was their team and they might have not realized it enough to take it over.

"I think people were still trying to find themselves and figure out their roles. What does Coach want from me? What do I have to do for this team to be really good? At times, people would step up in big moments, and other times you'd look out there and we'd have all these great players and no one is taking the team by the neck and forcing us to go a certain way. That's the one thing that frustrated Coach the most about this season. Sometimes, it didn't work. Sometimes, the more talent you have is worse."

Given the uncertainty and uninspired play engulfing the Greatest Team Ever Assembled, the seemingly solid fifty-five-point victory it achieved over Providence on January 13, in the final tune-up before the Notre Dame game in South Bend, would be but a hardwood mirage.

"There was a day [Auriemma] threw both Shea and Svet out of practice," Eagan said. "We [the press] came in and they were gone and it's like, What's going on here? That was part of the slog. When you beat the number three team in the nation by twenty-nine points in your first game, then what's the regular season supposed to be about? And then they discovered that it's not easy to just turn it on, and other teams got better.

"So they just were at a time where they were ready to be picked off. And they went into Notre Dame and they just got blasted."

Storrs, January 16, 1995

They started playing women's basketball at UConn in 1974, but for all intents and purposes, the program that came to dominate the women's sports landscape was born on Martin Luther King Day in 1995, when the Huskies hosted perennial powerhouse Tennessee at Gampel Pavilion in a made-for-ESPN Monday matinee.

Geno Auriemma was in his tenth season as coach of the Huskies and Gampel Pavilion had been in existence for five years. The combination of the two had revolutionized the way women's basketball was played—and watched—in New England, and eventually the nation.

Under Auriemma, who arrived in 1985, the Huskies went from an afterthought in a state that worshipped the men's program, to a national contender. When he arrived in Storrs, Auriemma barely had an office to call his own, and the team played in the dilapidated Field House. Even then, in the early years, Auriemma's team and staff often outnumbered the crowds that came to watch them play. It was not uncommon for a UConn practice to be interrupted by the track team circling them inside the multipurpose facility.

But as the decade ended, the fortunes of the program began to change. In 1988–89, led by a sharpshooting forward named Kerry Bascom, the Huskies won the Big East regular-season and tournament titles, earning the first NCAA Tournament berth in the program's history.

The next season, Gampel Pavilion opened in mid-January. The immediate benefactor of the new, modern facility was Jim Calhoun's men's team, enjoying a "Dream Season" in 1990 with its first Big East regular-season and tournament titles, and the miracle shot by Tate George to beat Clemson in the NCAA Tournament.

But the new building's curiosity factor also aided Auriemma's program. As Calhoun's team ascended to new heights of popularity with "HuskyMania" in 1990, tickets for men's games in the shiny new ten-thousand-seat arena became increasingly difficult to get.

In response, many UConn fans eager to see a game played in the new facility turned to Auriemma's up-and-comers. And what these new fans saw wasn't just modern building construction, but the architectural masterpiece that was Auriemma's program.

In 1991 the UConn women advanced to the Final Four in New Orleans, a shot across the bow of the women's game to signal that this tiny New England school was ready to take on the Southern stalwarts of the sport. By 1994 UConn was challenging eventual-champion North Carolina for another spot in the Final Four, falling in the regional semifinals to a team led by, among others, a speedy guard named Marion Jones.

But when ESPN tried to create a Husky Blue–Carolina Blue rematch in the 1995 regular season, Tar Heels coach Sylvia Hatchell balked. Undeterred, ESPN's director of programming for women's basketball, Carol Stiff, looked further south, to Tennessee, convincing coach Pat Summitt that playing at Gampel Pavilion in mid-January was just the tonic the sport needed to enhance its public profile. Summitt reluctantly agreed, and the top-ranked Lady Vols entered a hornets' nest.

The second-ranked Huskies, now led by player of the year candidate Rebecca Lobo, were 12-0 and had a sold-out Gampel crowd laying in ambush. As the ESPN cameras rolled, UConn throttled the Vols, walking off the court to a standing ovation after a 77–66 victory.

Later that night, as the women's players received a standing ovation from the men's crowd at the Hartford Civic Center, a special Associated Press poll—held back one day until Monday to await the outcome of the 1-vs.-2 showdown—confirmed the obvious: for the first time ever, the UConn women were No. 1 in the nation.

Forevermore, UConn and Martin Luther King Day

would be linked as closely as the Lions and Cowboys are with Thanksgiving. In Auriemma, the game had found its most dynamic personality in a rapidly changing media environment. For the first time ever, women's basketball had its Pied Piper.

Sherri Coale will never forget the night in December 1999 when Auriemma brought his circus to Norman. Coale's Oklahoma Sooners were an emerging power in the Southwest, a program just two seasons away from reaching the national championship game but averaging less than 1,600 fans at home games. That all changed on the night of December 29, when the Huskies arrived at the Lloyd Noble Center.

A crowd of 10,713 showed up to see this national sensation from Connecticut, accompanied by the pride of Norman, senior forward Stacy Hansmeyer. It was the first time ten thousand people had ever attended a women's basketball game in Oklahoma. It was neither the first time nor the last that UConn would draw a record crowd on the road.

"It was almost like counting down to the Final Four," Coale told the *Hartford Courant* in 2006. "We used to locker on the second floor and I was waiting there after the team did its preliminary warm-up. I could always hear them before they got to the locker room, and I could hear extra juice, extra life, extra noise. And before I could even get up to get to the door, Shannon Selmon comes busting through, her eyes as big as sil-

45

ver dollars, and she said, 'Coach Coale, you have built it, and they have come.'"

In September 2006, Geno Auriemma was enshrined in the Naismith Basketball Hall of Fame in Springfield, Massachusetts. In the twenty-five seasons through 2009–10—with the team coming off consecutive undefeated seasons and the fourth overall since 1995—Auriemma coached UConn to seven national championships and eleven appearances in the Final Four. He reached six hundred Division I victories quicker—by games and seasons—than any other women's coach in history.

Furthermore, while most coaches earn a place in Springfield by the sheer volume of their numbers and awards, Auriemma rightfully could add the title of "contributor" to his official Hall designation.

Like Red Auerbach in a different age, Auriemma has, since his arrival in Storrs in 1985, not only built a dynasty but developed a program that profoundly changed the landscape of women's college basketball. In the fifteen years that began with UConn's 35-0 season in 1994–95, women's basketball attained levels of popularity unheard of at any other time in the game's history.

Auriemma's influence led both directly and indirectly to the emergence of the Big East Conference as a national power, the filling of opposing arenas around the country for UConn's games, unprecedented national television exposure for the sport, and the formation of the WNBA.

"If I hadn't won five national championships and

coached Sue [Bird] and Diana [Taurasi] and Rebecca [Lobo] and all those guys, would I be going into the Hall of Fame? Probably not," Auriemma told the *Courant* on the eve of his induction in 2006. "But the fact I coached those guys and we did the things that we did, that helps me contribute to the game in other ways. The fact that we've been able to win so much has allowed us to contribute to the game as a team and me as an individual because of the resume those players helped me build.

"Put it all together and we'll be standing there [at the Hall of Fame], going, 'Who the hell thought this would happen?'"

The Tennessee game at Gampel in 1995 was considered such a groundbreaking event that the *New York Times* put its account of the game on the front page the next day.

Not the front of the sports section. *The front page.* This is believed to be the first time a women's regular-season game was featured so prominently in the *Times.* The coverage foretold the smothering attention UConn's program would increasingly receive.

"Once the *New York Times* got involved and once they put us on page 1, that's when I realized this wasn't so much about basketball anymore," Auriemma said. "Because they were writing about Rebecca Lobo and Jennifer Rizzotti and Nykesha [Sales] . . . they weren't writing about them as basketball players. They were almost like they were Globetrotters and were going to some Third World country and entertain them. It was really crazy."

An opening in the national consciousness cracked, UConn forced its way through in April, defeating Tennessee for a second time to win the national championship and finish the season 35-0. UConn was the second undefeated team in women's Division I history, but the first in the era of widespread ESPN coverage and an emerging Internet culture.

"I don't know if any of us were prepared for that," Auriemma said. "You never know when fate is going to tap you on the shoulder, but when it does, you better be ready, because it may never come again. Fate came into Gampel Pavilion and tapped us on the shoulder, and we were ready. We handled it, probably better than we thought we could."

In Rebecca Lobo, Auriemma had the national player of the year to help earn him his first NCAA title, and the women's game had its first superstar crossover into the mainstream. Lobo would appear on David Letterman's show the day after the championship, and her appeal would prove a godsend to the just-formed WNBA.

"She was our Mia [Hamm] when we started the league and she handled it beautifully," former WNBA commissioner Val Ackerman told the *Courant*. "When I look back, there were two primary developments in the 1990s that helped make the WNBA possible: the explosion of women's college basketball and the 1996 Olympics in Atlanta. With those two, the WNBA was teed up, and what happened at UConn in winning the championship was a seminal event.

"There's no question that the early victories and championship by UConn helped put women's basketball on the map. They caught people's attention and energized the Northeast media. And they captured a dormant public on the subject of women's basketball. Rebecca was an icon and still is. Once a household name, always a household name."

UConn began supplying a steady stream of players to the WNBA, then produced a gusher in 2002, with four of the first six picks in the WNBA draft. In all, UConn has had twenty players drafted by the WNBA, and will have two more top picks in 2010 and 2011 with center Tina Charles and forward Maya Moore.

"The players that come out of those top programs, in an unspoken way, they tend to be thought of as basketball royalty," Ackerman said. "They've trained under the game's best teachers, and it shows. Not just Sue and Diana, but look at an Asjha Jones or a Jen Rizzotti in her day. They come in and I think people respect what they've done, who they played under, and they come in with a certain confidence about them that serves them well. Not just the playing part, but the media, the expectations, things you're not always ready for."

Although UConn would not return to the national championship game until 2000, the Huskies were firmly established as one of the top draws in the country, along with Tennessee. And increasingly, Auriemma was a major part of the equation, with his good looks and Philadelphia wit attracting fans and television viewers.

"I don't know if it's something I set out to do or whether it's something that was thrust upon me because of the situation with our team," Auriemma said. "But there did come a point where everybody wanted to see us. Everybody wanted us to come to their building, and every TV event wanted us to be a part of it. Young programs wanted Connecticut to come to their building so they could test themselves. It got to the point where our kids looked forward to that."

As a result, the Huskies routinely set road attendance records.

"I was very well aware that wherever they go, the people go, too," Coale said. "And I think Geno understood really quickly, in the early stages of this phenomenon that is Connecticut basketball, that they had the power and the responsibility to take that product around the country, to jumpstart other programs so they could create something similar. I know that was the deal for us."

Oklahoma's program was never the same after UConn's visit in 1999. In 2001–2, when Coale and her best player, Stacey Dales, lost to UConn in the national championship game, Oklahoma's average attendance was more than 6,600, a fourfold upgrade from two seasons earlier.

"It was a huge moment for our players to play in their home arena in front of that many fans," Coale said. "It was a milestone for our program. It was so much more about getting those people there and that energy involved than it was about who won or lost. At that point in the building of our program, it was huge. I think it really helped Oklahoma fans on the legitimacy of women's basketball.

"We lost by sixteen, but it was one of those moral victories. It really was. It was a big deal. Heads were held higher, shoulders were pulled further back. If we can stay on the floor with Connecticut, we can stay on the floor with anybody. It was almost as if their body language said, Now we belong."

Auriemma himself was responsible for some of the opposing crowds' newfound curiosity. Never afraid to speak his mind, never shy about firing off a joke or a good-natured jab, Auriemma quickly became a personality to be reckoned with. Love him or hate him, few who encountered the Huskies' coach emerged with neutral feelings.

"Sometimes he's very controversial, and I know all about that," former Big East commissioner Michael Tranghese told the *Courant*. "But he knows who he is better than anybody does and that's part of the package. But when I look at the package, it's so overwhelmingly positive. I'm really pleased for him."

Tranghese was less than pleased on February 24, 1998, when L'affaire Nykesha (the controversy over the scoring record) generated more publicity on a national scale than any regular-season women's game in recent memory—even more than the 1995 game against Tennessee.

Although he regrets the fallout that descended on Sales, even Auriemma recognized the unintended boost the sport was receiving.

"If someone had done that at some other school, it would have generated zero discussion," Auriemma said. "But because we did it, then all of a sudden, it's going to generate a whole different level of response. I think anything that brings that kind of attention, as long as it gets people talking about the game, that's okay.

"I'm not okay with the way it happened, but if someone said would I do it again, I'd say yes, as long as I could spare what Nykesha went through. But Nykesha's agent later said to me, 'I don't know why you did that, but you made that kid a lot of money.' But I didn't want to put her through that."

Since then, Auriemma has had an ongoing hot-and-cold feud with Summitt, highlighted by Auriemma's "Evil Empire" crack in 2003, until Summitt called an end to the series in 2007, largely because of her personal dispute with Auriemma.

And there was the night in 2003 when Auriemma snapped at a UConn student newspaper reporter live on ESPN, for which he later apologized. All this has served to make Auriemma the most visible figure in a sport pining for colorful characters.

"I think his program, along with some others, he was fueling the fire," Stiff said. "Don't you love going to his press conferences? You don't know what's going to come up. He's never one to not have words. He's got a great personality and mind for the game. We'd much rather have a coach that has an opinion and doesn't state the obvious, and we get that out of him."

But Auriemma's brash public persona hides a different side to him, one he shows mostly in private. To many fellow coaches in the women's game, Auriemma is among the most generous with his time and advice, even if it means helping an opponent to beat him.

"People get to see his shtick," Coale said. "They see the celebrity Geno and they see him on TV and form their opinions by what they read. To a great extent, there's not a lot we can do to control how that comes across.

"But if you really know him, you buy into him, because he's real. He is willing to talk to you like your peers. When I was a high school coach, I would have conversations with him about the triangle offense, and he would talk to me like he was talking to his assistant coach or his best friend. His willingness to be open about his philosophy, the real stuff that matters, that's where I felt like I grew exponentially."

While Auriemma's Huskies were exciting crowds from Norman to Knoxville to tiny Ruston, Louisiana, another phenomenon was occurring closer to home. In 1995, when UConn raced to its perfect season, there was virtually zero competition coming from within the Big East. Since 1988, UConn has won seventeen Big East regular-season titles, including eleven in a row (1994–2004), and fifteen conference tournament championships, including nine in a row (1994–2002).

Still, as often happens in sports, when one team so thoroughly dominates its division or conference for an extended period of time, the other teams eventually began raising their own level of play in an attempt to keep up. By 2005, the Big East, with the help of additions like Notre Dame and Rutgers, had become an elite conference.

"Connecticut set the bar very high, and I know Geno has said a number of times, it's tougher to win the Big East than win the national championship," McGraw said. "He has really done amazing things for the Big East Conference. At one point, Connecticut represented the Big East almost entirely on its own.

"Now it's the most competitive it's ever been. People talk about the men's side, but the women's side is just as competitive. We have no easy wins. Everyone is tough at home. It's incredibly competitive."

Getting the conference to take women's basketball seriously was one of the greatest challenges Auriemma has faced in his twenty-four seasons at UConn. Schools lacked the financial and spiritual will to field competitive teams. The more UConn won, and the more revenue their success generated, the more other teams began focusing their resources on their own women's programs.

"There wasn't this urgency to be good at women's basketball [in 1995]," Auriemma said. "I think every team in the Big East was trying to make the NCAA Tournament and win in men's basketball. That's how the league was founded. Then we come along and we're in a situation where we have the ability to do something most teams couldn't.

"And after a while, people got tired of getting their

brains bashed in by Connecticut. It helped in recruiting. 'Why don't you come here and help us beat Connecticut's butt.' And with the schools that have come on board, everything's changed. We used to be the Big Least. Now, our coaches walk around and say, I dare you to find me a better league."

South Bend, Indiana, January 15, 2001

Ending the long winning streaks of its legendary opponents is nothing new for Notre Dame at the Joyce Center, their arena across the way from Notre Dame Stadium, in the shadow of Touchdown Jesus.

In 1974, the year they started playing women's basketball at UConn and three years before they would at Notre Dame, Digger Phelps's men's team stopped the greatest streak in NCAA history, knocking off John Wooden, Bill Walton, and the great 88 (wins in a row) of UCLA.

"Notre Dame has always been a funny place to play," Diana Taurasi said. "The minute you land, you're like, Where are we? The sun never comes up. The gym is underground. There's a whole weird vibe when you go there."

Muffet McGraw's women's team had an entirely different streak to contend with as the top-ranked Huskies came to town, and it wasn't UConn's thirty victories in a row. This day, the magic number was eleven, as in 0-11, as in Notre Dame's lifetime record against the Huskies.

But just as UConn had broken through on its Martin Luther King Day game versus Tennessee in the electric at-

55

mosphere at Gampel Pavilion in 1995, Notre Dame would benefit from the vibe at the Joyce Center as they faced the Huskies on this particular Monday afternoon.

"I wasn't even nervous," McGraw said in 2009. "That was one of the few games. I usually get nervous before a game. First of all, we were the underdogs, by a bit. This was one those games where, let's just have some fun.

"And the team, somehow, we all felt the same way. Nobody felt pressure. We weren't even thinking that we'd never beaten them. We just wanted to enjoy this moment. We went into it more with a businesslike approach. They [her players] were blue-collar kids and this was another game for us. We're playing well, we're undefeated, we've got nothing to lose."

As McGraw entered the arena that magical Monday, all thoughts of streaks and strategy took a momentary backseat. History would be made at the Joyce Center even before the teams took the court. For the first time ever, Notre Dame would play before a sellout crowd.

"I will never forget that day," McGraw said. "I still get chills. I walked into the arena and the first usher I saw said, 'Did you hear that it's a sellout?' And I thought, 'Oh my god, I've waited my whole career for this.' I was in the locker room, and Kevin White was our athletic director. He was awesome. He came in while I'm putting on lipstick and he wanted to say good luck and I said, 'I've been waiting my whole career for this.'

"I went out and the crowd was electric. And I walked from the locker room to the bench and it was so great, and I wasn't sure if I could coach the game. I was so hyped up and excited about the crowd, I just wanted to take it all in."

Muffet McGraw knew very early on in life that her career would be in basketball. After playing for coaching legend Theresa Grentz at Philadelphia's St. Joseph's University and graduating in 1977—the year before newly installed coach Jim Foster hired a young assistant from nearby Norristown named Geno Auriemma—McGraw took over the head coaching position at Archbishop Carroll High School in Radnor, Pennsylvania.

The school has many notable alumni, including a wide receiver named Gerard Phelan, who attended Carroll at the same time McGraw coached there and who would later catch a certain game-winning touchdown pass from Doug Flutie for Boston College in Miami's Orange Bowl.

Another student who graced Carroll's halls at the same time as McGraw was Kate Flannery, who later became an actress famous for playing Meredith on *The Office*. Carroll is also known for expelling another future actor, named Will Smith.

But the star from 1977 to 1979 was McGraw, who led Carroll to a two-year record of 50-3, including a Philadelphia Catholic League title in 1979 with a 28-0 record.

"I got that job and when I went to my first practice, I think it was right then, I was like, 'Well I've found my career,'" McGraw said. "This is it. One practice and I remember thinking, I love this. And you look back now, I knew nothing. How did I do that coming from being a player? But I loved it.

"I had a great experience with great kids. We were so good. I had like five Division I players. It was the luckiest move I ever made, walking into an amazing situation with good players."

McGraw's love of coaching knew no bounds. Not even her own wedding day stood a chance against the opportunity to hone her craft. The night before marrying her husband Matt, McGraw attended a coaching clinic.

"I loved to go to clinics and talk to coaches and write X's and O's on napkins. I loved it," McGraw said. "The guy checking us in said, 'You're just going to be here Friday?' And I said, 'Yeah, I'm getting married tomorrow.' And he didn't believe me. It does sound kind of funny now. But my husband was fine with it. 'Yeah, go ahead.' So, that kind of tipped him off to knowing that basketball maybe wasn't my first love, because he was, but it was pretty high up there."

After two years at Carroll, McGraw returned to St. Joe's, succeeding Auriemma, who left to coach his alma mater, Bishop Kenrick, before taking a job as an assistant at the University of Virginia. McGraw worked with Foster, who would become her coaching mentor, before making the leap to head coach, taking over the program at Lehigh in 1982 for five seasons.

Lehigh went 88-41 during McGraw's tenure, which included East Coast Conference coach of the year honors in her first season. In 1986 Lehigh went 24-4 and captured the East Coast Conference championship.

"[Foster] was such a great mentor," McGraw said. "He was philosophical. I learned so much from him, more than basketball: just how to work with the team, how to be hard on them. And then I went to Lehigh and got a chance to do things on my own at the college level and learn things and make mistakes in a good place to be. I always thought, When I get tired of practice, I'll know it's time to retire. I love practice. It's my favorite thing. I'd rather practice than have ten games. I love that part of it."

At the end of the 1986–87 season, McGraw was in Austin, Texas, for the Final Four, when her mentor, Foster, approached her. Notre Dame was looking for a new coach, Foster told her. She should apply. Muffet demurred. She loved Lehigh, she told Foster. She loved the East Coast, and Matt had a good job. What McGraw didn't say was that she feared a school like Notre Dame would have no interest in her.

"Typical of women," McGraw said. "Not enough confidence in themselves. My husband, he was relentless. He would not stop. 'Did you apply? Did you send in your resume?' We'd be on the golf course and I'd be in my backswing . . . 'Did you send it in?' So, I finally decided I'm going to send it in, but I didn't tell anyone."

To her great surprise, Notre Dame called back. Also to her surprise, she learned that Foster had already called Notre Dame on her behalf. Now it was McGraw's turn to surprise someone else.

"So I said to Matt, who used to go on recruiting trips

with me, 'Do you want to go on a trip this Thursday?' He said, 'Where are you going?' And I said, 'South Bend.' I think he was more thrilled than I was. I was so nervous, but he was so excited. He'd always been a Notre Dame fan, and so was my dad. A couple days later, when I came home, Matt had the ND mowed into the backyard. We had the victory march on the doorbell.

"Then they called me a couple days later and offered me the job. I remember exactly where I was on the phone and how the whole thing happened. It was the greatest thrill. I called one of the reporters [near Lehigh] and told him I was going to Notre Dame. He said, 'Notre Dame High School?' because there was one right in town. And I said, 'I guess you didn't think I could get the job, either.'"

Notre Dame announced the hiring of their third coach in the history of the women's program on May 18, 1987. In each of McGraw's first four seasons, Notre Dame won a minimum of twenty games. In the ten years of the program's existence before her arrival, Notre Dame had had four twenty-win seasons total.

In her fifth season, despite a 14-17 regular-season record, McGraw led the Irish to the Midwestern Collegiate Conference tournament title, earning Notre Dame its first ever NCAA Tournament appearance. In 1997 McGraw led Notre Dame to its first thirty-win season and the Final Four.

"It was like a dream," McGraw said. "And it still feels like one. The Dome and Touchdown Jesus, the band marching across campus in the fall, there's no place better. I remember when Kentucky's job came open, big basketball school, and I had no interest in looking there. Notre Dame was a dream job, and it still is."

With the sellout crowd still filing into the Joyce Center, McGraw could hardly contain herself. A year earlier, she had sent her Irish onto the court at the Hartford Civic Center believing they were finally ready to knock off their nemesis and claim superiority in the Big East. Two hours later, her hopes were crushed in a 77–59 defeat that literally left her in tears as she addressed the media after the game.

Now, with UConn struggling as they arrived in South Bend, Notre Dame found itself in the role UConn had played six years ago to the day. Notre Dame was the inspired challenger, spurred on by an electric crowd. UConn was the old guard, ready to be defeated, allowing Notre Dame to ascend atop the Associated Press poll.

"We could see they were ready to get beat," Niele Ivey said. "And the whole sold-out thing, I remember walking out on the court to do some preshooting, before the warm-up, and to see how many people were out there already . . . It was electric. Our fans aren't like football. They're not coming out for every game. But the whole student section was completely filled. I was like, 'This is going to be something special.' I got chills. I fed off that energy.

"Muffet didn't even have to say anything in the pregame. I'm like, Just roll the ball out. Let's go. Jump it up. There's too much excitement. I didn't want to wait another twenty minutes. We'd been ready for that game. We were undefeated at the time and everything was leading up to *that game*. That was the one that put us over the top. And to finally do it, to bring them down, when they've been bringing us down for years, and to do it at home, in front of a sellout, was one of the most exciting games ever."

UConn never had a chance. On the Huskies' opening possession, Ralph had her shot blocked by Ericka Haney and Ivey scored at the other end. Riley got a couple of easy scores on the blocks. Kelley Siemon, the daughter of Minnesota Vikings linebacker Jeff Siemon, showing her toughness and tenacity by playing with a broken hand, foiled UConn's attempt to rattle Riley by giving the big center a cutter to pass to when the doubles came. And when Siemon wasn't hitting inside, Riley was finding Alicia Ratay, the best three-point shooter in the nation, wide open for long-range bombs. Just like that, Notre Dame had a 23–12 lead.

"I remember our zone was unstoppable," Ivey said. "Obviously, we were clicking on offense, but I usually feed off our defense first. I came out and stole the ball from Swin Cash and made the layup with a strong finish. I was like, This is it. I'm ready. We were just in the zone. Ruth was in a zone. Kelley was in her own zone. Alicia was in a zone. Ruth was just so fundamentally sound. If you want to be a post player, watch that game. Inside out, it was a perfect game."

It was the first time all season UConn trailed in double figures.

"It felt like they outsmarted us," Bird said. "When we were doubling, they made the right pass. Everything we did, they countered right away. They knew exactly what was coming."

While the Notre Dame half-court game evoked the 1970 Knicks in sheer beauty and teamwork, the Huskies looked more like the Knicks of the late 1970s, a group of disjointed jump shooters. UConn was unable to score over McGraw's maddening 2-3 zone and unable to get inside it, with Riley the imposing last line of defense.

The Huskies would cut the deficit to 23–21, largely behind Svetlana Abrosimova, who had one of her best games of the season with twenty points and fourteen rebounds. Later in the game, after another Notre Dame run, UConn would get within 40–37.

But the Irish never relinquished the lead. With Riley leading the way with 29 points—21 in the second half, including 13 consecutive free throws—the Irish rolled to a 92–76 victory. The crowd of 11,418—which the media dubbed "The House That Ruth Filled"—stormed the court when it was over. Notre Dame was now 17-0 and would soon become the No. 1 team in the nation.

"It's kind of like when we played Tennessee six years ago, you know?" Auriemma told the media after the game. "We were number two and they were number one, and we beat them and the fans go crazy. It's a good thing for the game. It's good for Notre Dame. We need more sold-out buildings around the country. It's not a great thing for us, obviously, because you want to win every game. But we didn't deserve to win today. We didn't play well enough to win."

Even better for Notre Dame—like the 2004 Red Sox after they beat the Yankees in the ALCS on the road to their first World Series title in eighty-six years, the Irish no longer had to hear about never beating UConn as they pursued their first national championship.

"There were a lot of expectations and if we won that game, we would be ranked number one," Riley said. "Then coming out and playing so well and feeding off the crowd, it was definitely a huge accomplishment for us. It validated our team at that point in the season, that we're a contender. Any time you lose to a team that many times in a row, it's an accomplishment in itself."

The sixteen-point loss would be UConn's largest margin of defeat in a span of eleven years, from 1994 to 2005. Sue Bird joined Abrosimova with a solid seventeen-point effort, but Shea Ralph was held to a career-low two points. Taurasi scored just six before fouling out.

"We got our asses kicked," Bird said. "I remember in the locker room we had a little bit of a soul-searching situation where people were speaking and I remember thinking, This is what happens with teams that win—and this has happened with every team I've been on—you forget how hard it was when you won. You forget how hard the practices are. You forget how hard the games are. You forget how focused you had to be. You forget. You think you're just going to show up and it's going to happen again.

"We had never lost to Notre Dame up to that point. Every time we played Notre Dame in my two or three years, we kicked their ass. It wasn't even a question. And then you had a team in Notre Dame, they were not the most talented, but they had Ruth and they had all these pieces that just fit, and I feel like their whole goal in life that year was to beat us, no matter what. Even if they were playing other teams, I felt like they were preparing to beat us."

South Bend, January 16, 2001

The morning after the greatest victory in Notre Dame women's history, Muffet McGraw was a nervous wreck, more nervous now than she had been while coaching the game the day before.

Although it had waited for the outcome of UConn's historic game over Tennessee in 1995 so it could release its weekly poll, the Associated Press did not wait for the outcome of the Notre Dame game to release an update. Therefore, the Irish would have to wait six more days for the official declaration.

Not only would Notre Dame leapfrog both UConn and Tennessee to claim the top spot in the country, the Irish would now be considered an odds-on favorite to reach the national championship game.

On January 15, all that UConn lost was a game. But that same afternoon in Knoxville, Tennessee, the Lady Vols lost something far more important. In the second half of a victory over Mississippi State, Tamika Catchings, the Vols' All-American forward and daughter of former NBA player Harvey Catchings, tore the ACL in her right knee, ending her season.

Like that, Tennessee's six-year run of appearances in the national championship game seemed doomed. And the Irish, now 17-0, were poised to take their place.

For Niele Ivey, the dream scenario of ending her career at the Final Four in her hometown of St. Louis finally seemed attainable. For McGraw—on January 16, at least—that prospect seemed frightening.

"After that win, it was unbelievable," McGraw said. "You couldn't go anywhere because everyone wanted to talk to you, tell you what a great game it was, 'I'm making plans for St. Louis,' and I was like, Oh my god, I can't take this. I don't want to talk about St. Louis. We're not changing anything. But all of a sudden, everything got ratcheted up about three notches.

"And then a couple of days later, we were ranked number one in the poll. So a bunch of media people came out to talk to us—and I'm not sure the girls even knew—and I remember Kelley Siemon was being interviewed, they were like, 'What do you think?' And she thought they were asking about her broken hand. They're like, 'You're number one,' and the girls were like, 'Oh yeah?

What's that mean? It doesn't mean anything to us.' They handled it better than I did. They were amazing."

Ruth Riley had adopted that stance from the moment the UConn game had ended. In the joyous locker room, Riley set the tone for the remainder of the season.

"I remember saying to Coach, 'This isn't our goal,'" Riley said. "Even after that win, I stayed focused on the fact that the season wasn't over after a big win at midseason. We needed to stay focused. I didn't get that high because our goal wasn't beating Connecticut and being number one, it was winning a national championship."

There was also now the matter of possibly going undefeated. The Irish would not face UConn again in the regular season and had only one remaining regular-season game against a ranked opponent. That would be in mid-February against eleventh-ranked Rutgers, who would host Notre Dame at the Rutgers Athletic Center, known simply as the RAC because playing there was like being stretched out on one for opposing teams.

Rutgers was coming off a twenty-five-point loss to UConn when Notre Dame arrived for a Saturday night date. A month earlier in South Bend, the Irish had handled C. Vivian Stringer's team with little trouble, beating the 2000 Final Four entrants by twenty-one points.

But the rematch would not go as well. Behind its frenzied sellout crowd, Rutgers kept the game close throughout, largely because for one of the few times all season, Riley had gotten into first-half foul trouble. Riley eventually would foul out with a minute left to play, a particularly damaging foul because it came on Tammy Sutton-Brown's game-tying layup. Sutton-Brown then made the free throw to put Rutgers ahead by one, and when Ivey tried to split a triple-team on Notre Dame's final possession, it was Sutton-Brown to the rescue again, blocking Ivey's shot to secure the 64–63 victory.

It was Notre Dame's first loss since the meltdown against Texas Tech in the 2000 NCAA Tournament. After the game, McGraw kicked herself for not calling a time-out, which would have spared her team the chaotic final seconds, with Siemon screaming for someone to help Ivey, who had been swallowed up by Rutgers's notorious "55" press defense.

But if McGraw wanted to take blame for the defeat, she would have to get in line. In yet another example of the strength of their chemistry, each of her star players took turns accepting responsibility for the defeat.

"I thought I just completely blew it at the end," McGraw said. "We had the ball late to win it and I should have called time-out and didn't. They pressed us, we took too long and ended up not getting a good shot. I was like, I blew it, and there's Ruth crying, 'It's all my fault,' and Niele is crying, 'No, it's all my fault.' You had to love a team that was so accountable like that."

The road back from ruin began slowly for the Huskies after their stunning loss in South Bend. The problems that had plagued the team even before the Notre Dame game only seemed to magnify in its wake.

Shea Ralph was still struggling, following her two-point effort against the Irish with a four-game stretch at the end of January and early February in which she shot a combined 4-for-21 from the field, scoring a total of seventeen points, eclipsing four points just once.

"She wasn't 100 percent," Diana Taurasi said. "She was always trying to get through injuries and put the team on her back and lead us, because she was our vocal leader in the locker room, in the huddles. It's hard to do that when you're fighting your body and you're fighting your opponent and you're trying to carry the team. And that year, it was tough."

The Notre Dame game was Ralph's nadir. Not only was she held to two points on 1-for-4 shooting and one rebound, she was benched by Auriemma in the second half, as Riley led the charge to put the game away.

"I remember Coach sitting me and I remember thinking I was surprised he didn't do it earlier, because I was just awful," Ralph said. "We weren't even close to our top level, and I take responsibility for that day. I just didn't show up that day. And I knew it, and I could feel it that morning and tried to snap out of it, and I couldn't. The harder I tried, the worse it got. For me to play like that in a big game, it just shell-shocked some of the guys on the team. I didn't do a good job leading that day.

"I've never said anything to anyone about [her struggles] and I don't think I will, ever. It was just a struggle, and that's what it was. I tried to snap out of it and help the team. We all struggled toward the middle of the year.

69

We lost some games we shouldn't have lost. But it didn't matter why I struggled, I just did."

The more Ralph struggled, the more it appeared the torch of leadership was being passed from her and Svetlana Abrosimova to the junior class, led by Bird. But that, too, was a source of unease within the team, further clouding their chemistry.

"To some degree, we had a strong senior class and you had my class and there was a little bit of a changing of the guard happening, and you had Diana, who was probably the most talented player on the team," Bird said. "It was a unique situation trying to balance all that."

Still, the Huskies ended January having won their final three games by an average of thirty-three points over Big East bottom-feeders. Then it was on to Knoxville for a rematch with the Lady Vols.

For two seasons, 1999–2000 and 2000–2001, UConn and Tennessee met twice during the regular season, an unprecedented move for two nonconference opponents. The arrangement was made to allow both CBS, which had carried the women's Final Four through 1995, and ESPN, the current home of the women's tournament, to each carry one of the rivalry games, which were consistently the most-watched women's games of the season.

In the first year of the agreement, ESPN was the clear benefactor, televising a thriller at Gampel Pavilion. That night in early February, Tennessee handed UConn its only defeat of the season, with Semeka Randall scoring the winning basket with 4.4 seconds left in a 72–71 victory.

The conclusion of that game was as stirring as any in the history of the rivalry. Before Randall's basket, Bird had put UConn ahead with a baseline jumper. After Randall scored, Bird called a time-out, setting in motion one of the most controversial sequences in UConn history.

The Huskies trailing by one, Geno Auriemma instructed that the ball go to Abrosimova, the best-equipped player on the roster to rush the ball upcourt in less than five seconds to get a good shot at the basket. And Abrosimova accomplished the first part of the mission with ease, dribbling to the Tennessee foul line with two seconds remaining.

But there, Abrosimova deviated sharply from the game plan. Instead of pulling up and shooting, or finishing her own drive to the basket, Abrosimova stopped and passed the ball to Tamika Williams, who was stationed under the basket, anticipating a possible offensive rebound.

Surprised by the pass, with no time to square up to shoot and guarded closely by a Tennessee defender, Williams barely hit the underside of the backboard as the buzzer sounded.

"We got it right to where we wanted it with the person we wanted," Auriemma said. "That night might have been the only time in Sveta's career that she didn't take that shot when she had the opportunity, for whatever reason. Maybe she was pissed at me, maybe she was having a bad day, who knows?"

Whatever the reason, Auriemma could not contain his anger at his stubborn junior from Russia, benching her after one minute of play in UConn's next game. The tension between the two eventually lifted, to the point where the two would joke openly about their spat for the national media during the NCAA Tournament, like an Abbott and Costello routine.

But "Sveta's Pass" had far-reaching implications within the team. Just as Bird was increasingly becoming the team leader, she would now also find herself the shooter when last-second scenarios were played out in practice.

"The next day he put them in that drill and she ran it down and buried a little jump shot," Eagan said. "I think if Svet had shot and missed, Geno could have lived with it, but she didn't. She passed the ball. And you could say maybe that was the right basketball play. Maybe it was, maybe it wasn't. But he wants whoever has the ball in that situation to shoot it. And Sue Bird shoots the ball."

Although Bird had yet to experience anything close to a buzzer-beating scenario in an actual game with the Huskies, the concept was one she embraced fully.

"Those are situations that I like," Bird said. "I really enjoy them. They're fun. I mean, who doesn't want to have the ball with the game on the line? You know, when you play at Connecticut, fortunately or unfortunately, there's not a lot of those situations, so when they do come, you definitely want to capitalize on them, because there's not that many. If you can be one of those people, it's amazing. It's an amazing feeling.

"And I do remember in practice, when we would do those situations—and he would devise a lot of different things for a lot of people—I remember getting the ball a lot in those situations. I remember one conversation where he said, 'Okay, we're down one with the ball, what are you doing?' I'm like, 'I'm going to go to Svet.' And he's like, 'Why would you go to Svet?' So I said, 'I'll go to Swin, she'll definitely get fouled.' And I remember he said, 'Why not just keep it yourself?'"

Any debate over which of the two should get the ball in the final seconds became moot the night of February 1, 2001, in Knoxville. UConn and Tennessee delivered another classic for ESPN, combining to score 180 points in a back-and-forth contest. For the game's first six minutes, there were no whistles, meaning no stoppage in play, creating one of the most breathtaking sequences—especially for the exhausted players—ever seen in a women's game. Abrosimova was having yet another solid game, scoring eighteen points in her first twenty-five minutes. Her three-pointer with just over ten minutes left gave the Huskies a 64–63 lead.

But moments later, while going after an offensive rebound, Abrosimova felt a sharp, intense pain in her left foot and could not continue. UConn went on to lose its second game of the season, 92–88, in part because Taurasi was called for her fifth foul late in the game after

Tennessee guard Kara Lawson got away with a charge into Ralph. Enraged by the double whammy, Auriemma lost his cool on the sideline and was called for a technical foul.

All the free throws sealed the deal for Tennessee. For the second time, Taurasi had fouled out of a game that UConn lost. But the details of the final minute meant little. The injury to Abrosimova's foot was serious—just how serious, the team would not discover until a few days later. The senior forward from Russia, the fifth-leading scorer in UConn history, with 1,865 points, had torn ligaments in the foot. Her season was over.

Just like in 1997, 1998, and 1999, the Huskies had been dealt a crippling blow only weeks before the start of the postseason. Jeff Jacobs, the sports columnist for the *Hartford Courant*, compared Abrosimova's career-ending injury to the fate of another famous Russian, Doctor Zhivago. In Husky-mad Connecticut, the analogy seemed sadly apt.

"I hate the fact that I'm never going to be able to play with Svet again," Bird told the media after UConn's first game after the diagnosis was confirmed, a 90–38 drubbing of Virginia Tech. "That makes me upset, but at the same time I know that the only thing I can do for her, and the only thing my class can do for her, is win this for her. Things are expected of us now. A bulk of this has to come from our class. The seniors are going to have to do a great job leading and the younger guys are just going to have to play, and we are going to have to take some of the load off Shea's shoulders as far as leading and taking this team where it needs to go."

But if anything, the injury to Abrosimova finally jolted Ralph out of her season-long funk. The Tennessee game had been the sixth in a row where Ralph failed to score in double figures, and the same thing had happened in eight of her past nine games overall. But starting with the first game after the injury, Ralph would reach double figures in six of UConn's final eight regular-season games, and she'd have a 5-for-5 shooting performance against Villanova in the first official post-Svet game, before the extent of Abrosimova's injury was revealed.

"For Sveta, it was heartbreaking," Ralph said. "As good a player as she was and how important she was to us, it was hard to watch her go through that, but you can't dwell on it. She already feels bad enough, she doesn't need to see us all mopey as well. I knew that from having gone through it myself. That was the worst, to see your teammates upset. You hope they're inspired, because you feel bad as it is. It was hard to watch her go down, but I felt a greater sense of responsibility to step it up for her."

But what really freed Ralph from her doldrums and demons were the defiant, supporting words of a teammate. Even though the Villanova game had been her best of the month, Ralph was again quizzed in the postgame press conference about her struggles.

She offered a dismissive answer to a question about the health of her knees and the apparent end of her shooting slump, but Mike DiMauro, a well-respected—and not easily placated—writer for the *New London Day*, made an indignant observation about Ralph's recent scoring woes.

"He goes, 'Shea, what does 2-8-2-3-4-4 mean?'" Ralph said. "I was like, 'What does that mean?' He was like, 'Those are your point totals for the past six games. What do you have to say about that?' And I was so caught off guard. All those games, we'd won."

The always-intense Ralph, finally provoked beyond her limit, delivered a brief, angry rebuke by mocking the way DiMauro asked the question. But before the already-tense atmosphere boiled over into something uglier, junior Tamika Williams, seated next to Ralph on the podium, took the microphone and ended the matter for good.

Williams, an active leader in the student community, had long commanded respect among her peers in the program and the media for a wisdom and insight beyond her twenty years, and she was the perfect spokesman for Ralph at this moment.

"You guys have no idea all the things Shea does for us," Williams said. "There are so many more things that she brings to my game, to our game, that we don't even think about the points, because we know when we need that, she'll do that, too."

The lecture over, Ralph was left alone. The tension in

the room dissipated. So did the tension that had been coursing for weeks through Ralph's veins.

"I was so grateful," Ralph said. "She talked about how we'd been winning games and the seniors provided great leadership, and it just wasn't a good question. I remember being re-energized and wanting to be what she was saying, to even more of an extent. And when Sveta got hurt, there was more of that sense of urgency. There's plenty of reasons [for the slump], but it doesn't matter. I did struggle, but I came out of it."

For the first time all season, the Huskies began playing with a sense of urgency and purpose. Taurasi slid into the starting lineup and had a string of solid performances to end the regular season. At last, the Greatest Team Ever Assembled was playing like it, entering the Big East Tournament.

"All this crap is over. It's done with," Ralph said after the Virginia Tech game, three days after Williams's outburst and two days after Abrosimova's season had been declared over. "We've been in lulls and we've lost a couple of games, but it's not happening anymore. Everybody is coming alert to games and nobody is taking any more days off in practice. I just have a good feeling about this team right now."

Storrs, March 5, 2001

Led by Connecticut, the Big East had placed at least one team in the Final Four in four of the previous six seasons before 2000–2001. In 2000 the conference had

77

two entrants. While UConn would go on to win its second national championship in Philadelphia, defeating Penn State and Tennessee, the fourth team hailed from nearby New Jersey.

Led by C. Vivian Stringer, who previously coached Iowa to the Final Four in 1983 and Cheyney State College in 1982, the Scarlet Knights of Rutgers defeated Georgia in the 2000 West Regional finals to reach the Final Four, before losing to Tennessee in the semifinals.

For Rutgers and Stringer, the Final Four appearance, the first of two in the decade, was further validation of the claim she had made, upon her arrival in Piscataway in 1995, that Rutgers could supplant Connecticut as the "Jewel of the East."

This glowing prediction did not sit well with the defending national champions in Storrs. As it had with Notre Dame, UConn would dominate the early years of the rivalry with Rutgers, winning nine of the first ten meetings starting in 1996. However, the animosity between these two programs was far more palpable—even more uncivil than anything that had occurred to that point between UConn and Tennessee.

The style of play at Rutgers, in the mold of its head coach, was confrontational and unrelenting. In the middle of play in a game in the late 1990s, one of Rutgers's bolder players, Linda Miles, told Auriemma to shut up, after he had barked at someone on the court.

Miles, Shawnetta Stewart, Tasha Pointer, and Usha Gilmore were all talented players, good enough to hand

UConn its only Big East Conference loss in 1998 and good enough to reach the Final Four in 2000. But years before Don Imus would create a national controversy and lose his radio job after making racially insensitive comments about the Rutgers players' style and appearance, the perception that Rutgers was a "thug" program was very much alive and well, and seemed to find its most receptive audience in Connecticut.

When UConn played Rutgers on Valentine's Day in 2001, *Connecticut Post* columnist Chris Elsberry expressed that sentiment in his column published the day after UConn's 70–45 victory, a game that featured yet another confrontation, with Diana Taurasi picking up a technical for taunting Pointer: "All the tattoos, all the black uniforms and the headbands and the bravado you take to the court doesn't mean a thing when you don't have the talent, or the respect, to say that you can stand with the best. Even though they talk the talk, they don't walk the walk. . . . That street style has never meshed well against the Huskies' poise and depth."

Three weeks later, when the conference assembled at Gampel Pavilion for the Big East Tournament, everyone seemed to have forgotten the column—except Stringer. The first indication that this particular four-day tournament was going to be unlike any that had preceded it was revealed when Rutgers took the court for a Sunday night quarterfinal game against Providence.

When the Rutgers players came out of the locker room, their tattoos were covered with Band-Aids. As protests go, it was visually subtle but symbolically powerful. It was a direct shot at Elsberry, and, by extension, the UConn program.

One of the rules of decorum under which associate head coach Chris Dailey runs the UConn program is that the players must cover any tattoos that are not concealed by their uniforms during games. On the 2001 team, only sophomore guard Kennitra Johnson was affected by this edict, and for two years she had worn a Band-Aid on her arm to cover her art.

In having her players do the same thing as they beat Providence 69–58 on March 4, Stringer expressed her mockery of the perception that while UConn ran its program properly, Rutgers's "street style" was unsavory.

Whether anyone in Gampel Pavilion was paying close attention to this message was hard to tell. As Rutgers took the floor, most UConn fans were still preoccupied with an event that had occurred two hours earlier, in the Huskies' 96–53 quarterfinal victory over Boston College.

The victory over BC came easily, but at a high price. After wrenching her back in the first half, Bird spent the entire second half lying on the ground, with UConn's second-year athletic trainer, Rosemary Ragle, trying to work out the kinks.

Years later, Bird would attribute the injury to the stress she was feeling because her teammate Swin Cash had been slighted at the Big East banquet two nights earlier. Bird was named First Team Big East; Cash was second team—a result Bird felt should have been reversed.

"I remember having her on the floor with a heat pack on her back, then rolling her over and trying to stretch her out," Ragle said. "She didn't have an injury, it was just muscle spasms. People just tighten up, whether it's stress or someone knocking into them. She was one of these kids who didn't like hair in their face, let alone dealing with a tight back.

"She's a pretty intense individual and she takes things to heart. She doesn't seek the limelight. She thinks everyone around her makes her better, while recognizing that she makes other people better. I can see how that would stress her out. We weren't concerned about an injury to the bone, just a spasm related to stress."

Although not considered season-threatening, Bird's injury was severe enough that she would not play the next night in the semifinals against the defiant Scarlet Knights. Thus, the single-most bizarre evening in the twenty-year history of Gampel Pavilion would have to proceed without her.

Snowstorms, arena roofs, and UConn basketball have not had a happy history together.

On the night of January 17, 1978, the UConn men played the University of Massachusetts in front of 5,000 people inside the 10,000-seat Hartford Civic Center Coliseum, the game ending at roughly 10 p.m., while a heavy snowfall was underway outside.

Some six hours later, at 4:15 a.m., a thunderous roar shook the area, loud enough to be heard miles away in sleepy West Hartford. Under the massive weight of the snowstorm, the Coliseum roof had collapsed, destroying the seating bowl inside.

The arena, also home to the WHA (and soon-to-be NHL) New England Whalers, was rebuilt and reopened almost two years later, to the day, in 1980 as the 16,294-seat Veterans' Memorial Coliseum.

Ten years after that, a new 10,000-seat arena opened, this time on UConn's campus. Harry A. Gampel Pavilion, topped with an Epcot-like dome, would never suffer a fate as terrifying as that of the old Hartford Coliseum, but on the night of March 5, 2001, it met a formidable foe in Mother Nature.

In only the 429th day of the new millennium, the first "Storm of the Century" was bearing down on Connecticut. Weather forecasts called for upward of eighteen to twenty-four inches of powder starting in the afternoon, accompanied by high wind gusts. But despite the dire forecast—and a stern warning from Governor John Rowland, himself a hardcore Husky fan from Waterbury, to stay off the roads that evening—the Big East chose to conduct the women's tournament semifinals as scheduled. And just as fans had on that fateful night in 1978, some five thousand people braved the conditions to take in the doubleheader: Notre Dame–Virginia Tech in the opener, UConn–Rutgers in the nightcap.

So dire were the forecasts, some UConn players and media scrambled to make emergency sleeping arrangements. Shea Ralph and assistant coach Stacy Hansmeyer, who roomed together several miles off-campus, planned to spend the night in the players' lounge inside the arena.

Also making bedding plans for Gampel Pavilion were Matt Eagan and a *Hartford Courant* coworker, the two writers lugging blankets and pillows, as well as laptops, into the makeshift media area in the hallways outside the arena proper. The assumption was that the back roads leading in and out of campus would be impassible by the time the evening's second game came to an end, probably around 10 p.m.

That time estimate would prove overly optimistic.

The evening began uneventfully enough. In the opening game, a 67–49 Notre Dame victory, the biggest drama was that Ruth Riley, who had just been named Big East player of the year, was having an uncharacteristic off-night offensively: she was held by the Hokies to two points, both of them second-half free throws.

Riley found herself surrounded by two or three Hokies on virtually every possession. She attempted just two shots in the first half and went to the bench early in the second with three fouls. Riley didn't score until making two free throws with 9:30 left in the game.

"It was a bit of a rough go offensively for me," said Riley, who had averaged 20.5 points in Notre Dame's two regular-season victories over Virginia Tech. "They did a good job of double-teaming me, which I've faced all year. I didn't do so well handling it."

Kelley Siemon and Alicia Ratay each scored fourteen

points and Ericka Haney had twelve, proving that the Irish were more than just Riley and the Gang.

"Every time they play us they want to make the less-premier players do well," said Siemon, who added nine rebounds and four assists. "We're such a versatile team. On any given night, anyone can go off."

The Irish were also thrown off their game defensively, but that proved a blessing in disguise. Muffet McGraw had not intended to use her suffocating 2-3 zone in this game, preferring to play man-to-man. But early on, McGraw went to the zone for a brief look and discovered that the Hokies, who shot 6-for-34 from the field in the first half, couldn't handle it. So the zone stayed the rest of the way.

"It looked so good we decided to stay with it," McGraw said. "They had a poor shooting night, and when the shots aren't dropping, the basket gets a little smaller."

The stage was now set for another grudge match between UConn and Rutgers. The Huskies were already without Svetlana Abrosimova, and now they took the floor without Bird as well.

No matter. In a withering display, the Huskies raced to leads of 10–0 and 26–3. The lead was 41–20 with 3:31 left in the first half when, suddenly, whistles blew and play screeched to a halt.

As the UConn baskets rained down on the Scarlet Knights, rain of an entirely unwelcome kind began drip, drip, dripping onto the floor near midcourt. The combination of snow and wind produced by the storm raging outside had forced precipitation through a vent atop the Pavilion's dome. With nowhere else to go, the water slowly dripped onto the court, making the surface too dangerous for play.

Stringer, Geno Auriemma, and the officials huddled together. In an ominous sign of things to come concerning Stringer's mindset on this evening, the Rutgers coach initially declared, "This [is] intentional!" as if somehow UConn could (a) control the weather and the architecture; and (b) wanted this blowout victory to be stopped in progress.

Stringer's brief rant was quickly ignored. The focus instead shifted to getting the maintenance staff to plug the leak. As Auriemma would later quip to the media, there would be no ballboys rushing across the court, tennis-style, to wipe away the moisture while the game was being played. Either the leak would stop or the game would.

The leak won an early battle. The game was suspended while a battle plan to contain the moisture was plotted, and for ninety minutes, an indoor basketball game was subject to a rain delay. As they were leading by twenty-one points, UConn apparently felt that there was not much need for a strategy session inside the locker room.

"We watched *Kings of Comedy* for about an hour," Diana Taurasi would later say. "We used to watch that during study hall."

The fans were entertained with some live drama on

the court. Bill Sehl, the forty-four-year-old arena engineer, had been assigned the unenviable task of plugging the leak by any means necessary. While some enterprising reporters ventured out into the maelstrom, anticipating that Sehl would attempt to reach the source by scaling the dome from the outside, the plan eventually called for a more direct approach.

In a move worthy of a David Copperfield magic act, Sehl was to enter a small metal cage and propel himself up to a trapdoor in the ceiling. As he progressed, the 5,000-plus people in the arena chanted, "Bil-ly, Bil-ly!" Once Sehl reached the top, he disappeared into the ceiling, towels and plastic in tow. A few minutes later, he re-emerged victorious. The leak had been plugged. The show would go on.

Both teams returned to the court and the game resumed at 10:34 p.m.

"This is a very rare occurrence," Sehl, a reluctant folk hero, told an enthralled media. "But it's always interesting in athletics."

Sehl had no idea.

UConn picked right up where it left off, cruising to a 94–66 victory. But because of the delay, the game did not end until nearly midnight, and by the time the deadline-conscious media had gathered in the makeshift press-conference area where Stringer and others were slated to offer postgame comments before taking questions, the general hope was that the session would be quick.

Those hopes were dashed in a way no one saw coming. Stringer took to the podium, alongside some of her players, and made a brief statement in praise of UConn and Auriemma. Then, she looked out at her questioners, pulled out two pieces of paper, and asked a question herself.

"Is Chris Elsberry here?"

Writers seated before the podium turned to the back of room, where Elsberry was standing, then looked at each other quizzically. To the assembled media, whose unforgiving deadlines required them to churn out copy on a daily basis, the contents of a single piece written three weeks earlier—in a time before instant Internet saturation of news stories had fully taken hold—made little to no lasting impression.

Then, too, the media wasn't targeted in Elsberry's February 15 column. However, they were the targets now.

Having located the source of her anger in the back of the room, Stringer set the pages she brought with her on the podium. It was a letter of protest, one that would be distributed, along with the contents of Elsberry's column, to every media member in attendance.

But Stringer went one step further. She began reading out loud:

Dear Mr. Elsberry:

There are many items you mentioned in your column, "Rutgers teams have yet to earn Huskies' respect," after our last visit to Storrs several weeks ago. Instead of the many assumptions and generalizations you made regarding our program, our players, myself and my staff, I would like to supply you with just some of the facts that you failed to mention.

First of all, you are correct that we want respect. The way I see it, every team and every individual playing this game all across the country wants to be respected and every single person deserves that respect. The amount of work and sacrifice needed to compete at this or any level is substantial and that effort deserves to be acknowledged.

A ripple of unease swept through the interview room. It would be difficult enough to sit through a public scolding under ideal circumstances, and the present situation was far from that. Clocks ticked inside the heads of every writer in the room. It was already midnight, and the UConn players and Auriemma had yet to take the podium. Auriemma, in fact, was off to the side of the room, behind the blue curtains that served as a partition, studiedly trying not to make eye contact with the UConn writers; trying, it appeared, to suppress a smile.

Elsberry, better than anyone, understood the dilemma facing his colleagues, and for their sake, he tried to bring closure to the incident. Interrupting Stringer, he asked, gently, if she would prefer to address him privately so the rest of the room could continue working under their tight deadlines.

Stringer ignored this and continued reading—and the discomfort in the room began to border on panic.

Auriemma caught the eye of one distraught writer and gestured with his eyes sympathetically. Finally, Stringer completed the letter:

> . . . the "tattoos, black uniforms and the headbands" as you said in your article, those are all superficial things that have nothing to do with who we are as people. Those who know us know that our team is filled with some very special people. We attend church together regularly, we are involved in our community and we care very much about each other and those who care about us. . . . These are our student athletes, not the ones you think you know because you see them play once or twice a year. I believe in not judging a book by its cover. I hope that you feel the same way.

With that, the press conference moved forward, however rattled the writers may have been after this unprecedented public flogging. The storm in the room was over. The storm outside continued to rage.

"That was such a bizarre night," Eagan said. "So many different things happened. I remember most running outside under the mistaken impression that they were going to try and fix the leak in the roof from the outside, rather than the ceiling from the inside.

"But then there's obviously the bizarre circumstance of C. Vivian Stringer. After a surreal game, it was a surreal press conference, to have her come in and call out Chris Elsberry and take him to task. Regardless of whose side you took on whether his column was over the line or whether her argument had merit, that initial five minutes of her calling him out, for something that was old, was bizarre."

It was almost hard to remember that in less than twenty-four hours, the Storm of the Century would give way to the Rematch of the Century: No. 2 UConn versus No. 1 Notre Dame for the Big East Tournament title.

"You know how in 1978, the playoff game between the Red Sox and Yankees is always talked about as a Red Sox collapse?" Eagan said. "But the Red Sox had come back to force the playoff. It was two teams peaking.

"This game was two teams peaking. Notre Dame had been playing at an extremely high level all season, but Connecticut had just run Rutgers right out of the building. You had the sense that they're getting it and they're ready. It's March, they're ready, here we go."

Storrs, March 6, 2001

The snow was still falling across Connecticut as daybreak came on Tuesday, but the dire predictions of the day before would not be realized. About a foot of snow fell across Connecticut, enough to cancel school but not nearly enough to delay the proceedings set for that evening at Gampel Pavilion.

A cranky back would not be enough to keep Sue Bird off the floor for the biggest game of the season. Bird had sat out Monday's semifinal victory over Rutgers, but after a night of being hooked up to a stem machine—a pager-sized console that transmitted a steady current of stimulus into the muscles of her lower back—she was ready to return to the starting lineup.

Her teammates were ready, too. The doldrums of January had given way to a renewed energy and purpose in February, even with the sobering reality of Svetlana Abrosimova's season-ending foot injury.

"It was a more of a feeling that anyone that crosses us is going to get smashed," Shea Ralph said. "That was the general feeling, the Connecticut basketball feeling. We had the pep back in our step, that when we walk on the court, the other team is done before the jump ball. You look at them and see in their eyes that they're done. It was that kind of swagger and confidence that we had back, and you could feel it. It was palpable. In the locker room, on the bus, on the court, you could feel it."

A surge into postseason play had become a trademark of the Huskies during the Bird Administration. A year earlier, UConn had roared into March after an early February loss to Tennessee and dominated the postseason. It was all part of Geno Auriemma's master plan. The season he'd spent riding his players hard during practice had prepared them mentally and physically for the challenge of tournament play.

"The way Connecticut's run, the way he does things, the way we were designed, in some ways, there's no time for [egos]," Bird said. "He's such a perfectionist, you're not worried about [individual accomplishments]. You want to make plays, and you want to do the right thing, and you just want that to happen so bad, you don't care who gets what.

"He would drill that into us: Make a play. Make a play. Run the plays, but make a play. He was so demanding, had such high expectations, that there's nothing better than doing it right. That's the biggest 'Take that!' ever. And he loves that. He wants you to have that. Something he always drilled into us was if he's being hard on you and if you can continually make the plays, that's the best thing for your confidence. You know you're a big-time player if you can do that."

If the second-ranked Huskies were to extend their consecutive run of Big East Tournament titles to seven, they were going to have to draw on all the mental toughness they could summon against top-rated Notre Dame.

Like the Huskies, the Irish entered the tournament final on the strength of five straight impressive victories since their only loss of the season on February 17 at Rutgers. In their two Big East Tournament victories to reach the final, Notre Dame had outscored its opponents by an average of thirty-seven points.

"We are certainly prepared to play Connecticut," McGraw told the media the night before. "I think we've already proven that we are a great team. I think tomorrow's game, win or lose, doesn't change our number one seed [in the NCAA Tournament]. So I don't think that there is anything more that we need to prove."

By contrast, UConn felt it had much to prove. Although the two teams ended the regular season with identical conference records of 15-1, the Irish had been awarded the tournament's top seed by virtue of their January 15 victory over the Huskies in the teams' only regular-season meeting.

This meant that even though the game was to be played on UConn's home court, the Huskies would be relegated to the status of visitors. Notre Dame would wear their gold home jerseys and sit on what was normally UConn's side of the court. The Huskies, for only the second time in a nonexhibition game, would have to wear their road blue uniforms and operate from the visitors' bench.

"It was beyond strange," Bird said. "At least we used our own locker room. They couldn't take that away from us. But having to wear blue on the other bench, yeah, we were pissed. And the only reason we shared [the regular-season title] is because they lost to Rutgers. Otherwise, they would have had it alone.

"But this, the winner was taking it. So we wanted this. We didn't want to end the streak. We didn't want to be that team. We were ready to take back what was ours."

While Bird was making sure her back was in proper working order, freshman Diana Taurasi was going through her pregame routine. By March, Taurasi, the product of Southern California, had overcome the initial shock of living in a real-life snow globe, and was able on this day to settle into her normal activities. After morning shoot-around and film session, Taurasi took a nap, watched some TV, then popped some System of the Down into her portable CD player and headed over to Gampel three hours before the game. But even the carefree freshman knew tonight's game would be different than any of the twenty-nine that came before it.

"It was probably, up to that point for me, the game with the most at stake," Taurasi said. "As a freshman, I knew I had to mind my p's and q's. I think everyone else was feeling the pressure of the game, especially being at home."

As Notre Dame prepared to leave its hotel in Manchester, some fifteen miles west of UConn's campus, McGraw too was discovering, even before her team took the court, that this would be no ordinary night. The storm had created enough havoc on the roads to make travel treacherous, forcing the large Irish contingent to make a contingency plan.

"We called the NCAA to see if we would be allowed to take parents with us on our bus, because we didn't want anybody driving," McGraw said. "So we jammed the bus. I never would let people on the team bus, and we don't talk on the bus, and we had some highlights from the game when we beat them. The whole ride was like destiny. I remember sitting on the bus and not being nervous, but thinking, This is going to be a great game, and really looking forward to getting there and seeing what it was all going to be like.

"I'm sure all the people on the bus were nervous, mainly because they didn't want to do anything wrong, and it was a forty-minute ride from Manchester. So it was kind of a long ride, but we kept showing them good stuff, showing them winning. And we got there in time."

Broadcast on ESPN2, the game would be UConn's second 1-vs.-2 meeting of the season. In December, with another major snowstorm swirling outside, the top-ranked Huskies had knocked off No. 2 Tennessee at the Hartford Civic Center. That was two weeks before Notre Dame, ranked No. 3 at the time, stunned the Huskies and ended their thirty-game winning streak with a sixteen-point victory in South Bend.

As the Irish prepared for the rematch, they had no illusions about what was waiting for them on the court. Unlike the night before, at the height of the storm, when only five thousand people had made it to Gampel, this was to be a full house, and an angry one.

"It felt eerie to me," Niele Ivey said. "I felt that crowd was on our back that entire game, because we did beat them. I really wanted to beat them there. That's what I was thinking. And I knew they were going to come out harder and stronger against us."

In the UConn locker room, Auriemma barely had to say anything. One look at his silently seething players told him they were ready.

Maybe too ready.

"You can sense it," Auriemma said. "A lot of times, you may have to say or do something to get their minds where they need to be. Sometimes you walk into the locker room and you can feel it. It's like every kid in the room had an electrical cord and they were plugged in and the energy was shooting out of them. And you're like, Oh boy, I hope they're not crazy. I hope they don't go out there and just lose their minds because they want to win and kick their ass so bad."

Nobody's engine was running harder than Shea Ralph's. In January, when she had scored only two points and been benched by Auriemma, she'd taken the loss personally, and had carried that burden for the next six weeks.

"Going into that game, I thought we were going to kill them," Ralph said. "I didn't even think it was going to be a game, and I was intent on making it that way. I couldn't even see straight, I was so ready to play that game. I wanted to kick their butts so bad. In my mind, I was thinking this was going to be ugly for them."

As game time approached, both coaches went over their last bits of strategy. In the Notre Dame locker room, McGraw prepared her team for the onslaught they were about to experience and discussed how best to counter it.

"Having beaten them [in January], we were thinking, They're going to come at us with everything they have now," McGraw said. "Maybe they hadn't been playing well in January, but now we're both at the top of our games, and they're ready for us. And maybe we had caught them a little by surprise, they didn't expect that we'd ever beat them, and now they're ready for us.

"We talked about their pressure and that we wanted to go to Ruth. That was the biggest thing. We wanted to get Ruth and Alicia on the same side of floor as much as we could. Just get the ball down into Ruth. That was the game plan for every game, but we felt that if they were going to press us, our best chance was to go to Ruth at the end of the press."

Ruth Riley was a hot topic of conversation on the UConn side as well.

"Coach had a game plan and we did it over and over," Bird said. "It was defensively, how we were going to trap Ruth and rotate. They killed us with that at Notre Dame. And on offense, it was how we were going to attack that zone. That zone was a pain in the ass. How could we find the weak spots? And I remember we worked on that even before we were going to play them. We were working on that for a long time."

Ivey remembered that one of McGraw's final words of advice was to ignore the crowd. Treat Gampel like a neutral court. Easier said than done.

Maybe it was the significance of the game. Maybe the snowstorm had limited other entertainment options. Whatever the reason, for one of the rare times for a women's game on campus, the student section was out in full force. Historically, their contributions had been limited to the men's home games. This time, especially with the UConn team residing on the bench closest to their end-zone enclave, the students set the tone for a fully engaged audience.

"The students were the best," Bird said. "I remember during the Notre Dame introductions, they'd have newspapers in front of their faces, ignoring them, and when they'd announce, 'At center, Ruth Riley . . .' they'd yell 'SUCKS!' and then they'd put the newspapers back up. We were right there. That, I remember."

The UConn women's fan base has long had the reputation—mocked by some, admired by others—of being composed primarily of grandparents and grandchildren, a genteel group that adores its girls, takes in forty-point blowouts with aplomb, and lacks the killer instinct most often seen in the UConn men's crowds.

But the women's fans are a fiercely loyal following, a fan base the UConn media jokingly refers to as "the blue-haired jihad" for its combination of age and enthusiasm; a group that flooded the *Hartford Courant* mail room after columnist Jeff Jacobs chastised Nykesha Sales and the "gift basket" in 1998 that gave her the school scoring record.

Jacobs dismissively referred to Nykesha as "Soupy Sales" for contributing to the mockery of the sport, and the result was the most intense public backlash the paper had ever seen, before or since, culminating with a death threat called into Jacobs's home. So many letters of protest flooded in that the *Courant* ran a special section devoted solely to printing all the hate mail.

They had braved the snowstorm in December to fill the Civic Center for the Tennessee game, and five thousand fans had ignored the pleas of the governor to stay

Table 1. Starting Player Lineups, Coaches, and Game Officials, Big East Women's Tournament Final, March 6, 2001

CONNECTICUT (27-2; NO. 2 SEED)

POSITION	PLAYER	HEIGHT, CLASS RANKING	POINTS PER GAME	REBOUNDS PER GAME
F	Asjha Jones	6-2, junior	8.4	5.1
F	Swin Cash	6-2, junior	12.4	6.9
G	Diana Taurasi	6-0, freshman	10.5	2.8
G	Sue Bird	5-9, junior	10.1	5.2
G	Shea Ralph	6-0, senior	9.7	4.0

Head coach: Geno Auriemma, 16th season (420-97)

NOTRE DAME (28-1; NO. 1 SEED)

POSITION	PLAYER	HEIGHT, CLASS RANKING	POINTS PER GAME	REBOUNDS PER GAME
F	Ericka Haney	6-1, junior	11.5	5.4
F	Kelley Siemon	6-2, senior	10.9	7.2
C	Ruth Riley	6-5, senior	17.6	7.5
G	Alicia Ratay	5-11, sophomore	13.0	5.0
G	Niele Ivey	5-8, senior	12.2	6.9

Head coach: Muffet McGraw, 19th season (404-157)
Game officials: Dennis DeMayo, Lisa Mattingly, Angie Lewis

off the roads on semifinal Monday to see the roof leak and the Huskies rout Rutgers.

Now, despite the continuing poor driving conditions and the fact that the game will be broadcast on ESPN2, another ten thousand fans have filled Gampel to capacity and, along with the students, they have brought their A game to the proceedings. Notre Dame is the home team in name only as the crowd rises in unison for the jump ball—a UConn tradition that will see them stand and clap until the first UConn basket is scored. They are loud, and after what happened in South Bend on January 15, they want blood.

"It was at a crescendo right at this moment," the *Cou-*

rant's Matt Eagan said. "At that point, there was, between a fan base and a team, there was such a union of affection. And it always seemed that way when there were opportunities for the fans to show how much they cared about this team. They were into it. There was a heightened sense of what this game was, and you could feel it. So there was this sense of something special ready to happen."

2

First Half

0–0, 20:00 remaining

Notre Dame wins the opening tip and goes to Ruth Riley on its first possession, but unlike in the January game in South Bend, Riley cannot take quick advantage, fumbling the entry pass at the top of the key and losing the ball, with Shea Ralph swooping in to make the game's first steal.

Now it's UConn's turn to reveal a little stage fright. Ralph feeds the ball to Bird, who starts the Huskies on a fast break. But Bird, perhaps a bit anxious, perhaps a bit stiff in her first minute of action since Sunday's quarterfinal, throws a lead pass meant for Taurasi deep into Notre Dame territory; the freshman isn't ready for it and the ball bounces harmlessly out of bounds.

Auriemma might be coaching in unfamiliar territory, situated as he is along the visitors' bench at Gampel Pavilion, but he is still the same man with the same Philly personality, and he reacts to Bird's turnover with his patented incredulous laugh.

The Irish take over and go right back to Riley in the low post. This time, the big center handles the entry pass flawlessly and is in perfect position to make her patented low-post move against Jones, who at 6-foot-2 is giving away three inches. Riley gives a quick shoulder shake to the right, then the hard spin to the left, and Jones is helpless to stop the layup. Notre Dame leads 2–0.

At the other end, the Huskies look to return the favor, hoping to draw the big center into early foul trouble just as they had done a little more than a year earlier at the Civic Center. And when Cash makes her post-up move into Riley's chest, a whistle sounds, eliciting a cheer from the Gampel crowd.

But things are not what they seem. Cash has taken an extra step in her attempt to power her way past Riley, also three inches her superior, and has been called for traveling. That makes two turnovers in two possessions for the Huskies, hardly the emphatic opening statement they are looking for seven weeks after South Bend.

The Irish continue to pound into the low post, feeding Riley the ball for a third straight possession. After spinning to her right for her first basket, Riley changes it up for her second. The Huskies have made the tactical decision not to double-team Riley, leaving her to make any move she wants against her shorter defender. This time, Riley fakes to her left then turns back to the right and shoots a fallaway over Jones, nailing the jumper for a 4–0 lead.

The last time Riley had faced the Huskies in the state of Connecticut was the previous February at the Civic Center. That afternoon, Kelly Schumacher and a swarm of double-teaming guards had frustrated her into a miserable game, with more fouls and turnovers than points.

"It's funny, in the four years she was at Notre Dame, the previous three years, we just destroyed them because she couldn't handle the physical play and the way we attacked her," Auriemma said. "Swin, Tamika, and Asjha weren't big enough to handle her, and a lot of our success came from swarming at her from all over. We had guys who were just as big and guys quicker and more athletic than her, and she struggled with all that.

"And to her credit, whatever happened that year, whether it was a coaching move or something she did, they handled the double-teams better, she didn't get frazzled as easily, she stayed within herself and kept her composure, and it made it very difficult to defend her one-on-one, and if you doubled, they were good enough that someone else was going to be open."

It was from the ashes of that February afternoon that Riley rose to the pinnacle of her sport. With the help of assistant coach Carol Owens, whose responsibility was improving the post players, Riley spent the summer of 2000 refining a post-up move she learned from watching NBA star Shaquille O'Neal, using her upper body to fake one way, then spinning the other way toward the basket.

"I was never the most talented and Carol was a very demanding coach," Riley said. "We did a lot of technical stuff. She really drove me to become a better player. As a post player, especially in high school, you don't have a lot of good position coaches. There aren't many high school coaches that played the post position and can teach you how to become a post player. She worked with me every day and continued to push me. Coach McGraw was always a steady teacher and Carol was the one that drove me in the post.

"It depended on whether I was single covered or doubled. I think as I became double-teamed more frequently, it was splitting the double before it got there. Coach didn't want me dribbling at all, if possible. So it was trying to figure out how to get a shot off over a single defender, so I would shake one way and go the other. I worked a lot with Coach Owens the first couple of years, and after that it was a lot of me working in the gym, a lot of repetition. I think that was how you get better, moving in both directions, and by my senior year I was able to go both ways, on either block."

Perhaps more important, Riley learned to avoid spinning out of control when facing double-teams. With Siemon working as a cutter and Ratay spotting for threes, Riley made herself a bigger threat by passing out of the double teams to the open teammate.

"Throughout my career, I'm the kind of player that

was going to recognize my weaknesses and try to work on them," Riley said. "And turning the ball over and being foul prone were definitely two of them. To be effective at what I was doing, and with a lot of the offense going through me, I needed to be as efficient as possible. Learning how to pass out of the double-team and making me more effective was definitely something that I worked on. And I had a great connection with Kelley and some of the other players, where they were going to be when they spotted up."

Riley also continued to develop a strong bond with Ivey, who was responsible for getting the ball to Riley when she was in position to score, utilizing set plays with names like "Power Game" and "Gray."

"We would talk X's and O's," Ivey said. "I wanted to know where she wanted the ball. We had a good working relationship. She would point, if it was a high-low for her, 'Okay, I'm ready now.' She was good at communicating with her hands and letting us know where she wanted it.

"'Power Game' was something where we would screen down and get Ruth a shot on the block. It was something where we had everybody involved. It wasn't a play where everybody stood outside and I just threw it in. It was a continuous play. That was my money play. I knew I could get a high-percentage shot with that play. With 'Gray,' I would pass to the wing and get the ball back and Ruth would dive and be one-on-one on the block."

As Notre Dame's magic 2001 season went on, particularly after the UConn victory in mid-January, Riley was forced to learn a new aspect of the game: handling a national media eager to promote the talented and telegenic center as the new "it girl" of the sport.

But when they were on the court, the Irish did not let the extra attention Riley received off it create a distraction.

"I talked to her all the time," McGraw said. "I would say, 'Ruth, you can't go anywhere. You're 6-5 and everyone knows you. I have people protecting me and you can't. You're going to be mobbed and how can I help you embrace it.' And she handled it. And she loved it. She never let it get to her."

The year before, Riley's increasing public profile had nearly torn the team apart. In the midst of the late-season meltdown that ended with the team's Sweet Sixteen collapse against Texas Tech, one of the Notre Dame coaches suggested to the players that jealousy of Riley's growing popularity had affected the team's performance.

"That hurt me, because one thing I've never been is jealous of my teammates," Ivey said. "That's not who we are. I took that to heart. If that's happening on the team, then that falls back on me. I remember telling her after that, 'I'm one of your biggest fans.' Your teammates have to be your biggest supporters. I wanted her to know that. And I was a big fan. When she was doing USA Basketball, even though it was stuff I wanted to do, I would always say, 'Man, that's awesome.' We're a family."

Trailing 4–0, the Huskies remain determined to counter inside. Again, Cash tries to slither her way around the mountainous Riley. Riley is holding firm, forcing Cash all the way to the baseline but leaving her a tiny sliver of space to put up a shot.

However, Cash's glimpse of the rim is fleeting, and Riley swats her attempt into the hands of Ivey, sending Notre Dame racing the other way for its first fast-break attempt.

Ivey quickly spots Siemon, who has sprinted behind the back line of the UConn defense, and lofts a pass to her over the retreating UConn defenders. Siemon catches the ball in stride and scoops in a lefty layup, all in one motion. Just like that, seventy-five seconds into the rematch, it's all Notre Dame again, 6–0.

A ripple of unease makes its way through the crowd, which is still standing and clapping, waiting for UConn to score before sitting. In three possessions, the Huskies have yet to even put the ball on the rim. Could this be January 15 all over again?

"We wanted to get the ball inside," Taurasi said. "They weren't the deepest team, so we wanted to get it to Asjha and Swin and work inside out, because we knew the threes were going to be there, but we wanted to get Ruth and Siemon and Haney into some kind of foul trouble. Sometimes you try to do something so much, it works against you, and those first few possessions, we really didn't execute."

Notre Dame 6–0, 18:45 remaining

Undaunted by Notre Dame's fast start, the Huskies again attempt to work the ball inside. This time, the ball goes to Jones, pitted against Riley. But instead of taking the ball strong, as Cash had tried twice without success, Jones attempts a fallaway jumper. The ball at least catches some iron, but misses, going out of bounds, possession going again to Notre Dame.

While the shot is the closest UConn has come to scoring thus far, it is not the kind of shot Auriemma wants. Fallaways will never get Riley in foul trouble.

"Go at her!" Auriemma screams from the bench.

"We were a little bit goofy in this particular game," Auriemma said. "Everything was just happening way too fast. For whatever reason, we wanted to hurry up and win the game. It's a big game, you want to win, and your emotions just get the best of you. There wasn't much you could do about it. You end up playing way faster than you want to play.

"Swin gets double-teamed and she takes bad shot after bad shot. That was three possessions in a row where we walked, had a shot blocked, and took a bad shot. You can tell there's not enough patience. You can't take fadeaway jump shots against a kid like [Riley]."

Notre Dame now has a chance to go up eight, maybe nine points, and with it take the "neutral" crowd out of the game early. But Siemon, who had just made a nice athletic play on the fast break, can't convert a runner in the lane—Notre Dame's first miss—and the Huskies control the rebound.

Now the momentum begins to swing the other way. And it is the freshman, Taurasi, so often the sparkplug on offense—especially in the wake of Abrosimova's injury—who gets UConn started.

For the first time in four tries from their half-court set, the Huskies do not look to pound the ball inside. Instead, the ball kicks out to Taurasi, who calmly fires a three-pointer from the right wing, a few feet from the Notre Dame bench, and buries it, cutting the deficit to 6–3 with 17:54 left in the half.

UConn's first field goal sends a charge through the arena, and the pace of the game begins to pick up.

"That's one of those shots that if it doesn't go in, we're like, 'Uh-oh,'" Bird said. "When it goes in, you're like, 'Whew.' The thing that was cool about Dee, she knows what a team needs, when it needs it. That whole year, she knew that she could take over any time she wanted, but she also knew there was a hierarchy, and she fit in where she could. But in this tournament, she knew and she stepped it up."

For the first time since the opening tip, the Notre Dame offense loses a bit of its precision. Siemon takes a pass from Ivey at the foul line and is open, but she hesitates with the ball for a split second, perhaps surprised to find herself alone with the ball in scoring range. Siemon is open because Cash, attempting to double-team Ivey as she brought the ball over half-court, has gotten lost defensively. But inadvertently, this helps UConn retain possession.

Unsure what to do with the ball, Siemon considers a pass to Riley in the post, but for the first time in the game, UConn is doubling the center down low, so that avenue is closed. Instead, Siemon squares up and fires a jumper, but the shot hits the back of the rim with a thud. Taurasi grabs the rebound and gets it to Bird, who pushes the ball upcourt.

Taurasi trails her point guard, who is rushing into the frontcourt along the left sideline. Because of Bird's penetration with the ball, the Notre Dame defense, already in retreat after Siemon's miss, has backed down too far into the paint, leaving Taurasi wide open at the top of the key and Ratay too far away to offer an impediment to a shot.

But despite Taurasi's furtive clapping, demanding the ball, Bird does not see her and instead fumbles the ball out of bounds, a basketball version of an unforced error. Bird falls down as the ball bounces away, but luckily for the Huskies, Siemon touches the ball on its way out, allowing UConn to retain possession.

Bird's second bobble in three minutes is enough for Auriemma, who makes the game's first substitution, removing Bird and Cash in favor of Tamika Williams and Kennitra Johnson, the fastest player on UConn's roster.

And KJ uses her speed to make an immediate contribution, driving along the baseline from the right corner as play resumes, drawing Riley away from Jones to help on a double-team. But as Riley slides down and leaves Jones uncovered, Johnson slips the ball to Jones for a wide-open eight-footer, cutting Notre Dame's lead to 6–5.

The past two possessions, Taurasi has been an agent of good for the Huskies, hitting the three-pointer and grabbing the defensive rebound that led to their second bucket. But now, Taurasi's undisciplined side shows itself.

Haney takes the ball from Ivey on the right wing, with Taurasi defending her. Haney fakes a move to her left and Taurasi bites for it, exposing a path along the baseline that Haney exploits, driving the ball hard to the basket and blowing past Taurasi in the process.

Freed from her defender, Haney pulls up at the edge of the lane for a short jumper. But Taurasi, who has recovered from the fake and now trails Haney as she stops-and-pops, refuses to accept that she is beaten, reaching up for the ball from behind and knocking it away.

A whistle blows. Referee Dennis DeMayo raises one arm, then the other, banging his wrists together. His next move is to extend his outstretched hand toward the scorer's table and hold out three fingers: shooting foul on No. 3, blue team. Taurasi's first foul of the game.

"I don't think she's been as focused on the defensive end as maybe she needs to be," Doris Burke says to Robin Roberts and a worldwide ESPN audience.

Diana Taurasi didn't have to wait until the official start of practice in mid-October 2000 to start playing for Geno

Auriemma. That summer, before Auriemma headed to Sydney, Australia, as an assistant coach for the gold medal–winning U.S. National Team in the Summer Olympics, he coached Taurasi on the U.S. Junior National Team, which would compete in the summer of 2001 for the World Championships in the Czech Republic.

"I got a taste of it," Taurasi said. "He had to be nice to me then."

That would change dramatically once everyone gathered inside Gampel Pavilion that fall. Taurasi arrived in Storrs as the most heralded freshman in the history of the women's game. Perhaps a tad too heralded. Even before she played her first exhibition game with UConn, she found herself at the center of a media brushfire.

In the college basketball preview section of ESPN: The Magazine that October, Taurasi was on the receiving end of a withering assessment of her game—and gamesmanship—by acclaimed sportswriter Sally Jenkins. The Washington Post columnist, who also contributed to ESPN and, perhaps not coincidentally, authored both of Pat Summitt's literary ventures, ripped Taurasi, describing her as "giggly, turnover-prone and lack[ing] a conscience with the ball. Even worse, her ego needs its own zip code."

Certainly, Taurasi was not in need of confidence. Clearly, she had a shooting range unlike anything the game had seen before, and—not lacking for confidence—believed she could score from virtually anywhere on the floor. Yes, she was a fun-loving jokester who drew comparisons in the UConn coaching offices to Eddie Haskell.

1. Ruth Riley (00) and Kelley Siemon (50) are all over Shea
Ralph and the Huskies at a sold-out Joyce Center in mid-January,
as Notre Dame defeats UConn for the first time in twelve tries,
92–76. (Michael McAndrews/*Hartford Courant*)

2. Riley and Swin Cash (32) jump center to start the Big East Tournament championship game at Gampel Pavilion. By virtue of its January victory, Notre Dame is the tournament's top seed, making UConn the "away" team on its home court—complete with road-blue uniforms. (University of Connecticut Division of Athletics)

3. Shea Ralph writhes in pain as trainer Rosemary Ragle places a hand on Ralph's injured left knee late in the first half. After twice tearing her right ACL as a freshman, this final ACL tear ends Ralph's career. In the foreground, Cash realizes her teammate's fate and bows in despair. (Michael McAndrews/ *Hartford Courant*)

4. Sue Bird, referee Angie Lewis, and the Gampel crowd all give the signal: Bird's half-court bomb at the halftime buzzer is good, giving UConn a six-point lead and an emotional boost after Ralph's injury. (Michael McAndrews/*Hartford Courant*)

5. Hurting Huskies: All-American Svetlana Abrosimova, *left*, saw her UConn career end with a foot injury in February. Ralph, her injured left leg immobilized, is also out for the season, putting Geno Auriemma's guarantee of back-to-back titles in jeopardy. (University of Connecticut Division of Athletics)

6. Ruth Riley transformed herself into the national player of the year in 2001, in part by learning how to effectively handle double-teams, like this one from UConn's Tamika Williams (34) and Asjha Jones (15). (Michael McAndrews/*Hartford Courant*)

7. Diana Taurasi lifts a triumphant Bird into the air
as the celebration begins after Bird's coast-to-coast
basket at the buzzer gives UConn a 78–76 victory in
the Big East Tournament championship game.
(Jay L. Clendenin/*Hartford Courant*)

8. Arch rivals? UConn coach
Geno Auriemma, *center,* and
Notre Dame coach Muffet
McGraw, *right*—longtime friends
from Philadelphia—share a
laugh with Robin Roberts on
ESPN's pregame show before
their national semifinal
showdown in St. Louis.
(University of Connecticut
Division of Athletics)

9. Bird looks to pass the ball after being stopped along the baseline by Riley in the second half of the national semifinals. Notre Dame stopped UConn cold in the second half, outscoring the Huskies by twenty-seven points to win 90–75 and advance to the championship game. (University of Connecticut Division of Athletics)

10. Niele Ivey grimaces after turning her ankle on this second-half collision with Diana Taurasi, who shot 1-for-15 in UConn's semifinal loss. Ivey, who overcame two knee injuries in her career, would recover and go on to win the national championship in her hometown of St. Louis two nights later against Purdue. (Michael McAndrews/*Hartford Courant*)

And like any freshman, she would make mistakes, committing more turnovers per minute than any of the regulars on the 2001 team.

"There were a lot of battles," Auriemma said. "With all of her talent and god-given ability and the way she plays the game, it almost was like a young pitcher who throws 98 and comes into the Majors and can't find the strike zone and doesn't care. 'I'm just going to throw it as hard as I can and I don't care where it goes'—just undisciplined and not caring about being disciplined.

"Coaching her was easy and it was hard. It was easy because she could do things that you didn't have to coach. And it was hard because you're trying to coach her into understanding there's more to this game than who makes the last three, and how much fun it is. And thinking that winning is easy."

But the characterization by Jenkins, written before Taurasi had even played a college game, seemed wholly unfair. Taurasi would go on to commit seventy-two turnovers as freshman, not because of an outsized ego but because of a desire to create scoring opportunities for teammates unprepared for her array of no-look passes.

What bothered Taurasi and the coaching staff even more about the article was that Taurasi had never even spoken to Jenkins.

"I'd never met the lady," Taurasi said. "I was taken aback, because for someone that I'd never talked to or met, those were some strong words. Everyone has their own opinion, and she's a Tennessee gal, so it's all good.

It only gets to you if it's true. She said that, but it didn't bother me, because I knew it wasn't true. All my teammates, people I had played with, they knew I wasn't like that."

In fact, Taurasi's new teammates couldn't wait to see what kind of dynamic she would bring to the defending national champions. Auriemma always hopes his incoming freshmen will push the veterans in practice, to keep the older players on their toes. Not a problem with Taurasi.

"She had that thing about her where you're like, Are you serious?" Ralph said. "Talking to the refs and laughing and making thirty-footers in somebody's face. She just had that thing where you knew she was special and she didn't back down from anything. She came right in, was like, 'I'm here,' and that was good. We needed that.

"For me, I just wanted to be a good teammate. I wanted her to see how, when she was a senior, how to treat the freshmen, to continue Connecticut tradition. In order for young guys to do that, they need to be taught by the older guys how to do it. She was really special. I was kind of amazed, around the middle of the year, that I was still in the starting lineup. She was really special and brought a lot to the team. Those kind of players don't come around very often."

What teammates and coaches also knew was that for all her abundant talent, Taurasi was very much a freshman, prone to mistakes more costly than turnovers. By the time of the Big East final, Taurasi had already fouled out of three games, including the only two games UConn had lost. Taurasi's penchant for committing bad fouls had become blackboard material throughout the Big East.

"I would try to go at her because she would make mistakes on defense," Ivey said. "Defense was the one area that she had to get better at. We definitely tried to challenge her, because she was a freshman and she was going to have off-nights."

The foul against Haney in the opening minutes of the Big East final is Exhibit A.

"That was a dumb, freshman, stupid foul by Diana Taurasi," Auriemma said. "That kid isn't going to make that shot. Why foul her? And even if she does make it, what does two points matter at this point in the game if it keeps you in the game a little bit longer?

"I've always said your greatest strength is your greatest weakness. Her greatest strength is her emotion. That's why she'll get hit with a technical, or if her man gets by her, she'll smack 'em in the back of the head, because her passion and emotion just takes over. She's not content to just get a layup. She wants to go in and elbow you in the face and make the layup, and then get an offensive foul call and scream at the ref."

Eight years later, Bird will say of her good friend, Olympic teammate, and fellow WNBA All-Star that foul trouble is the only thing preventing Taurasi from going down as the greatest women's player ever, a title Taurasi may likely claim regardless.

"She takes risks," Bird said. "Dee doesn't get that her

presence alone is enough to scare people [into thinking] that they're not going to make that shot. They're going to think she's going for it. The thing is, Dee's a really good shot-blocker, so you don't want to take it away from her completely. You have to pick and choose."

Even Taurasi, in direct contradiction of Jenkins's assessment, admits that she still had much to learn in 2001.

"I could have been a little more disciplined," Taurasi said. "In reality, that's what we would always do: we would force them baseline and make them take a tough shot. And I would always think that I could block it. I still want to block it all the time. I'm a natural shot-blocker. I've learned to pick and choose. I had to learn how to be more disciplined. Not always go for the home-run pass. As a freshman, I wouldn't even think about making a 50-50 pass. Now, it has to be 80-20. Those are the little things you learn as a freshman, especially with Coach, who wants everything to be perfect."

Notre Dame 6–5, 17:09 remaining

As a result of Taurasi's foul, Haney goes to the free-throw line for two shots. But Haney misses both and the second is rebounded by Williams, giving the Huskies a chance to take their first lead.

The Huskies go right back to attacking Riley inside. Jones gets the ball in the post, figuring to go at Riley as Auriemma had demanded moments earlier. But Jones gets some unintended help to clear a path to the basket.

As Jones takes the entry pass, Ratay slides over from

her position at the top of the zone to double-team. But what she actually does is set a pick for Jones, screening Riley away from the ball handler and leaving the diminutive Ratay alone against Jones, who does not hesitate, scoring over Ratay to give the Huskies a 7–6 lead at the seventeen-minute mark, their first lead of the game.

After scoring their first two baskets, UConn had applied token pressure to Notre Dame's guards in the backcourt, allowing Ivey to bring the ball up with minimal difficulty. Now, after scoring for the third time and taking the lead, Auriemma calls for full-court pressure, forcing Riley to help handle the ball in the backcourt rather than setting up camp under the UConn basket.

The ball eventually makes its way to Ivey, but she is forced to advance the ball across midcourt along the left sideline, with Williams riding her the entire way. Under such pressure, Ivey never notices Ralph rushing at her. Catching Ivey unaware, Ralph pokes the ball away, then tracks it down in the corner by the UConn bench.

Ralph quickly wheels around and starts UConn's first fast break of the night. Ralph feeds Taurasi in the middle, then Diana passes to Williams under the basket, where Riley has no choice but to foul, picking up her first with 16:39 left.

But Williams misses both of her free throws and Ivey pushes the rebound ahead to Haney with position on Taurasi. This time, Taurasi plays solid fundamental defense and Haney misses the shot, the ball going out of bounds off UConn.

The follow-up possession goes even worse for Notre Dame. Siemon was the X factor in Notre Dame's victory in South Bend, but facing a hostile crowd at Gampel Pavilion, she's having her problems.

After taking the inbounds pass at the top of the key, Siemon dribbles toward the lane, then stops to pass back out to Riley. But as Siemon lets the ball go, Riley starts to move down the lane and the ball sails untouched into the backcourt, where Jeneka Joyce touches it for a violation.

Taurasi then makes Notre Dame pay dearly for its mistake, taking a pass at the top of the key a good five feet behind the three-point circle and firing. The ball lands with a thud on the front of the rim but takes a shooter's bounce off the backboard and in.

UConn now leads 10–6, having scored ten straight points, and they get a chance for more when Ivey, pressured by Ralph and Williams in the backcourt, dribbles the ball off her foot out of bounds at the 15:59 mark, triggering a TV time-out.

"One thing I remember is that we turned the ball over a lot because of their press," Ivey said. "The way we were turning the ball over and missing easy shots, it was uncharacteristic of us that year, because we usually were so sharp. We didn't look as sharp as we normally did. No matter what generation, they're going to bring the heat defensively. UConn, they bring the pressure, full-court pressure, and it seemed like they stepped it up this game."

The time-out allows the crowd to fully express itself, the noise inside Gampel growing to its loudest point thus far. There's more to cheer about on the other side of the time-out: UConn runs a play under the Notre Dame basket that results in Jones knocking down a foul-line jumper eight seconds into the possession for a 12–6 lead.

"We must have worked on this set all week long," Taurasi said. "Out of bounds against the 2-3 zone, we worked on this all week. Pop them out, screen them in, Tamika pins the middle guy, throw it in [to Jones]. Coach just breaks down a defense. In the zone, you had to be calculated in spacing and where to cut and who to screen. So basically, we would bring Tamika outside to screen for Shea. Then I would pop out and they would cheat out to cover Shea. Then Tamika would pin the middle man and [the inbounder] has the option of Asjha, Kennitra on the far side, or me."

So far, the options have been Taurasi, with six points on a pair of three-pointers, and Jones with three baskets in the low post. Combined, they have put together a 12–0 run to counter Notre Dame's six-point start, making it clear that there will be no repeat of the January debacle.

"That might have been one of the things that helped us, was them jumping out to a six-point lead," Auriemma said. "Had we gone up 10–0, we may have used up all of our emotion and energy, and then they would have made a run and it would have brought us back down. Looking back, they get the six right away, and we're like, Okay, let's calm down, one possession at a time, and boom, boom, boom, next thing you know, we go on a run and everybody's throwing counterpunches and no knockout punches are being thrown."

But just as UConn appears poised for an early knockout, Notre Dame responds. Again facing full-court pressure off a made basket, Notre Dame struggles to get the ball over half-court, with Joyce barely able to corral a high pass from Ivey at the midcourt line that Williams briefly gets a hand on.

But with the ball finally back in Ivey's hands, the Irish run their best half-court set since the opening minute. Ivey passes left to Ratay, with UConn settling into its defense. Lost in the defense, however, is Taurasi, who tangles with Siemon as Ratay dribbles toward the middle, then remains on the strong side of the court while Joyce slides unnoticed—except by Ratay—into the corner on the weak side. By the time Taurasi realizes she's out of position, it's too late to race across the lane and bother Joyce's shot, which she bangs in for a three, cutting UConn's lead to 12–9.

Taurasi compounds the mistake by trying to answer with her own three and leaves it short, allowing Notre Dame to advance the ball without pressure. The result is the first attempted post-up by Riley in almost four minutes, and she easily scores on Jones to make it 12–11.

But Jones, off to a terrific start at the offensive end, takes it right back at Riley, splitting a double team from Riley and Ivey, losing the ball momentarily, then regaining it and shooting in one motion with four gold jerseys surrounding her to give UConn a 14–11 lead.

"If I'm Geno Auriemma," Burke shouts, "I like to show her the first five minutes of this ballgame and say 'Asjha, please do this every single night, because you have the skills to do it.'"

Siemon gets fouled at the other end and makes both to cut the lead to one point again. At this point, Bird returns to the game, replacing Taurasi but leaving Johnson in. KJ rewards Auriemma's trust by nailing a three-pointer from the left elbow for a 17–13 lead.

UConn's pressure defense almost forces another steal, but Ralph, who knocks the ball free from Joyce, is called for her first foul. Ivey then draws the first foul on Bird, which in turn draws a sharp rebuke for the point guard from Auriemma, who calls a twenty-second time-out with 14:04 left, allowing him more time to chew Bird out.

Out of the time-out, Notre Dame goes back to Siemon, who takes Cash off the dribble for a layup, knocking Shea to the floor with an elbow in the process. It was the kind of takedown that would have made Siemon's father, former Minnesota Vikings linebacker Jeff Siemon, proud.

But Ralph and Cash get instant revenge, with Shea threading a perfect entry pass through three Notre Dame defenders to Cash, whose quick lefty spin leaves Riley flat-footed and allows for a layup and a 19–15 lead with 13:29 left.

Notre Dame tries quickly to get Ruth a post-up, but

Jones disrupts the entry pass, forcing Ruth to her knees to retrieve the ball. Down among the little people, Riley fights with a diving Ralph for possession. Riley wins the battle and passes the ball back out, but the entire sequence takes place with Riley's knees planted on the blue paint of the lane, and she is called for a three-second violation.

During the stoppage in play, Taurasi returns, giving Jones her first rest with 13:17 left. The move gives UConn a three-guard look with Cash and Williams inside. The new look also spreads out Notre Dame's 2-3 zone, allowing Bird to drive the middle for a pull-up jumper that puts UConn up 21–15. But the smaller lineup also opens up opportunities for Notre Dame, as Siemon makes an easy layup at the other end, cutting the deficit to 21–17.

Cash, who had made good on a post-up moments earlier, tries again deep on the left block. In the game's opening minutes, this move resulted in a Riley block. Now, with Ivey coming to double, Cash gets a similar result, the ball hitting short of the rim with Riley easily rebounding and starting Notre Dame the other way.

With the UConn defense unable to reset quickly enough off the miss, Ratay, the nation's top three-point shooter, is left wide open to cut the lead to 21–20.

Their inside game not working as well with Jones out, UConn goes back to letting Bird create at the top of the key, and she again finds the weak spot in the zone, driving just inside the foul line and pulling up for a twelve-foot jumper and a 23–20 lead.

"That's what [Auriemma] told us," Bird said. "'Do that all night.'"

Bird has been making the pull-up jumper in the lane since her earliest days. Her ability to score off the dribble makes Bird a unique double threat as a scoring point guard.

"One of the major differences between men's and women's basketball is the ability to break people down off the dribble, and she could do it," Eagan said. "She could always get her shot. And then you spread her out all over the court and it's even more difficult to stop her.

From the moment she arrived in Storrs in the fall of 1998, Sue Bird was thrust into a world of sky-high expectations. Bird's incoming freshman class was touted as the best—and most diverse—of Auriemma's career. Bird and Walters were the guards, while Swin Cash, Tamika Williams, and Asjha Jones manned the post. Of the five, Bird was considered the lowest-ranked—at seventeenth—in the national recruiting surveys. The other four were considered top-ten prospects.

Such a collection of talent begged for a nickname. Some called them the Fem Five, a play on the great Michigan men's class of the early 1990s, led by Chris Webber, Juwan Howard, and Jalen Rose and self-titled the Fab Five.

But a borrowed nickname wasn't good enough for Cash, the 6-foot-2 forward from Pittsburgh with the athleticism of a track star and the looks and charisma of a supermodel. Cash took the first letters of their first names (Tamika, Asjha, Sue, Swin, and Keirsten) and dubbed them the TASSK Force.

The task facing them as they arrived on campus as freshmen for the 1998–99 season was simple: return the Huskies to the Final Four for the first time since 1996.

But the plan was derailed early on. After playing eight rather pedestrian games to open her career, averaging just 5.1 points and 3.1 assists, Bird was running in a practice on December 14 when she came to a sudden stop.

As her left foot planted, her knee wrenched violently and she fell to the ground. The diagnosis was unforgiving. Bird's season was over: she had torn her ACL. Even worse, because she had already played in eight games, she was not eligible to redshirt. The entire season was a loss.

But as painful as the experience was for Bird, the lessons it taught her proved invaluable. In the two months prior to the injury, Bird had done little to establish herself as a player, either in practice or in games, her passivity limiting her potential. Auriemma called her "Suzy the Cruiser," an unflattering portrayal of a player failing to push herself hard enough.

"I think it was in part my personality," Bird said. "When I would enter a situation, I would like to stand back a little bit and assess the situation. And with college basketball, with my position and the expectations, there was no time for that. I wasn't really living up to my potential. Cruiser is the right word, because I was just there. I wasn't the worst player in the world, but I wasn't doing anything, either.

"I think that injury was a wake-up call and brought a lot of things to the forefront. I didn't have basketball in my life for the first time since I was six. It was a wake-up call in that regard, and I also got to watch and learn by seeing and realizing what it took. And the minute I was able to play again, I vowed never to be in a situation where I regretted it. I look back on the games that I did play, and in a way I regret the way I did play, because I know I could have done a lot more. I mean, it's hard when you're a freshman. You don't know any better. But I vowed that I would never want to play that way again."

Further motivating Bird were the expectations placed on the team as she entered her sophomore season. With Ralph a full year removed from her two knee injuries and Svetlana Abrosimova establishing herself as one of the top scoring threats in the nation, the Huskies were installed as the preseason No. 1.

Only one question mark about the team remained.

"I remember there was a Street and Smith [magazine] thing where they said, 'Connecticut's good, they have this, they have that, but the one question is at the point guard spot," Bird said. "It was directed at me. That was the big question mark of the team. I wanted to take away all those question marks. That's what drove me.

"I played in a handful of games [as a freshman] and whether it was the coaches, my teammates, the fans, the

people who saw us on TV, I felt like they based everything they thought of me on those games. I knew that
wasn't me. So at the start of my sophomore year, I had
a lot to prove."

Bird started strong in her sophomore season, register-
ing a career high ten assists in the season's third game,
against Old Dominion. But the true breakthrough game
was in Knoxville in early January.

The Lady Vols had handed UConn its first loss of
the 1998–99 season at Gampel Pavilion, largely because
Walters, whose career would end prematurely because
of various injuries, struggled in Bird's absence, going
3-for-14 from the field as Tennessee dared her to shoot
in a 92–81 loss.

Bird would have no such difficulties at Thompson-
Boling Arena, hitting eight of ten shots from the field
and scoring twenty-five points, the second-highest total
of her UConn career. And the points did not come easy:
at one point she was sandwiched by a pair of Tennessee
defenders and had to come out of the game briefly. But
when it mattered most, Bird was the word. With UConn
clinging to a 55–50 lead, Bird drained a pair of three-
pointers and hit a tough pull-up in the lane to push
UConn's lead to eleven points. Bird also held Tennessee guard Kristin "Ace" Clement scoreless and forced
her into seven turnovers.

"There was a point in time where our team had to make
a decision," Auriemma told the media. "We had watched
as our lead went from thirteen to twelve to eleven and

right on down, and I asked them if we were going to let them take it away from us.

"Sue Bird is the kind of kid who wants that responsibility. She loves the pressure. She loves the intensity of the game. That's when she's at her best. But like everybody else, she has to go through the process before you believe it."

The process was something that went on behind the scenes. Before she came to UConn, Bird had watched an HBO documentary about the 1997 Tennessee team that had lost ten games but still won the championship. One thing that stuck out for her in the program was how much abuse Tennessee's point guard, Abby Conklin, took from Coach Pat Summitt over things that, on the surface, weren't Conklin's fault. Bird found herself laughing at Conklin's misfortune.

But Bird was not laughing when Auriemma called her into his office before the start of her sophomore season and gave her the same ultimatum that Conklin received in Knoxville.

"Coach Auriemma, obviously he's one of a kind and has a unique ability to manipulate," Bird said. "It sounds harsh, but he knows what buttons to push and he pushes them in the best ways possible. I remember sitting in his office and he asked me if I was ready. And I'm like, 'Yeah, of course, I'm ready, I can't wait to get back.' And he said, 'Okay, everything that goes wrong is your fault. Are you ready to accept that responsibility?'

"He definitely lived up to that. There's no doubt that

my experiences here, starting even before the injury, have shaped me as a player and as a person, how I am in my everyday life. A lot of that is because of Coach Auriemma and the rest of the coaching staff."

By the end of the 2000 season, Bird had not only quieted the doubters, she had evoked a new line of questioning from them: how high in the 2002 WNBA draft would she go? Bird won the Nancy Lieberman-Cline Award as the nation's top point guard and propelled the Huskies into the national championship game by thoroughly outplaying the other top point guard in the nation, Penn State's Helen Darling, in the semifinals, hitting five three-pointers and scoring nineteen points.

"Sue was tough," Ralph said. "She was a lot tougher than me, in her own way. She came back from a lot, too. I have so much respect and admiration for Sue. She came back and she came back even better and played such an invaluable role on the team, in so many ways.

"I know how hard it is to come back from that injury and become an even better player. The player that is that tough and mentally strong and physically strong and that determined to do that, they're few and far between."

Often, the only player who was capable of stopping Bird was Bird herself.

"As a player, I liked to get my teammates involved and do the right thing," Bird said. "It's a balance between doing that and being aggressive, and I always leaned towards the team side. But at the same time, if the game was on the line or the shot clock was running down, or we're in a big game, something clicks. That's always how I've been. I wake up all of a sudden."

UConn 23–20, 12:10 remaining

Nearly eight minutes into the game, both teams are shooting lights-out. UConn is 10-for-14 from the field (71 percent) while Notre Dame is 8-for-11 (73 percent). Riley makes it 9-for-12 with a spin move around Williams for a layup and a foul. But Riley, who is now 4-for-4 from the field, misses the free throw that would have tied the score, and Ralph nails a three-pointer at the other end for a 26–22 UConn lead.

Bird pumps her fists in celebration at the sight of Ralph's three ripping through the net, but that was just the warm-up for UConn's fifth-year senior. After Joyce misses a three-pointer in the corner, Shea releases ahead of the field and takes a long lead pass from Bird to give UConn a 28–22 lead with a 11:15 left, prompting a twenty-second timeout from McGraw.

Ratay stops the bleeding with another three, and the game enters its first ragged period. Jones, back in the game, misses a jumper from the foul line, leading to a Notre Dame break. But Ivey, driving into a triple-team, can't connect on a layup, and UConn comes storming back. Bird pulls up for a three-pointer and front-rims it, giving both teams three straight misses after combining to make 21 of 29 shots to start the game.

It appears Ratay will make it four misses in a row as Taurasi blocks her layup attempt out of bounds. But referee Lisa Mattingly blows her whistle and Taurasi has picked up her second foul with 10:24 remaining.

As Ratay makes the first free throw, McGraw takes Riley out of the game. In the January game, Riley played all forty minutes, but because of the tournament format, this is both teams' third game in three nights, and with a TV time-out automatically coming up once Ratay makes the second free throw, the move will give Riley an extra few moments of rest.

But Ratay misses the second free throw and the game continues on without Notre Dame's big weapon. But even with UConn center Kelly Schumacher replacing Taurasi and her two fouls, UConn cannot take immediate advantage.

Johnson misses a three and Siemon rebounds. At the other end, Ivey and Ratay work a perfect backdoor play, with Ivey leaving Johnson flat-footed and scoring the layup that ties the score at 28–28 with 9:54 left, prompting another twenty-second time-out from Auriemma.

The time-out affords McGraw an opportunity to put Riley back in but she chooses to keep her center on the bench, and now UConn attacks inside. Ralph drives the lane from the right wing, takes a swipe from Ivey, and hits a short pull-up as the whistle blows. Ralph makes the free throw for a 31–28 lead and the whistle blows again, this time to signal the twelve-minute TV time-out with 9:38 remaining.

With the Huskies back in front, the Gampel crowd has

roared back to life, and with eight straight points scored, so has UConn's vocal and emotional leader.

"We depended a lot on Svet and Shea, especially Shea," Bird said. "With Shea, we looked to her for everything. I remember before that year, she could have left [for the WNBA]. And I remember all of us being like, 'Oh my god, I can't imagine Shea not being here. What are we going to do?' We depended a lot on her, maybe almost too much.'"

Diana Taurasi credited Shea Ralph with having influenced her decision to come to UConn. But barely into her first week of official practices, Ralph had Taurasi wondering what she had gotten herself into.

"We had this drill where Coach would throw it off the bubble [covering the rim] and you had to rebound it," Taurasi said. "And we would compete against each other. So he throws it and I grab it as I'm falling out of bounds. I chuck it off Shea, so it goes out of bounds off her, and it hits her right in the stomach.

"She gave me this look. And I'm like, 'I'm going to get my ass kicked on the next possession.' So he throws it up and boom, forearm to my chest. I didn't go for a rebound the rest of the day. She throws the forearm, then smiles, 'You okay, Dee?' I could barely see."

Ralph's unbridled competitive spirit and physical nature made her an instant fan favorite in Storrs. She played the blue-collar game much like that famous blond-haired baller from Indiana did for Boston. And like Larry Bird, Ralph did it despite playing with a debilitating injury.

Bird's back never stopped him from diving into the crowd for a loose ball, never kept him from backing down an opponent, and Ralph played the same way. When a player from Hampton University tried mixing it up with Ralph toward the end of a first-round NCAA Tournament game in 2000, Ralph answered with a body block that sent her challenger sprawling. End of confrontation.

Messing with Ralph in the month of March (or April) was never a good idea. The year before, in the only NCAA title game she would play in, Ralph scored 15 points on 7-for-8 shooting, handed out 7 assists, made 6 steals, and thoroughly embarrassed Tennessee by scoring on backdoor layup after backdoor layup.

"She was always able to dial it up at the end of the year," Auriemma said. "That's what the great, great competitors do. They just find a way at the end of the year. No matter how much she was struggling, no matter what was going through her mind and her body, Big East Tournament time, that's the start of Tournament Shea. 'It's my time now.' She was able to do that in the biggest games."

Tournament Shea. Originally coined by Ralph's fellow senior Marci Czel, the phrase reappeared at the onset of the 2001 Big East Tournament. After ending the regular season with 44 points, 15 rebounds, and 14 assists in her final three games, Ralph put up a 16-5-5 line against Boston College in the quarterfinals. Against Rutgers, she scored just 6 points but had 7 rebounds and 7 assists, the latter matching her season high.

"I'm very competitive and those are my favorite times of year," Ralph said. "Any kind of championship we could win, I wanted to win. I had a couple of years where I couldn't play in them, so there was that sense of urgency. I love tournaments, I can't lie about that."

Now, seeking redemption against Notre Dame after her January benching in South Bend, Ralph has taken over the tournament final, scoring UConn's last eight points, including the three-point play for a 31–28 lead.

"To this day, I don't think I played with anybody who could complete a three-point play the way she could," Bird said. "I don't think I will, either. Drawing the contact, body control, she goes into you and boom, and still has enough to put it in. So strong.

"She was ready. I do remember once the tournament started, Shea was playing really well. Whenever the tournament came around, Tournament Shea came around. And I remember thinking that finally, here's Shea."

Ralph's performance is all the more remarkable considering the condition of her right knee. Nearly four years to the day since the first of her two ACL tears, Ralph had struggled all season to overcome their lingering effects, working daily with trainer Rosemary Ragle, then supplementing the rehab with her own, almost fanatical, workout regimen.

"Even with everything I did with her to try and make sure that her knee was strong enough and she was ready to go, she on her own would do extra," Ragle said. "She's one of these fierce personalities with a tremendous work ethic that never sees an end. She's constantly working on making herself feel better and be better in general.

"I worried about her doing too much, because I knew she was going to do stuff on her own, even if we told her what we did was enough. And I worried because of her intense nature. I had to tread lightly, because if I told her she couldn't do something, she'd turn around and do it. She just had a tremendous fierceness about her that made it difficult."

Ragle, who joined the UConn staff before the 2000 season, sat at the end of the bench for every game, watching Ralph throw her body across the court, worrying that each night might be the last.

"Knowing her work ethic, knowing how hard she pushed herself, knowing that she was going to dive over scorer's tables to go after a loose ball, of course I worried," Ragle said. "That's what athletic trainers do. There are some things you watch a player do, and after seeing enough, you're okay. But with Shea, I constantly worried about her. I tried not to think that way. I tried to be comfortable knowing that I've done everything that I can possibly do for an athlete and they've been as compliant as they possibly can. Once that's said and done, you just sit back and hope they can enjoy the game and play as hard as they can and pray that nothing happens."

Although she was able to relegate such thoughts to her subconscious, even Ralph was philosophical about a premature end. She had already injured her knee twice. Don't such things always happen in threes?

"Toward the end of my career, my knees were always an issue and there was more I had to do to take care of them," Ralph said. "But to have Coach and my teammates, I would do anything for them. That was my motivation to play and push myself and that's how I got better and recovered. I focused on wanting to do better for them.

"I'm not going to be able to do this forever, and every day is a gift, even more so when you get back on the court, which is hard, because you're dealing with fear. Is it going to happen again? How much time do I have?"

UConn 31–28, 9:38 remaining

Out of the full time-out after Ralph's three-point play, Riley remains on the Notre Dame bench, but the ball still goes into the low block as Siemon posts up Cash for a layup, cutting UConn's lead to 31–30.

At the other end, UConn's offense loses its rhythm and Cash is forced to take a twelve-footer with four seconds on the shot clock that misses, giving Notre Dame a possession to retake the lead.

It is Ratay, who has already buried a pair of threes, who takes a shot to try and put Notre Dame ahead, but her foul-line jumper is well contested by both Jones and Johnson and back-rims, with Jones clearing the rebound. Jones then contributes again on offense, knocking down a jumper just below the foul line for a 33–30 lead with 8:22 left.

At the other end, Siemon again crosses signals with

a teammate, and her pass to Ratay is stolen by Johnson, who passes ahead to Ralph in the corner in front of the Notre Dame bench.

Ralph feeds Williams on the block, but Williams misses the post-up over Amanda Barksdale, subbing for Riley. But the hustling Ralph, running the baseline after making the pass, retrieves the miss and passes out to Johnson, who front-rims a deep three-pointer. The ball goes out of bounds, but UConn retains possession as the game stops for another TV time-out at the 7:50 mark.

Bird takes the ball on the ensuing possession and tries to get it to Cash down low, but Cash can't handle the pass and the ball goes out of bounds, back to Notre Dame. The Irish set up in their half-court offense, but Le'Tania Severe, trying to hit Joyce on a curl pattern along the left sideline, throws the ball too high and out of bounds, and UConn gets the ball back with 7:33 left.

Still leading by three, now it's UConn's turn to work the half-court, with Bird, Ralph, and Johnson passing the ball back and forth on the perimeter before Ralph finally makes the entry pass to Cash on the low block one more time. Cash tries yet another lefty spin on Riley, who has returned to the game, and one more time her path to the basket is denied, her altered shot going over the rim.

Notre Dame rebounds and brings it back up the floor with Joyce attempting a three-pointer from the right wing that misses wildly. But Riley gets the rebound and

Notre Dame completes its prettiest play of the half, cutting UConn's lead to 33–32 with 6:56 remaining.

After grabbing Joyce's miss, Riley kicks the ball out to the top of the key to Ivey, who quickly sends the ball right back toward the basket with a diagonal lob pass. Joyce, having missed the shot, has cut to the basket behind UConn's defense, catching the Huskies unaware and completing the alley-oop play with a layup.

UConn tries to return the favor at the other end with Johnson firing her own diagonal pass over the top of the Notre Dame defense, finding Cash on the right block. But for the second straight possession, Cash fails to score over Riley. Her shot is short but Jones swoops in for the offensive rebound, only to miss the putback. This time the ball goes out of bounds, but UConn retains possession.

Given a third chance, the Huskies decide to go outside, throwing the inbound pass from under the basket to Bird at the top of the key. They are rewarded for their decision as Bird knocks down her first three-pointer of the game, putting UConn up 36–32 as the crowd erupts.

The Irish go right back inside to Riley, but as Riley attempts her spin move from the top of the key, three UConn defenders swarm around her. Sensing the pressure, Riley swings the ball around her midsection as she looks to pass out, but Ralph swipes at the ball, knocking it free, then takes off up court for another UConn fast-break attempt.

Johnson retrieves the loose ball and fires ahead to Ralph, who has a step on her defender. Ralph takes one dribble and then goes into the lane, taking the contact from Joyce and scoring to giving UConn a three-point play and a 39–32 lead with 6:15 remaining.

This is the Shea Ralph that UConn fans, players, and coaches have been waiting to see all season. When Shea knocks down the free throw, it gives her 11 points on 4-for-4 shooting, along with 6 assists and 3 steals. It is easily her best all-around effort of the season, and her intensity fires up the crowd even more.

What the crowd doesn't know, what no one knows, is that Shea Ralph's brilliant game—and career—has less than a minute remaining.

UConn's pressure defense continues to give the Irish fits as they try to bring the ball up the floor. Harassed by Bird, Ivey nearly loses the ball at the top of the key. Siemon comes over to help, taking the ball from Ivey along the right baseline and barely keeping it from being poked away by Cash.

But the pressure on the ball leaves the middle exposed, and once Siemon is able to set herself and find Riley alone in the lane, the Huskies are doomed. Instead of shooting over Jones, Riley instead loops the ball to a cutting Ivey, who uses Riley as a screen to get an unfettered look at the basket and a layup to make it 39–34.

UConn again counters by sending a guard along the left side, then trying to feed the post player in the lane.

In this instance, it's Bird that drives toward the left baseline before trying to slip a pass inside to Jones. But Bird has driven in too deep and Ivey is able to step in front of Jones and knock away the pass, sending the Irish back up the floor.

The Irish once again send the ball into Riley, posting up against Jones. But as Riley makes her patented spin move to the left, Ralph hustles over to double-team, forcing Riley to kick the ball out to Ratay, standing beyond the three-point line along the sideline in front of the UConn bench.

Ralph quickly switches back out to guard Ratay, but her frantic rush allows Ratay to pump-fake and elude Ralph with a dribble to her left. Seeing Ratay get free for a fifteen-footer on the baseline, Cash leaves Siemon alone in the post and rushes out to defend. But Ratay shovels a pass to the uncovered Siemon, who then attempts a wide-open lefty layup.

But Siemon leaves the ball short and Riley, attempting to keep the possession alive, slaps the ball all the way out to the top of the key. The ball finds its way, as it so often does, into the hustling hands of Ralph, who turns and storms up court for yet another fast-break opportunity

"I remember we were supposed to trap the post and I was at the top of the zone and Ruth Riley got the ball and I stuck my hand in and swiped it out and we ended up on the break," Ralph said. "That's what I remember. I can see that like it was yesterday . . ."

UConn 39–34, 5:27 remaining

Having gathered the loose ball after Riley slaps it toward the top of the key, Ralph drives into the frontcourt, hesitating for a moment at the Notre Dame three-point line to make a cross-over dribble, then plunging forward with her left hand toward the basket.

The cross-over allows Ralph to get a step on Joyce, and believing she has beaten her final obstacle to the basket, Ralph makes her final thrust from the left side. But as she starts to go, Ivey rushes across the lane from the right side through Ralph's blind spot, trying to impede her path to the basket. At this last moment, Ralph plants hard with both feet and twists her legs before rising up to avoid Ivey and take the shot.

Suddenly, an agonizing scream pierces the air inside Gampel Pavilion.

Even before the shot has left Ralph's right hand, her left hand reflexively reaches for her left knee, which has twisted horribly from the impact of the final course correction. As Ralph releases her shattering scream, she collapses to the floor.

Now crumpled on the ground, Ralph lets out a second, stricken wail, clearly audible over the shocked and hushed crowd. Ralph pounds the floor angrily four times with her right hand before rolling onto her back and covering her contorted face with her hands. The ACL in her left knee, the one good knee, has torn, and Ralph, engulfed in pain, knows it.

"Shea Ralph, oh goodness, oh no," Robin Roberts

cries into her microphone, knowing full well what has just occurred. "You know the injuries she's had with her knees . . ."

Even as Ralph falls to the floor, the game continues for three surreal seconds before the whistle blows, with Cash and Riley stepping unaware over Ralph while battling for the rebound. After the whistle, Cash looks down to see her teammate crumpled in agony. The sight causes Cash to bend over at the waist, hands on her face, as if she's been punched in the gut.

"You just know," Diana Taurasi said. "The minute she went down like that, we knew. You really feel sick when something like this happens. You feel sick."

Sue Bird, who had been trailing the play around the foul line, is the first player to rush to Ralph's aid. She leans over her fallen teammate, placing a gentle hand on her back, trying to stop Ralph from writhing back and forth.

For a moment, Ralph clasps Bird's hand in hers, but the pain is so intense, and the anguish so overwhelming, that Ralph cannot hold on, and she rolls over again, this time into the waiting arms of trainer Rosemary Ragle, who required an extra few agonizing seconds to make it across the court and attend to Ralph—another byproduct of UConn's unusual distinction this night as the road team.

"There's a woman who knows what this injury is," a subdued Burke says on the ESPN telecast. "Obviously, her reaction is from experience."

"She has worked so hard," says Roberts. "You don't want to speculate, but someone who's had two severe knee injuries . . ."

"You come to understand," Burke says, finishing Roberts's thought. "And any woman who's had that ACL torn understands what that feeling is. You know that sensation. And there are women's college basketball fans around the country looking at this and just absolutely shaking their heads at the number of times this happens to premier athletes."

Ragle leans over Ralph, placing her hand on Ralph's back for comfort, trying to ascertain the exact nature of the injury. But Ralph's only form of communication is a heaving sob and scream, while tugging for a moment at Ragle's skirt before rolling over one more time, now into the waiting arms of associate head coach Chris Dailey and head coach Geno Auriemma.

"I remember just reacting and being beside her, and once I knelt down beside her, I usually let them gather themselves," Ragle said. "And she just was devastated. She'd done the ACL so many times before that when she went down this time, she knew exactly what had happened."

As Ralph is finally able to regain some of her composure and lie prone on the floor, Auriemma, kneeling over her, slumps his shoulders and rubs his temple as the heartbreak of the moment washes over him.

For two minutes, Ralph remains down on the floor, while Ragle and team doctor Thomas Trojian attend to her, with Auriemma and Dailey alongside. There is no examination, really, just an attempt to console Ralph, to get her prepared to stand back up and be led into the trainer's room, where the inevitable diagnosis can be confirmed.

"Anytime I see an injury like that, you try to get an examination in on the floor, before the swelling starts to set in," Ragle said. "But in that situation I made a conscious decision not to, because she was so upset. She was so adamant that she had torn her ACL again, and I just wanted her to get some composure and get off the floor on her own and then have me examine her in the training room. I remember her anger, pounding her fists on the floor. She knew what happened and she saw her senior year flash before her eyes.

"It was letting her get her emotions out. By the time the coaches got there, she was still saying, 'I did it again, I tore it again.' And she's just hitting her fists on the floor. And as a coach, when you've seen her go through it before, what can you say? You just let her get the emotions out and we'll do what we can after the fact. I didn't say anything. Usually you try to console and get them off as quickly as possible. I remember not saying anything besides, 'When you're ready to get up, I'll help you off the floor.'"

While Ralph lies at one end, her teammates huddle with the other assistant coaches at the other end, trying simultaneously to keep their minds on the game while agonizing over the plight of their teammate and leader.

Maria Conlon bites down on her hand, trying to stave off a wave of nausea. Jessica Moore, the redshirt freshman, claps encouragement to her teammates, then stops and looks at the huddle around Ralph, then claps again.

Tamika Williams, who has come to respect Ralph deeply after three seasons together, who came to Ralph's defense against the media in January to help turn Ralph's season around, can only stare blankly at the sad tableau, her thoughts almost visible just behind her eyes.

"When she got hurt, everyone was like, 'What do we do now?'" Bird said. "The thing about injuries, when they happen in games, you don't really have time to think. You wonder how she is. But at the same time, you're in this game, so you can't really worry about it. It's like when players get subbed in and out, you don't think about it, you just keep playing. We had to just play.

"Everybody knew immediately what is was. It was very sad. For me personally, Shea meant a lot to my UConn experience, as a friend, as a teammate. The bond that we had, in regards to our injuries, meant so much. So, to see that was hard. It was difficult. She is everything that UConn is, and for it to end that way, that's not how it's supposed to end."

On the Notre Dame bench, just feet from where Ralph is lying on the floor, the team gathers to pray. Niele Ivey, whose innocent defensive play indirectly led to Ralph's injury—and who has injured her own knees twice before—is particularly shaken.

"I remember just feeling sick," Ivey said. "I can't believe she's going through this. This is our complete rival and it's the most important game of the season for the conference, but that reality for her . . . you don't want your worst enemy to experience that once, let alone three times. I remember feeling horrible for her. I know you have to move on, but it took me a lot of time. It took me a minute to get my thoughts back, Okay, we have to finish this game."

As Ralph is finally helped to her feet, Ragle under one arm, Trojian under the other, the stunned Gampel crowd, which had been struck silent by the terrible turn of events playing out in front of them—save for a few shouts of encouragement to Ralph—rises in an emotional standing ovation.

The UConn women's players have always been viewed as daughters—and granddaughters—by their loyal fans, and Ralph's odyssey has touched them like few others since the team's rise to prominence in 1995. Perhaps only Svetlana Abrosimova and Nykesha Sales, both teammates of Ralph, both of whom also had their careers cut short with injuries, could claim a similar outpouring of affection.

"What was sort of ironic about this game—not ironic, but sad—is that she had just figured it out," the *Courant*'s Matt Eagan said. "It was so clear this game that she had figured out: 'This is how I play.' She had played such a great half and she was once again the leader of that team. And for it to happen right before the half, it was more sad than anything.

"The building is just silent. Everybody knows. They're all hoping for something else, but everybody knows it's not something else. When she goes down right here, you could hear the air go out of the building."

But once Ralph is escorted off the floor and the teams emerge from an officials' time-out, the crowd's ovation becomes equally about the players Ralph has suddenly left behind. Now down two All-Americans, the Huskies will need all the help they can get to navigate the rest of the game. The crowd recognizes this, and accepts the challenge.

"Once this happened, in the building there was a sense of, 'Boy, that may be the end of the national championship, right here. We may have just seen it. But maybe we can get this game,'" Eagan said. "You could hear almost a defiance in the crowd. The crowd suddenly became like, 'We can still get this one and we'll help.' That's how people felt about it.

"It was the all-hands-on-deck moment. Let's face it, this is why we watch sports, for moments exactly like that. They don't come along often, but that's why we watch. We watch to see Willis Reed come limping onto the court. Every so often, there's something a little unique that we haven't quite seen. Little gestures. Curt Schilling, Kirk Gibson.

"You look at Sue Bird's face, and she's like, 'Okay, we're getting this one.' That injury, in a way, made this game all about winning this particular game."

Ivey hears the crowd and thinks the same thing. The

Huskies were already playing an inspired game after the January blowout. Now, the emotions are sent completely off the charts.

"You have to think they're going to rally around her," Ivey said. "You're curious to see how they're going to respond. I think we were thinking, Shoot, that's their girl, their leader that's been playing so well in this game. They're playing for more than just the game now."

UConn 39–34, 5:18 remaining

Out of the time-out, the Huskies take possession of the ball underneath the Notre Dame basket, the previous sequence having ended with Riley knocking the ball out of bounds while Ralph lay on the floor injured.

"Right now, you just concentrate on closing the half," said Taurasi, who replaces Ralph in the lineup. "Let's stay focused until we get into the locker room. But it was hard. You could feel the whole energy of the building just get sucked out of you. It's the hardest thing in the world to play the game when someone gets seriously injured, and you know it."

Taurasi inbounds the ball and the Huskies again work the ball on the perimeter instead of trying to find a shot inside. With the shot clock down to eight seconds, the ball works its way back to Taurasi, who is left unguarded on the left sideline for a three-point attempt.

Taurasi's shot is slightly short, bouncing high in the air off the front side of the rim. The high bounce gives the UConn post players the opportunity to carve room for an offensive rebound, with Jones doing a superb job of boxing Riley out of the lane, leaving the 6-foot-2 Cash to battle one-on-one with the diminutive Ratay.

Cash easily wins the mismatch, grabbing the carom and going straight back up. All Ratay can do is grab Cash's arm to try and deny the shot, but Cash is too strong, absorbing the blow and making the layup for a three-point opportunity with exactly 5:00 remaining.

The aggressive rebound and putback are a perfect response to Ralph's injury. The play not only creates another burst of emotion from the crowd but steadies the Huskies after the shock of seeing their teammate sprawled in agony before them.

"It's definitely a high-emotion situation," Bird said. "I think the next couple of minutes were out-of-body-like. You're thinking about who it was. That was a huge part of it. You talk about wanting to win games for people, and I don't know if it was said—Coach Auriemma isn't a big believer in that stuff, writing numbers on your shoes— but for what she always gave to us, there was definitely a sense of what we wanted to give to her."

Cash makes the free throw to complete the three-point play and give UConn its biggest lead of the half at eight points, 42–34.

The inspired Huskies nearly force Ivey into a turnover at the other end, with Johnson harassing Ivey toward the sideline near midcourt and forcing her to pick up her dribble. But Joyce rescues her beleaguered teammate by rushing at Ivey to take the ball and dribble out of harm's way.

But the Huskies will still get a turnover before the possession is over. Joyce lobs the ball deep into Riley, who fakes a pass to a cutting Siemon, causing Johnson to get confused and lose track of Ivey, who waits for Siemon to clear the lane and then cuts to the basket unguarded.

Riley hits Ivey in stride, and it appears Ivey will make an easy layup. But Cash, having shadowed Siemon into the lane, makes a late jump into Ivey's path, causing Ivey to shuffle her feet before passing the ball to an open Siemon for a layup. As Siemon puts the ball off the glass, the whistle sounds and Dennis DeMayo signals the travel. UConn has the ball with 4:37 left and a chance to go up double-digits.

But what Cash giveth, Cash taketh away. On the offensive end, Cash gets the ball in the post against Ruth and dribbles to the strong side, trying to elude her low-post nemesis. Bird is momentarily open on the weak side, beyond the three-point line, and Cash tries to pass it to her. But Siemon, at the bottom of the zone, reads the play from the beginning and easily picks off the cross-court pass.

Siemon dribbles up court and passes to Joyce in the corner by the UConn bench. Joyce hoists a three-pointer but leaves it short, the ball caroming toward the middle of the lane, where Siemon is on the spot again, tipping the ball out to Haney, who hands back to Ivey. Before the UConn defense can reset, Ivey feeds Ruth, who is fouled by Jones. Ruth makes both free throws, cutting the deficit to 42–36 with 4:05 left.

The Huskies respond by getting Bird an open baseline jumper from fifteen feet, but Bird comes up short and Siemon clears the rebound. The Irish go right back to Ruth, this time with Siemon throwing high over the top of the defense to get Riley an easy layup. Like that, UConn's lead is down to 42–38.

A jump ball is called on the ensuing UConn possession, with the arrow favoring the Huskies. Bird inbounds under the Notre Dame basket and passes to Jones, who shoots over Riley but misses. Jones manages to get the rebound, but so does Ivey, and the two wrestle for control before DeMayo signals another jump ball, giving possession back to the Irish.

Having scored the past four points, the Irish work the ball on the perimeter, trying to get Riley set up in the paint alone against Jones. Finally, after UConn nearly pokes the ball free on two separate occasions, Joyce is able to pass the ball into Riley, and almost simultaneously, Jones is called for a pushing foul, her second.

Jones and Auriemma cannot believe the call. Not because it went against UConn, but because it ignored the fact that Riley had been camped in the lane. But in fact, Riley had not been in the paint for longer than three seconds at any one time.

Riley heads to the free-throw line, making both shots to cut UConn's lead to 42–40. At one point, just before Ralph's injury, the Huskies seemed poised to take a double-digit lead. Instead, the Irish have taken advantage of a rattled team and have clawed back within a basket.

The Huskies need some kind of spark to get going again, and Tamika Williams provides one. Williams, so shaken by Ralph's injury minutes earlier, gets prime position on Siemon in the lane and converts a short hook while Siemon drapes over her and is called for a foul with 2:50 left.

But Williams cannot complete the three-point play, leaving UConn ahead by just four. And that lead is momentary, as Riley works a perfect high-low play with Ericka Haney to cut the deficit to two points once again.

Back comes Williams, taking an entry feed from Taurasi and wheeling around Riley for her second straight basket for a 46–42 lead, only to have Riley go again into the lane with just over two minutes remaining, drawing Jones's third foul and forcing her to the bench.

Jones and Ralph have been UConn's two most productive players in the first half. Now both are out of the game for the final 2:07. In Jones's case, there is a second half to be played. But back in the trainer's room, the prognosis for Ralph is grim. No second half. No NCAA Tournament. The ACL in her left knee is almost certainly torn, with only an MRI left to confirm it. Ralph's UConn career is over.

"It was a different experience," Ragle said. "The minute we got her in the training room, the doctor that had done her surgeries [Dr. Michael Joyce] was the first to examine her. He came right in and got his hands on her knee. I remember her crying and being angry. I think she was going through the five stages of grief. The tears didn't stop.

"It was just a lot of people standing around, not knowing what to say. What do you say to somebody who has had as many ACLS as she's had, has had as many arduous rehab sessions, knowing she's a tough kid and a great leader. What do you say? You know as well as she does that her season is over. It's devastating for everyone involved."

After Jones's foul, Riley misses her first free throw of the game before making the second, cutting UConn's lead to 46–43. As the clock slips under two minutes, Johnson uses her speed to blow past two Notre Dame defenders at the top of the key and attempt a running layup over the outstretched arms of Riley.

But the wingspan forces the diminutive Johnson to overcompensate the loft of her attempt, and the ball hits too hard off the backboard and into the arms of Siemon, who feeds Ivey and sends the Irish back up the floor.

UConn denies the fast break and Siemon attempts a twelve-foot hook shot over Williams. The shot misses, but Riley, now being defended by Schumacher, gets position for the offensive rebound and kicks the ball back out to Ivey at the top of the key. Ivey makes a thrust toward the lane, then passes to the sideline, where a wide-open Joyce squares up and buries a three-pointer, tying the score at 46–46 with 1:35 remaining. It is Ivey's eighth assist of the first half.

It didn't take long for Niele Ivey to imprint her personality on the Notre Dame program, both off the court and on it. While Riley was the team's best player, she was quiet. It was Ivey that grew on everyone.

"She was the emotion," McGraw said. "She was definitely the fire. She was the team clown. She would make me laugh. But when she got to practice, she would flip the switch and she was all business. She was fiery. She would get them going.

"In the Connecticut game [at Notre Dame], we were up a lot, and all of a sudden they hit a bunch of threes and I took a time-out and said, 'We've got to go man-to-man. We have to guard the three-point line.' And Niele, who would never come close to being disrespectful or even say anything in a huddle, she went 'No!' And I said, 'What?' And she said, 'We're tired. We can't do it!'

'And I said, 'Okay, we'll stay in the 2-3, but would you guard the three-point line?' And she said, 'Yeah, we'll think about it.' And everyone laughed and took a breath and we stayed in the zone and won the game."

Ivey arrived at Notre Dame in the fall of 1996 and felt comfortable immediately in her new surroundings, having been joined in the freshman class by an old friend, Julie Henderson. The point guard and the post player had originally met during Ivey's junior year of high school at an All-American camp in Saginaw, Michigan.

Ivey and Henderson became pen pals, but it was not until Ivey's recruiting process that she learned something significant about her long-distance buddy. While making her official visit to Notre Dame, Ivey spotted a picture of Henderson on the desk of assistant coach Carol Owens.

"I was like, 'You know her?'" Ivey said. "And Carol said, 'Yeah, she committed here.' So we always had that bond, and then we picked the same school. It was perfect."

Henderson's friendship would prove invaluable to Ivey over the course of their first two years in South Bend. Just five games into Ivey's freshman season, while going up for a layup in a game at Bowling Green, Ivey was fouled from behind, causing her right leg to buckle. The diagnosis was a torn ACL.

Like that, Ivey's first season at the college level was over. But because Ivey had played in such a small percentage of Norte Dame's games that season, she was awarded an extra year of eligibility should she choose to return for a fifth season in 2000–2001. But for the remainder of the 1996–97, it was hardly a consolation.

"I hear about it happening with other people, but I never expected it would be me hurt and sitting," Ivey said. "Not being able to be active was very hard. I was depressed at one point. I remember being devastated, and [Henderson] was definitely one who knew how talented I was and knew that I would get back to that level. I was worried that I would never be the same. How much is this going to affect me, long-term? She was my constant support who built me up. My family was six hours away, but she was my support system here."

Further compounding Ivey's sense of loss was the fact

that her teammates went on to enjoy the finest season to date at Notre Dame. The Irish lost just one game in the Big East (to Connecticut, naturally) and finished the regular season with a 25-5 record.

After losing again to UConn in the Big East Tournament final, Notre Dame ripped through the first three games of the NCAA Tournament, then advanced to the program's first-ever Final Four with a 62–52 victory over George Washington.

All the while, all Ivey could do was watch.

"I had to get through my own selfishness, especially at the beginning," she said. "It was a long season and at the beginning it was hard for me to watch our point guard and not think, 'I would be starting.' I thought very selfishly at first. I guess anybody would. I had to check myself early, because it was a long season and this was out of my control. I had to really focus on getting ready for the next year. But I went through that period of feeling sorry for myself and not feeling a part of it.

"But towards the end, I lived through Julie. We would be checks and balances for each other. By the Final Four, going through that ride, I was the number one fan of my own team. I loved being a part of that.

"Having that experience, I expected us to be there every year. You don't know how attainable it is until you get to the Sweet Sixteen, then two more games and you're in."

In Ivey's first full season in 1997–98, the Irish were eliminated in the Sweet Sixteen. Ivey became a full-time starter in 1998–99, averaging 13.1 points and 6.5 assists, earning her third-team Big East honors. But for the second time in three years, there would be no NCAA Tournament.

Before facing rough, tough Rutgers in the Big East Tournament semifinals on the Scarlet Knights' home court in Piscataway, New Jersey, Ivey got into it with two of Rutgers's more demonstrative players, Tasha Pointer and Linda Miles. The war of words inspired Ivey to raise the level of her game, which had finally gotten back to the level she expected two years removed from her injury.

"Before that game, I felt like I was in my element," Ivey said. "The year before, it usually takes a year to feel normal. Now, I felt like I was there, I was ready. I was like, No one can stop me right now. I had like sixteen points at halftime."

In the second half, lightning struck for the second time. Ivey tore up her left knee, the good one.

"This one was more painful than the other one," Ivey said. "I remember just screaming and the whole gym was silent. That one really hurt, physically, mentally, and spiritually. I'm like, You have to be kidding me. I felt like I had learned my lessons, that you can't take things for granted.

"I didn't know what to say about the second one. I knew I had my body ready, I was in shape. It was nothing I'd done rehab-wise. But after the first one, I knew I could come back. I knew I'd be fine. But now I'm like,

Why do I have to be the strong one all the time? Why are these things happening to me?"

As was so often the case with UConn in the same period of time, the loss of Ivey on the eve of the NCAA Tournament was too much for the Irish to overcome. Notre Dame lost in the second round, its earliest exit since 1996. For Ivey, it meant another off-season of rehab.

"She had so much adversity," McGraw said. "We had a student manager one year and Niele would tell her, 'You've played in more NCAA Tournament games than I have,' because she got hurt at the end of one year, missed another year. She considers herself the oldest player to ever play here and she jokes about that. But that is so hard to come back from. Once is hard. Twice, you wonder if she can come back. And I knew she would because she was so determined and dedicated and disciplined."

Ivey did return to full strength in 1999–2000, earning Big East second team honors before faltering against Texas Tech in the NCAA Tournament with a 1-for-9 shooting night in the four-point loss. But all her struggles finally proved to have some meaning.

Because of the timing of her first injury in 1996, Ivey had been awarded a fifth year of eligibility. Had that injury taken place three games later—as proved to be the case for Sue Bird in the winter of 1998—Ivey would not have been eligible for the extra season.

Given the extra chance to compete as a redshirt senior, Ivey was suddenly afforded a remarkable opportunity. Should the Irish advance to the Final Four, the games would be played at the Savvis Center in St. Louis. The girl who had wowed the crowds at high school games in St. Louis with her long-range shooting would have the chance to do it again, this time for a national championship.

"It was complete motivation," Ivey said. "I remember after that summer, realizing it was going to be in St. Louis, I had a talk with Muffet and I said, 'What an awesome way to end it.' I thought about it once or twice and then I was like, I know what I have to do to get there and I don't want to talk about it anymore. I see the light at the end of the tunnel and I know I have to put in the work to get there."

As much as Ivey tried to downplay it, the reminders that season were everywhere. Even before the season opener against Valparaiso, the prospect of a heroic homecoming was scripted for her—quite literally.

"We had a commercial shoot here to highlight our upcoming season," Ivey said. "They said, 'I want you to dribble the ball and shoot it and do what you would do if you won the national championship.' I remember thinking, I don't know what I would do! But I realized later that I was preparing for that, even if I didn't know it as I was doing it."

Score tied 46–46, 1:35 remaining

UConn's eight-point lead now evaporated, the crowd anxiously urges the Huskies to close the half strong.

Once again, the ball works its way down low to Williams, and once again, Williams makes something good happen, drawing Riley's second foul with 1:18 left. The foul forces McGraw to take Riley out of the game, not willing to risk a third foul with just 1:18 left.

But Williams makes just one of two free throws, giving the Irish their first possession with a chance to take the lead in almost eight minutes.

"Now everybody's like, 'Oh boy,'" Eagan said. "It's 47–46 and there is a sense that they could go under. They've lost their best player on the court from the first fifteen minutes and here comes Notre Dame and then somehow this becomes suddenly the number two team in the nation, in their own building, is a tremendous underdog."

On this critical possession it is Joyce, not Ivey, who mans the point, guarded by Bird. Ivey, guarded closely by Johnson, shakes free as Johnson dives to the floor in a failed attempt to steal a hand-pass from Joyce, allowing Ivey to reset the offense.

As the clock goes under a minute, Ivey passes to Joyce, who dumps the ball down low to Siemon, who touch-passes the ball back out to Haney on the sideline. The ball moving with alacrity, Haney passes back inside to Siemon, but this time, Notre Dame is called for three seconds, as Barksdale, a seldom-used backup pressed into service with Riley on the bench, gets caught standing in the lane too long. A chance for Notre Dame to take the lead goes by without even as much as a shot attempt.

UConn inbounds with 56.8 seconds left and Bird takes

her time working the ball up the floor. The Huskies work the ball along the outside, with Bird, Johnson, and Taurasi all handling it before Taurasi gets the ball at the top of the key, a good three feet beyond the three-point line, and fires with forty-one seconds on the clock.

The ball bounces hard off the back the rim, but with no Riley on the court, the 6-foot-5 Schumacher is able to swoop in and grab the offensive rebound, then easily take the ball back up for a layup with the three smaller Irish players helpless to stop it. The basket gives UConn a 49–46 lead with 36.9 seconds left and guarantees the Huskies will get one more possession before the end of the half.

"Now we have them playing the way we want them to play," Auriemma said. "We have the tempo going the way we want it. We wanted them to get a little bit frazzled. It's like every time somebody made a mistake, either team, it cost you a bucket. In a game like this, you can't make mistakes."

Schumacher's electrifying rebound and putback get the crowd the most fired up it's been since Ralph's injury. Drawing strength from the commotion, the Huskies put together their most intense half-court defensive sequence of the game so far, harassing Ivey at the top of the key, then swallowing up Siemon on the low block and forcing a pass out to Haney, who takes a rushed shot with five seconds left on the shot clock and front-rims with a thud. The carom is so severe, the ball winds up near the foul line, bouncing off Taurasi's foot before Haney touches it last. It finally goes out of bounds by the UConn bench with 1.9 seconds left. The Huskies will have time for a final shot.

During the morning shootaround, the Huskies continued their tradition of ending the brief practice session with a prayer. Not the spiritual kind, but the half-court variety.

"Every day at shootaround, that particular group, there was a contest to see who [could] make a shot from half-court first," Auriemma said. "Even in the NCAA Tournament, because you're timed, and the clock is running and at the forty-five-second mark, guys are lining up. And it has to be at the buzzer, so you don't get multiple shots at it. So you see guys standing there, dribbling, 3 . . . 2 . . . whoosh! And fifteen basketballs fly at the basket.

"Invariably, someone will make one. That day, Sue made one. And you're like, hmmm."

If Niele Ivey was the half-court champion of grade school, Bird is the champion of the college and professional level.

"I like to consider myself a proficient half-court shooter," Bird said. "In the WNBA, we shoot them for money. I've made a lot of money."

With 1.9 seconds left, the Irish retreat on defense, leaving Ivey alone to guard Bird in the backcourt as Schumacher inbounds the ball. As the ref hands the ball to Schumacher, Bird and Ivey are only three feet away from the sideline and seventy feet from the basket. Like a wide receiver on the line of scrimmage, Bird pushes Ivey to create space and moves laterally across the floor, while Schumacher loops a lead pass over Ivey's head, taking Ivey out of the play.

Bird tracks the ball down about sixty feet from the goal, as Siemon rushes up to block her path. But Siemon is more worried about drawing a foul than guarding Bird closely, and she stops in her tracks, raising her arms, signaling no intent to create contact. As she does, Bird gathers the ball and takes one long dribble to her left, careening out of Siemon's path and activating the clock . . . 1.9, 1.8, 1.7 . . .

At 1.3 Bird regains the ball and takes one final dribble . . . 0.7, 0.6, 0.5 . . .

Her legs straddling the half-court line, Bird gathers the ball one final time, takes her last step into the front-court, and releases a two-handed forty-five-footer toward the basket with 00.3 showing on the clock.

The halftime buzzer sounds as the ball arcs its way past the three-point line, past the foul line, its trajectory taking it directly toward the rim. Even before the ball comes down, a fan several rows up behind half-court has already made the instantaneous geometric calculation: the shot is perfect. His arms raise upward, then ten thousand others join him.

"I covered them for two years, and they used to run

that five-second drill, and I never saw her miss," Eagan said. "Never, never, ever saw her miss. Never at the end of a game. Never at the end of a practice. I've never, in that situation, seen her miss. I'm sure she has. I've just never seen it."

The ball rips clean through the net, not even touching the rim. Three points. UConn leads 52–46.

"Will not . . . ," Roberts starts, as the ball leaves Bird's hand. "Ohhhh! Ohhhh! It counts! Are you kidding me?! Sue Bird, bad back and all, knocks down the prayer at the end of the first half!"

Bird watches the ball go through, then raises her arms in victory, skipping her way along the sideline opposite the team benches. But before she gets too far, Marci Czel, Maria Conlon, and the rest of the UConn bench engulf her while the crowd reaches a frenzy. Bird jumps into freshman Morgan Valley's arms, and the hopping amoeba heads off to the locker room.

"I let it go and I'm thinking, 'This has a chance, this has a chance . . . yes!' It's momentum. Something to smile about. Everyone was hyped, very excited. I remember in that Tennessee game [in 2000], when we lost at home, how pissed [Auriemma] was because we let somebody score right before the half and how it gave them momentum. Those shots, they do play a role."

Indeed, the reaction on the Notre Dame side is not a happy one. Ivey in particular cannot believe the turn of events. One minute, the Irish are setting up to take the shot that would give them the lead again for the first time since the score was 6–5. Next thing she knows, her team trails by six points again.

"That was ridiculous," Ivey said. "First of all, with the last two possessions, Ruth is on the bench and we don't get a good shot. I'm not really being aggressive offensively. I've got Ericka taking a bad shot. I've got Amanda Barksdale, who doesn't play many minutes, getting a three-second call, so I'm already frustrated that we're down one and we're not getting good looks and it looked like we had no offense.

"So we completely lost our focus and had a lapse defensively. I didn't keep her in front, and there was no recognition that if I did get screened, somebody [else] stay on the ball so she doesn't get a wide-open look like she did. That's my lack of focusing on defense and it carried over from not executing on offense and being frustrated. That's completely on me. That's just lazy. And it gives them momentum going into the second half and the frustration carried over on defense."

Walking off the court as the crowd celebrates Bird's bomb, McGraw is hoping that last sequence doesn't come back to bite her team.

"That was one of those where you go into the locker room and think, I hope we don't lose by two or three," McGraw said. "What are you going to do? It was a great shot. We could have picked her up earlier and done certain things. We'd actually worked on some things like that, and then it happened again in the end."

Halftime, UConn 52–46

Sue Bird's half-court buzzer-beater is a lightning bolt that energizes the crowd and sends the Huskies into the locker room with giddy delight.

But no sooner have the players reached the tunnel than the euphoria vanishes. Immediately, all thoughts turn to their fallen teammate. Where is Shea?

"Immediately when we left the court, we went to the room," Bird said. "We didn't even go to the locker room."

Inside the trainers' room, a small group has gathered around Ralph to sit vigil. Trainer Rosemary Ragle, who has spent countless hours working with Ralph to keep her right knee healthy enough to play, is devastated. The worst-case scenario she always feared might happen has come to pass. Could she have done more to prevent it?

"It was difficult for me on a couple of levels," Ragle said. "Once you work with these college students, you're invested in them professionally and emotionally. Knowing what was probably running through her head, my heart went out to her. When it's something like that and their season is on the line and someone like her, who takes so much pride in the effort she puts into practice every day, it's very hard.

"And on the other side of that, as a professional, you think, Did I do everything that I could have done? I don't question how I do my job, but I think that's the natural reaction. You take personal responsibility for your kids."

There are roughly fifteen minutes before the teams must head back out to the court, so time is short. But Geno Auriemma, among the first to arrive in the room, intends to make the most of it.

Auriemma has witnessed every setback and comeback of Ralph's career. This final injury, at a time when it appeared Ralph had rediscovered herself as a player, seems particularly cruel. While the doctors and trainers attend to Ralph on a table in the training room, Auriemma stands at Ralph's side, putting his hand carefully on her tattered left knee.

"To have happen what happened, it was like being on a magic carpet ride and it's pulled right out from under you," Auriemma said. "I would say of all the moments in my coaching career, that one probably stung the most, from a personal standpoint. To the point where—I don't remember ever doing this—I never went into the locker room. I stayed there, and they came and got me and I walked out to the bench and [the players] were already out there.

"I just couldn't pull myself out. I couldn't go in there and talk to my team knowing what I just saw and where she is and what she's going through. And I didn't say anything. I just stood there shaking my head and staring and I had my hand on her knee and I couldn't move. I couldn't move. I couldn't walk away. I remember a manager coming in to get me."

Inside the Notre Dame locker room, the focus is on the

final twenty minutes. The Irish are not playing as crisply as they did in the rout of Connecticut in January, having committed ten first-half turnovers to UConn's five. Despite the fact that Notre Dame is shooting a higher percentage (60.7 to 52.5), UConn has managed to take twelve more shots and owns a 12–6 advantage in points-off-turnovers. Not coincidentally, the UConn lead is also six points.

"Things aren't going our way, when we were used to having things go our way all year," Ivey said. "We're not responding. We're not getting crucial stops. We're not taking care of the ball, not even getting a shot, which is completely controllable. We can't control them going in, but not even getting a look and committing turnovers and not doing the job defensively was what she was focusing on."

McGraw has seen her team wilt against the Huskies too many times in her career not to be concerned that it might happen again. Beating UConn at the Joyce Center before a raucous sellout crowd was one thing. Doing it in the belly of the beast, Gampel Pavilion, would require much more mental toughness than the Irish had displayed in the first half.

"We probably talked about that at halftime," McGraw said. "We're relentless. We're not backing down. We're in a big fight here and we're going toe to toe and we're throwing punches. We're not backing down from anyone. Just stay with everything we're doing and keep doing it."

Table 2. Box Score, First Half, Big East Women's Tournament Final, 2001

Official Basketball Box Score—GAME TOTALS—1st PERIOD—00:00 REMAINING
CONNECTICUT vs NOTRE DAME
3/6/01 7:30 p.m. at Harry A. Gampel Pavilion, Storrs, CT

VISITORS: CONNECTICUT

## Player Name	TOT-FG FG-FGA	3-PT FG-FGA	FT-FTA	REBOUNDS OF	DE	TOT	PF	TP	A	TO	BLK	S	MIN
15 Jones, Asjha........ f	5-9	0-0	0-0	1	3	4	3	10	0	0	0	0	15
32 Cash, Swin......... f	2-7	0-0	1-1	1	1	2	0	5	0	2	0	0	13
03 Taurasi, Diana...... g	2-5	2-5	0-0	0	1	1	2	6	2	0	0	0	13
10 Bird, Sue.......... g	4-6	2-3	0-0	0	1	1	1	10	2	3	0	0	17
33 Ralph, Shea......... g	4-5	1-1	2-2	1	1	2	1	11	6	0	0	3	14
11 Schumacher, Kelly...	1-1	0-0	0-0	1	1	2	0	2	0	0	0	0	3
23 Johnson, Kennitra...	1-4	1-3	0-0	1	0	1	0	3	3	0	0	1	16
34 Williams, Tamika....	2-3	0-0	1-5	0	1	1	2	5	1	0	0	0	9
TEAM..................				2	1	3							
Totals.................	21-40	6-12	4-8	7	10	17	9	52	14	5	0	4	100

TOTAL FG%	1st Half: 21-40	52.5%	2nd Half: 0-0	0.0%	Game: 52.5%	DEADB
3-Pt. FG%	1st Half: 6-12	50.0%	2nd Half: 0-0	0.0%	Game: 50.0%	REBS
F Throw %	1st Half: 4-8	50.0%	2nd Half: 0-0	0.0%	Game: 50.0%	1

HOME TEAM: NOTRE DAME

## Player Name	TOT-FG FG-FGA	3-PT FG-FGA	FT-FTA	REBOUNDS OF	DE	TOT	PF	TP	A	TO	BLK	S	MIN
03 Haney, Ericka....... f	1-3	0-0	0-2	1	0	1	0	2	1	0	0	0	11
50 Siemon, Kelley..... f	4-8	0-0	2-2	0	5	5	1	10	1	2	0	2	20
00 Riley, Ruth......... c	5-5	0-0	5-7	1	2	3	2	15	2	3	2	0	17
22 Ratay, Alicia....... g	2-3	2-2	1-2	0	1	1	2	7	2	0	0	0	13
33 Ivey, Niele........ g	2-3	0-0	0-0	0	3	3	0	4	8	3	0	0	20
04 Severe, Le'Tania....	0-0	0-0	0-0	0	1	1	0	0	0	1	0	0	2
05 Joyce, Jeneka.......	3-6	2-5	0-0	1	1	2	1	8	0	0	0	0	14
31 Barksdale, Amanda...	0-0	0-0	0-0	0	0	0	0	0	0	1	0	0	3
TEAM..................				1	2	3							
Totals.................	17-28	4-7	8-13	4	15	19	6	46	14	10	2	2	100

TOTAL FG%	1st Half: 17-28	60.7%	2nd Half: 0-0	0.0%	Game: 60.7%	DEADB
3-Pt. FG%	1st Half: 4-7	57.1%	2nd Half: 0-0	0.0%	Game: 57.1%	REBS
F Throw %	1st Half: 8-13	61.5%	2nd Half: 0-0	0.0%	Game: 61.5%	2

Officials: Dennis DeMayo, Lisa Mattingly, Angie Lewis
Technical fouls: CONNECTICUT—None. NOTRE DAME—None.
Attendance: 10027

Score by Periods	1st	Total
CONNECTICUT.................	52	52
NOTRE DAME....................	46	46

Points in the paint—UCONN 30, ND 24.   Points off turnovers—UCONN 12, ND 6.
2nd chance points—UCONN 8, ND 7.   Fast break points—UCONN 7, ND 5.
Bench points—UCONN 10, ND 8.   Score tied—2 times. Lead changes—4 times.

3

Second Half

UConn 52–46, 20:00 remaining

The UConn players and coaching staff leave the trainers' room and head back onto the court for the second half. Ever the warrior and emotional leader, Ralph refuses to remain behind.

"I remember she was very adamant about getting back on the court," Ragle said. "She didn't even want ice. She was like, 'I don't want an [expletive] icepack on my knee.' We made her do it anyway and put her in an immobilizer. She wanted to go out there on her own free will and be a part of that game and the rest of the season.

"Shea was vocal. She's a leader. She wasn't going to feel sorry for herself too long. By the time she got back on the court, her priority was her team coming out with a victory. She was coaching from the sidelines."

In one of the many heart-tugging moments of this night, Ralph limps over to her fallen teammate, Svetlana Abrosimova, adorned in a pink sweater and silver crutches, and the two warriors embrace.

"I'm so sorry," Abrosimova says, dissolving into tears as Ralph reaches out her arms.

"It's okay," Ralph whispers into Abrosimova's ear, and the two hold the hug.

"It is what it is and it's part of the game," Ralph said. "You have the cards you're dealt and that's what you have to deal with. I don't think we were in our own world. It was more about our team and what could we do to help them."

For UConn, now without their two All-Americans— the two players best equipped to lead the Huskies to a repeat championship—the show must go on.

When Auriemma finally addresses his team, he implores them to slow things down, stop rushing, stop taking the first available outside shot.

"We want to go up and down and we can't, so now we're pissed and we're like, 'How did we get ourselves into this mess?'" Auriemma said. "And [Notre Dame is] like, 'Yeah, this is how we want the game to be.' You know when you're in a shootout and you just have to outscore them. And you also know when you're in a dogfight and every possession means a lot, you better get a stop."

UConn takes the first possession of the second half, with Schumacher, earning the second-half start with Jones in foul trouble, joining Bird, Taurasi, Cash, and Kennitra Johnson, who is earning extended minutes this night with the injury to Ralph. Notre Dame counters with its usual starting five of Riley, Ivey, Siemon, Ratay, and Haney.

The first shot of the second half belongs to Taurasi, who attempts a three-pointer from the top of the key. But the long-range dagger is missing the mark in this game—an ominous portent—and this first shot of the half clangs hard off the rim and caroms out to Johnson, who slips the ball inside to Cash.

The change of sides has not altered the equation in the paint, and Cash, who was repeatedly denied by Riley in the first half, cannot connect to start the second. But this time it is Ratay, not Riley, that has stymied Cash, stripping the ball from her hands before Cash can elevate for the shot. But the alert defensive play is trumped by an equally alert reaction from Schumacher, who reaches out for the loose ball under the basket and scores the layup to give UConn a 54–46 lead twenty seconds into the half—matching the biggest advantage either side will enjoy the entire night.

"Schumacher made some plays in the first half, so it's interesting [Auriemma] comes right back with her here," Burke says. "The size of Schumacher, I think he's trying to get a look at what that will do defensively."

"But she doesn't have the agility of some of the other post players for Connecticut," Roberts counters.

But for a moment, Schumacher's size thwarts Riley in the post. Instead of shoulder-shaking her way past Schumacher to the basket, Riley passes out to Ratay behind the three-point line. But then Schumacher's lack of agility shows itself. Ratay drives into the lane, drawing Schumacher and Cash away from the basket to help Bird prevent the penetration. As they move, Siemon makes a backdoor cut, leaving Schumacher and Cash out of position to defend it. Ratay then fires a jump-pass over Johnson and into Siemon's arms for an easy layup.

Schumacher has an even worse experience on UConn's ensuing possession. In a rare breakdown of the 2-3 zone, Notre Dame leaves Schumacher alone at the foul line with the ball. But Schumacher, anticipating some sort of harassment that never comes, seems unsure of what to do, despite having essentially a wide-open free throw. She pump-fakes the ball once, then a second time, while the crowd implores her to shoot. Finally, Schumacher releases the ball, but all the faking has thrown off her timing, and the shot barely catches the front of the rim, falling into Ivey's hands.

Now, on Notre Dame's second possession of the half, Riley gets prime position against Schumacher in the post, no more than three feet from the basket, and there is nothing Schumacher can do to prevent two more points on a double-clutch shot, cutting UConn's eight-point lead to 54–50 with 18:54 left.

UConn quickly gets a chance to grab two of the points back as Cash manages to beat the retreating Notre Dame defense down the court. Bird spots the developing mismatch of Cash against Haney alone underneath and fires a perfect pass from half-court to Cash under the basket.

All Haney can do is reach out and hope for the best, knocking the ball into the arms of Siemon on the baseline. Luck of the Irish? Nine times out of ten, a reach-in like Haney's is called a foul, regardless of whether the defender has gotten all ball.

But this time, there is no whistle, only the sound of Cash crying out and the crowd moaning its displeasure. Lisa Mattingly, the official on the weak-side baseline, thought Haney made a clean block, and Dennis De-Mayo, watching from the strong side—along the sideline in front of the UConn bench—was screened at the last moment by Johnson and could not see the play.

Despite their good fortune, the Irish cannot convert. After being abused by Riley on the previous play, Schumacher tries fronting this trip up the floor, positioning herself between Riley and the passer at the top of the key, hoping to deny the entry pass.

The gambit pays off as Siemon fails to loft her pass high and far enough, allowing Schumacher to jump up and intercept it.

"Not a great pass by Siemon," Burke says. "You've got to understand that's 6-foot-5 fronting her, not 6-foot-2."

At the other end, Johnson, having advanced the ball herself, pulls up for a three-pointer and misses, but Siemon, blocked out nicely by Cash, knocks the ball out of bounds. Ratay then fouls Schumacher attempting a shot off the inbounds under the Notre Dame basket and Schumacher makes both free throws, pushing UConn's lead back up to 56–50.

In some ways, the best night of Kelly Schumacher's UConn career was also the worst. On the night of April 2, 2000, Schumacher picked the game's biggest stage for a dominant individual defensive performance. While her teammates were dismantling Tennessee in the national championship game at the offensive end, Schumacher was a one-woman wrecking crew on defense, blocking a championship game–record nine shots in the 71–52 victory.

That was the final game of a breakout season for the junior from Quyon, Quebec. Schumacher started fifteen games and came through with some critical defensive efforts, including a five-block afternoon in a gut-buster of a 50–45 victory over Rutgers at the RAC.

But her monster performance in Philadelphia brought monster expectations for her senior season. And as would many of UConn's players in 2001, Schumacher struggled to meet those expectations. A stress fracture in her right foot caused her to miss six games early in the season, and after her return, she failed to play with the same killer instinct she had showed in the NCAA title game.

Nowhere was the disparity more evident than in her two previous games against Ruth Riley and Notre Dame. In the regular-season finale in 2000, Schumacher throttled Riley, forcing her into turnovers and fouls, while scoring eight points, grabbing eight rebounds, and blocking four shots in twenty-six minutes.

But when Riley turned the tables in South Bend in January, Schumacher was a nonfactor, playing just thirteen minutes, with two points, three rebounds and not a single blocked shot.

"I think there were big expectations," Schumacher said a few days after the January game. "But I think they are expectations I can follow through with, that I could definitely do. I just think, you know, I haven't done it yet. I'm still working on it."

The following game, Schumacher scored a career-high 20 points against Pittsburgh, grabbing 6 rebounds and blocking 4 shots. The next seven games combined, Schumacher scored 34 points with 19 rebounds and blocked 6 shots.

"Schuey isn't exactly Muhammad Ali in terms of confidence level," Auriemma told the *Courant* during the season. "So, playing time, being out there, doing things, those are real important to her. And she missed a lot of that. So now it's going to take awhile for her to get all that back. In the meantime, I'm trying to throw her out there and let her play, and you know, it'll be all right. She'll get back. Schuey's come a long way. But [confidence] is a delicate thing. You don't know where it comes from, you don't know where it goes."

Auriemma had apparently lost his confidence in Schumacher entering the Big East Tournament final. Although Riley was having her way inside against the smaller Jones—scoring fifteen points on 5-for-5 shooting from the field and 5-for-7 from the free-throw line—Schumacher played just one minute of the first seventeen.

Even when Jones picked up her third foul with 2:07

left, Auriemma wasn't sure who to put in to replace her. Auriemma wasn't sure, but Schumacher was. She angrily stared her coach down, prompting a reaction.

"What are you looking at?" Auriemma snapped.

"Put me in," she said back.

"Why, are you gonna play?"

"Yeah."

So he did, and she did. Before the half ended, Schumacher made a spectacular offensive rebound and put-back, putting UConn ahead 49–46, moments before Bird's buzzer-beating three-pointer. That was good enough for Auriemma, who started Schumacher to open the second half.

"I was a little bit angry the whole game, I'd say," Schumacher told the *Courant* days later. "Part of it was easy layups that they were scoring, which was driving me absolutely nuts. I don't think it was hard for them to score against us. Their whole offense was driving me crazy. I was irritated on the bench. I was irritated it was such a close game. I thought that I could make a difference. So I finally spoke my mind."

It was a rare display of defiance from Schumacher. And she would prove critical to UConn's success in the second half, adding eight points and four rebounds in fifteen minutes.

"[Red Sox manager] Don Zimmer would say that Bill Lee didn't have a killer instinct, but Bill Lee would pitch his guts out to win a game and Zimmer never understood that," Eagan said. "Schuey wasn't Shea Ralph. But in fairness, she's on a team with Shea and Svet and Diana and Sue Bird and Tamika Williams, and how much of the foreground is she supposed to have? She's on a team with people who can really score. I'm not sure I'm going to dial up a play for Schuey.

"In those games, they only wanted one thing from her. The thing about Schuey, sometimes we try to attribute things to attitude that are simply talent. I don't mean to denigrate her talent, but there's a level. Every team needs a Marc Iavaroni. You can't have five players who want the ball all the time. It's just not going to work. So that's what Schuey was."

UConn 56–50, 18:16 remaining

Siemon redeems herself for her turnover on the previous possession, blowing right past Tamika Williams for a layup to make it a four-point game again. Bird counters at the other end with a pull-up jumper on the baseline, but the shot bricks off the side of the rim. Riley clears the rebound, passing to Ivey to start an Irish fast break that ends with a layup by Haney, pulling the Irish within 56–54—one possession away from the lead for the first time in the second half.

The easy Notre Dame basket prompts Auriemma to call a twenty-second time-out with 17:39 remaining. The shooting statistics early in the half explain Auriemma's concern. The Huskies are 1-for-6, while the Irish are a perfect 4-for-4.

Taurasi reverses the trend for the moment, connecting

on a wing three-pointer out of the time-out to give UConn a 59–54 lead. It is Taurasi's third three-pointer, but just her first since the opening minutes of the game.

Taurasi's first three-pointer stopped a 6–0 Irish run to start the game. This triple comes early in the second half, after an 8–2 Irish run.

Trailing by two possessions again, the Irish return to their bread and butter, getting Riley the ball down low against Schumacher. But the lanky Canadian remains equal to the task, bothering Riley's shot attempt and forcing a miss, something the smaller Jones was unable to do in the first half.

But instead of grabbing the rebound, an off-balance Schumacher tries swatting the ball in Taurasi's direction. The freshman is not looking, however, and the ball sails past her into the backcourt, where Riley, who had given up on the play after her miss and was already retreating on defense, is able to control it.

Riley hands the ball to Ivey, who drives all the way from the three-point circle to the basket unmolested and hits the lefty layup to make it 59–56 as the clock ticks inside seventeen minutes.

Bird, who had no trouble connecting from forty-five feet to end the first half, is having issues with her patented pull-up jumper in the second. For the second time in a row, Bird maneuvers herself free for the shot, this time from the top of the key, but the ball front-rims and Jeneka Joyce grabs the rebound.

Bird makes amends by stepping in front of a lazy pass by Joyce, but then Joyce herself gets redemption. After staying stride for stride with Bird down the court, Joyce gets herself into the set position under the basket as Bird collides with her upon releasing a layup attempt.

Both Bird and Joyce tumble to the floor as the shot hits the backboard hard and misses. Remarkably, despite the obvious contact, no foul is called in either direction. It's either a blown noncall by both Mattingly and DeMayo—in perfect position on each side of the basket—or the height of discretion, the ultimate example of "no harm, no foul."

Burke, never shy with her opinions, chooses the latter interpretation.

"Good, solid no-call by Lisa Mattingly and Dennis De-Mayo. No advantage-disadvantage in that block/charge situation, so no whistle."

While the announcers and crowd focus on the carnage under the basket, Johnson makes a brilliant defensive play to retain possession for the Huskies. After Bird's miss, Haney outleaps Johnson for the rebound and starts to head up court for a four-on-three fast-break chance.

But just as Haney starts to make her move in the corner of the court, Johnson reaches in and pokes the ball free, forcing Haney to regather it along the sideline in front of the UConn bench. Johnson then harasses Haney, who is trying to pass the ball to Ivey in the middle of the court. Johnson denies this, too, knocking the pass attempt back off Haney and out of bounds, giving the Huskies possession with 16:34 left.

An opportunity for a quick, easy basket denied, Riley stands in the paint at the UConn end of the court, placing both hands atop her head in frustration. Since UConn went ahead 12–6 in the opening minutes, the Irish have continually clawed their way back, only to be denied just short of retaking the lead, often as a result of their own mistakes. This is not the recipe for success in a hostile environment.

During the stoppage in play, Auriemma replaces the frustrated Bird, who has now missed three shots in a row. By sending in Jones, Auriemma gives UConn a more traditional and balanced lineup, with Taurasi and Johnson alone in the backcourt.

Bird, still upset at the combination of the no-call and her own wayward shooting, plops down next to Dailey and vents steam, practically taking the arm off a team manager handing her a water bottle.

While Bird simmers, the Huskies stumble.

First Cash, then Williams, miss inside, with Notre Dame able to come away with the second rebound. Cash has tried all night to score on Riley and simply cannot do it. This time, Cash gets prime position on the right low block and has Riley out of position. But Cash can't handle Taurasi's entry pass cleanly, the hesitation allowing Riley to reposition herself and tower over her.

Her open road to the basket now closed, Cash tries a spin move into the lane, but the shot is off the mark.

Williams rebounds but gets swallowed up by Riley and Siemon and misses from underneath the basket.

But once again, Notre Dame cannot capitalize. Haney grabs the rebound off Williams's miss and lobs a perfect fifty-foot lead pass to Siemon, who has beaten the Huskies up the floor. But Taurasi gets back into the play just in time to alter Siemon's release of a running layup and the ball hits the glass too hard, bouncing away into the arms of Williams, who sends the Huskies back down the floor with sixteen minutes left.

"Both of these teams need to settle in here," Burke says. "Quick shots by Connecticut."

As the word "Connecticut" escapes Burke's lips, UConn attempts yet another quick shot. Again, it is the undeterred Cash, trying one more time to climb Mount Riley for a layup. One more time, the irresistible force is turned away by the immovable object. Cash starts to go, only to have Riley swallow her up. At the last moment, Cash tries a fadeaway shot, falling backward as she attempts a midcourse correction.

Haney grabs the miss, and Johnson again tries to harass the ball back into UConn's possession. This time, KJ is too aggressive, banging into Haney and drawing a whistle from DeMayo with 15:50 remaining, triggering the second half's first TV time-out.

Given the extra time to collect his thoughts, Auriemma turns his back to the players heading over to the sideline, then turns around, his gaze catching its intended target: Cash.

"Hey Swin, that's okay," Auriemma starts in mock empathy. "There were only three people around you."

Out of the time-out, the Irish, still trailing 59–56, go for the tie immediately, with Ivey attempting a three-pointer from the left wing. But her shot is long and UConn starts back the other way. After trying—and failing—to score inside on its past two possessions, the Huskies now try working the perimeter against the Irish zone, with Cash only handling the ball when it's eighteen feet from the basket.

Taurasi finally attempts a pull-up jumper from the left baseline, but Siemon stays with the freshman step for step, forcing Taurasi to overshoot the target. But with Siemon and Riley both on the strong side of the zone where Taurasi released the ball, Jones is free to grab the offensive rebound on the vacant weak side. Haney is the only Irish defender within reach, and all she can do is reach in. This time, UConn gets the call, sending Jones to the free-throw line with 15:19 remaining.

Jones misses the first shot, as Bird returns to the lineup, then connects on the second shot, UConn's first point in just over two minutes, pushing the lead back to 60–56.

After Cash nearly comes up with a steal from Siemon in the backcourt, Siemon outfoxes her tormentor for an easy layup, expertly using a pick by Ratay to curl through the lane with a full two-step advantage on Cash.

For Haney at the top of the key, it's an easy entry pass to the cutting forward, and all Cash can do is lunge in vain at the lob pass, which Siemon gathers with ease and scores to make it 60–58 with exactly fifteen minutes left to play. Siemon now has sixteen points on the night, including six of Notre Dame's first twelve points of the second half.

Jeff Siemon played linebacker for the Minnesota Vikings for eleven seasons, going to four Pro Bowls and playing in three Super Bowls between 1974 and 1977. But Siemon, who won the Butkus Award at Stanford in 1972 and was a 2006 College Football Hall of Fame inductee, played primarily in the shadow of the fabled Purple People Eaters—the Vikings defensive line of Jim Marshall, Carl Eller, Alan Page, and Gary Larsen.

So it was perhaps inevitable that Jeff's daughter, Kelley, would find herself in a supporting role in the frontcourt at Notre Dame in 2001. While Ruth Riley earned all the press accolades as she put together an All-American season, it was the inspired yet oft-overlooked play of Siemon that propelled Notre Dame toward a national championship.

Siemon, who grew up in Edina, Minnesota, and wore her father's jersey number (50) at Notre Dame, was even overlooked by the Irish coaching staff in high school. Recruited the same summer of 1996 as Riley, Siemon was helping to lead her AAU team its second national championship in three seasons when McGraw and her coaching staff came to watch her team play.

Siemon wasn't the object of their affections, but she quickly drew McGraw's attention.

"I went to see another player on her AAU team and I came away thinking, 'She's okay, but what about that Kelley Siemon!'" McGraw said. "I started talking to her and she was so positive and upbeat all the time. She was fun to be around. She was a hard worker, but she wasn't all about basketball. She had other interests and she was very religious. She was always really levelheaded. Maybe because she grew up with an athlete in her family, they weren't always heaping praise on her head, the way some kids get spoiled that way.

"So she came in and she was the best freshman in that class, better than Ruth. She was so athletic, she could run the floor and bang around and liked to be physical. She wound up having a great career because she could play off Ruth. They would double-team Ruth and she had a big game. If Ruth didn't score a lot of points, Kelley probably had eighteen or twenty, because that's what they gave her. She didn't force things. She was fine with her role."

Over her first three seasons, Siemon averaged 6.8 points in twenty-one minutes per game. A deeply religious woman—Jeff Siemon serves on the Fellowship of Christian Athletes Advisory Board and is Minnesota's Search Director for Search Ministries—Kelley played an invaluable, behind-the-scenes role as trusted teammate and friend.

"She was my rock," Ivey said. "I was the closest to her that season. She's just as bubbly as I am. She has a great personality, big Christian. Together we prayed and she would lead. She was a great listener. She would give you good advice, good Christian advice. She would just be there for you. If you needed to talk to somebody, good or bad, you would talk to Kelley. She was that type of girl. Outside of Ruth, I would want to play with Kelley. She's the one you want to be around all the time. All we did was laugh. She was a good-hearted person."

Siemon emerged from the shadows as a senior, earning Big East Most Improved Player honors by averaging 11.3 points and 7.1 rebounds, while playing an average of 30.1 minutes per game, all career highs by a significant margin.

"Kelley came in really focused our senior year and she really understood the role we needed her to play and she was willing and excited to do that," Riley said. "She was so great at getting out in transition and playing off the double-teams, doing all the little things that we needed done. She was an integral part of our team. We needed everyone to be a part of it, and Kelley was a pretty big piece, especially that game against the Connecticut, even with the broken hand."

On January 13, two days before UConn arrived in South Bend, Siemon broke the lower part of her fourth metacarpal bone in her left hand late in a game against Virginia Tech. She had gone in for a layup and got hacked, but it wasn't until Sunday's practice that the severity of the injury became apparent. After practice, McGraw informed the media that Siemon was "very doubtful" and was originally scheduled to have surgery on Tuesday, the day after the UConn game.

Very doubtful? Not the daughter of an NFL linebacker. Not only did Siemon play against the Huskies, she dominated them. Foiling UConn's plan to double-team Riley, as it had done so successfully in previous meetings, Siemon expertly provided Riley with an open cutter, making 6 of 9 shots to score 15 points, all the while playing with her left hand wrapped in a protective pad. Siemon added 8 rebounds and 5 assists, helping Notre Dame to a stunning 92–76 victory.

"One of the unsung heroes on that team was Kelley Siemon," Geno Auriemma said. "And nobody was paying much attention to her. The guards were good and Ruth was Ruth, but I thought that kid made all the difference in the world that year. Every time we doubled Ruth and there was a big play to be made, she made it, whether it was a fifteen-footer, or a drive to the basket, or a rebound. At the end of the game, you'd look at the stats and say, 'Yeah, she played pretty good.' But if you watched the game, you would say, 'Wow, that kid played great.'"

When the 2001 season was over, Siemon was drafted in the third round by the Los Angeles Sparks of the WNBA. But Siemon never played a game for them, instead choosing to follow her religious calling, and ended up playing for Athletics in Action, an international Christian sports ministry.

"She always went with her heart," Ivey said. "She always thought of others more than herself. She chose to run camps for underprivileged kids and teaching the Bible. She would read verses at night. She was very active with campus ministry. That's who she was. She was a very outgoing girl, but she went wherever her heart went. If that wasn't where the Lord wanted her to go, then that's what she felt. Maybe the WNBA wasn't right for her. She lived by her faith."

UConn 60–58, 15:00 remaining

UConn's subsequent possession, after Siemon's layup cut their lead to two points, results in a Jones miss from the foul line with 14:42 left, providing Norte Dame with its first opportunity to take the lead on a three-pointer since late in the first half.

Instead, the Irish go for the tie, working the ball down to Riley on the left side of the lane. This time, it's Cash who issues Riley a denial, moving her feet to force Riley almost beyond the end line. Riley can only attempt an awkward, double-clutch fadeaway jumper and the ball falls well short of the rim, into the waiting arms of Bird, who starts the Huskies on a fast break.

Bird attempts a one-handed bounce pass through a thicket of players to Cash under the basket, but the pass lacks touch and does not bounce high enough for Cash to gather. Instead, the ball slips through Cash's fingers and out of bounds. The Irish retake possession with 14:25 left, still looking for that elusive tie or lead.

Again the Irish try to get it done with Riley, and again

the prohibitive national player of the year cannot convert, missing a turnaround jumper over Schumacher from twelve feet with Williams grabbing the rebound.

As the clock goes under fourteen minutes, Williams passes to Taurasi on the wing. Taurasi dribbles to the half-court line, then succeeds where Bird had just failed, threading a perfect lead pass to Jones, who only has Siemon to beat for a layup. But Siemon holds her ground, nearly drawing a charge, which would be Jones's fourth foul.

But though there is no whistle, the hustling Siemon forces Jones to take a highly contested running layup, the ball glancing off the rim into the arms of Haney, who hands off to Ivey, giving Notre Dame its third straight chance to tie or take the lead.

"They're letting them play," Roberts says.

Since falling behind 7–6 in the first half, Notre Dame has had seven possessions in which they are trailing by one or two points. The results have been four missed shots and three turnovers, including back-to-back misses by Riley on Notre Dame's first two possessions while trailing 60–58.

Now, on possession number three, Ivey slows the pace down, allowing the other nine players to advance up the floor before she makes her way up court. The previous two possessions resulted in Riley taking shots out of her comfort zone. But at least those possessions resulted in a shot. This third time is hardly the lucky charm for the Irish.

Ivey passes to Ratay on the right wing with Taurasi in pursuit. This time, Riley is not looking for the ball on the low block: instead, she drifts into the right corner, while Haney pops out to the top of the key to take the pass from Ratay.

But as Ratay begins the passing motion, Williams races out and blocks her path. The set play busted, Haney fakes cutting to the basket, then fakes popping back outside, trying to throw Williams off the scent.

But all the zigzagging has the opposite effect. Ratay sees Haney start back out to the top of the key, as the original play called for, and throws the ball in her direction. But Haney has already started back the other way, and the pass sails untouched into the backcourt, where Haney can only touch it for a backcourt violation with 13:38 left, Notre Dame's fourth turnover of the half and fourteenth overall.

All game long, Cash has tried to power her way to the basket, driving into Ruth Riley's gut to score points. Virtually every thrust has been denied, either with blocked or altered shots.

Finally, with 13:20 left in the game, Cash discovers the weak spot in the Irish zone. Instead of putting her back to the basket and trying to post up, Cash drifts out to the perimeter, where the only defenders are guards such as Ivey and Ratay, both giving away as much as five inches to the 6-foot-2 pogo stick from Pittsburgh, instead of the three-inch advantage they enjoy with Riley.

After Johnson drives the baseline to pull the bigs even farther away from Cash, Johnson skips a pass back out to the foul line, where Cash has all day to line up an uncontested fifteen-footer, putting UConn ahead 62–58.

Riley has had no such difficulty finding the sweet spot in the post to do her scoring damage. But in the second half, Schumacher has presented the same type of challenge she did in the game at the Civic Center the year before, muscling Riley in the lane, fronting at times, making both the entry pass and the move to the basket far more difficult than when the 6-foot-2 Jones was guarding Riley in the first half.

And now, the frustration level begins to rise for the Notre Dame center. So focused is she on battling for position with Schumacher on the ensuing possession that Riley loses track of her positioning on the floor, spending three, then four full seconds in the painted area.

A whistle blows. For the second time in the game, Riley is called for three seconds. Even though play around her has stopped, Riley continues to attempt a turnaround jumper over Schumacher. Even though play has stopped, Schumacher emphatically swats the ball back in Riley's face, then gives Riley an icy glare.

Riley looks back and laughs, as much about the call as Schumacher's intimidation tactics. Muffet McGraw is not laughing. With exactly seven minutes gone in the second half, her team has committed five turnovers, for a game total of fifteen. With UConn leading by four points, McGraw chooses not to wait the additional minute for a TV time-out and signals for one herself.

All the turnovers have helped UConn maintain essentially the same lead they held at halftime, despite shooting just 3-for-16 in the second half.

And after the time-out, the Huskies continue struggling to find a quality shot in the half-court against the 2-3 zone. Bird and Johnson work the ball on the outside, with Bird dribbling and dribbling, unable to find an open player on the interior. For one of the few times all night, the shot clock dips into single digits with the ball not in a shooting position.

Finally, with eight seconds on the clock, Bird slips the ball inside to Williams, who has the ball stripped away by Ratay, coming over to double from the weak side with Williams oblivious to her presence, contending with the more formidable Riley in her path. One more time, the Notre Dame zone has frustrated the Huskies into a turnover.

The funny thing is, Muffet McGraw never set out to coach the 2-3 zone at Notre Dame. Although a self-described defensive-minded player, when McGraw arrived in South Bend to coach in 1987, she fancied herself more as a Paul Westhead than a Jim Boehiem.

"I started out always wanting to run and score a lot of points," McGraw said. "I turned into a zone coach once I got out here. Bill Fennelly [now head coach at Iowa State] was my assistant, and I think he talked me into it. I've changed so much since I got here. You start out as Bobby Knight, it's my way or the highway, and you finally realize that's not working with kids today. And you wind up morphing into someone you want your own kids to play for."

The 2-3 zone was a perfect recipe for the 2000–2001 Irish, who led the nation in field goal percentage defense (33.6 percent) and ranked fifth in scoring defense, allowing just 55.8 points per game (UConn ranked third in both categories, with totals of 34.3 and 54.9).

"That zone was a pain in the ass," Bird said. "I remember we worked on that even before we were going to play them. We were working on that for a long time. They were quick in their rotations. They had size and they had speed and they really clogged it up. And [when facing the] zone, at times, if you're not hitting shots, you can get numb. You get stagnant and you're just standing and it builds up and it can force you to look like crap out there."

With 6-foot-5 Ruth Riley putting up a roadblock in the middle, the other four players would be free to cover more ground on the fringes of the zone, unafraid of the consequences if an opposing player got by them toward the goal. Riley led the nation with 113 blocked shots in 2001, averaging just over 3 per game.

"Ruth made it work," McGraw said. "We had great athleticism on the wings with Kelley Siemon and Ericka Haney in the back. They could cover a lot of ground. And Niele could cover a ton of ground. And Alicia was really smart and could figure out who she needed to guard. And if they got by somebody, Ruth was going to block it. It probably hasn't been as good since she left. She was a dominating presence in the middle."

And with McGraw using a rotation of just six players for much of the season, the zone allowed the Irish to slow down the pace of games, giving her players a chance to rest and recover for the next offensive thrust.

Notre Dame's zone was the perfect foil for UConn's motion offense. The contrast of styles elevated the battles between the two teams to grand theater, like the Lakers–Celtics matchups in the 1980s that pitted Showtime against the original Big Three.

"Aesthetically, this particular game was a very pleasing game to watch," Eagan said. "And in some ways, it's because you have teams that are opposites. At this point, although they had some low-post scoring, UConn was a perimeter, push team. And it's not that Notre Dame didn't want to run, or couldn't run effectively, because they could. But their whole thing was built inside-out. And, really, Muffet had very little choice. You cannot, with that team, play UConn man-up. They'd get killed."

In the first meeting in South Bend, the Irish had done all the killing, forcing UConn to shoot 36.7 percent from the field, one of its worst shooting efforts of the season. Cash, Jones, Williams, and Schumacher, UConn's four primary post players, combined to take 26 shots, while the guards attempted a season-high 33 three-pointers, making just 11 of them.

"I think when you're facing a team that plays zone all the time, it puts pressure on you to score inside, so you don't just become a perimeter-shooting team," Auriemma said. "But because they were so big inside, we had Asjha, Tamika, and Swin, and we can't match up with their size. Too many times, we settled for jump shots, and Schuey wasn't a good enough offensive player at the time to throw the ball into her [so that] the zone has to collapse, and we get wide-open shots. So they were able to keep their zone extended and keep us from attacking it the way you're supposed to attack it.

"Now, they come here and we don't have Sveta and we lose Shea and we can't run as much as we want to. We can't press and trap them as much and get them into a game where our depth will take over. Now we have to play the way they want us to play. All the stars were lined up exactly right. They only have six guys and they have to play zone. We lose two guys and now we can't run. It's amazing how things work out like that."

UConn 62–58, 12:35 remaining

The Irish are shooting 6-for-11 in the half, but now, after Ratay's steal from Williams, they too see their half-court offense break down. Siemon, trying to run the right baseline as the shot clock winds under 10, puts up an off-balance lefty layup too short off the glass, the rebound going to Cash.

Even worse for the Irish, Riley reaches in to try and take the ball back from Cash and is called for her third foul with 12:13 remaining. The crowd, which has not had much to cheer about for the past few minutes, roars to life at the prospect of Riley fouling out.

And UConn goes right at the big girl on its next possession. Bird passes the ball into Williams in the post, then Williams makes a terrific drop-down bounce pass to Cash making a backdoor cut, hoping that Riley, who is out of position, will make another foolish foul.

But Riley is not falling for it. As Cash goes in for the layup, Riley emphatically blocks it with her right hand, showing no hesitation despite her three fouls, then grabs the rebound to send Notre Dame the other way.

The Irish wait for Riley to take her position in the post against Schumacher and feed her the ball. But after two previous failures to score against her nemesis, Riley passes out to the left corner, where the sharp-shooting Ratay is open for a three-pointer.

Johnson, who had been guarding Ratay, had momentarily paused in the lane as the ball went into Riley, then was screened off by Siemon as she scrambled to get back to Ratay in the corner.

By the time Johnson is free, Ratay has the ball in the firing position, and all Johnson can do is leap in her direction to try and harass the shot. Seeing Johnson commit, Ratay fakes the shot and starts to drive the baseline. But the airborne Johnson, still in Ratay's path, catches Ratay in the shoulder with her hip and sends her hard to the ground for a foul.

With the ball dead and the clock at 11:44, both teams

retreat to their benches for a TV time-out. McGraw takes the opportunity to get Riley and her three fouls out of the game, saving her for the stretch run.

"Where does your scoring come from right now, if you're Notre Dame?" Burke rhetorically asks her ESPN audience. "Riley on the bench, you can't work it through her."

The answer is Ratay, although it doesn't go smoothly at first. Out of the time-out, Ratay handles the ball, even with Ivey still on the floor. From either side of the court, Ratay, normally a stand-still shooter, tries driving into the lane, only to be rebuffed by the Huskies' post defense.

As the shot clock dwindles toward single digits, Siemon drives the left side of the lane, then looks to pass back to Ratay at the top of the key. Sensing the pass coming, Johnson dives and knocks the ball free, but Siemon is able to pick up the loose ball and get it to Ratay, who is now ridiculously wide open with Johnson sprawled on the floor.

Cash makes a late rush to try and bother the shot, but Ratay doesn't lead the nation in three-point shooting for nothing, and she buries her third three of the game (on three attempts) to pull Notre Dame within a point at 62–61 with 11:21 remaining.

Alicia Ratay grew up a fan of Larry Bird, so it's fitting that the guard from Lake Zurich, Illinois, would become a deadly accurate shooter from three-point range.

"I'm a big Larry Bird fan," Ratay told the *Chicago Sun-*

Times late in the 2001 season. "I watch his video before all of our home games. I just get motivated watching him play with so much tenacity."

As the late *Manchester (CT) Journal Inquirer* columnist Randy Smith said after one of Ratay's threes during the Big East final, "She's a one-trick pony, but that's one hell of a trick."

"She's the best pure shooter that I have ever seen," Siemon said. "That shot is so effortless. It's just a matter of whether or not she wants to shoot."

No one was better at shooting threes in 2001 than the 5-foot-11 sophomore. Ratay connected on 54.7 percent of her three-point attempts, the only player in women's Division I to shoot over 50 percent.

"I really don't think about stats," Ratay said. "If I need to shoot three-pointers, I'll shoot them. But if it's better passing it in to Ruth or blocking out, that's what I'll do. Whatever it takes for the team to succeed."

Ratay's long-range bombing allowed the Notre Dame offense to succeed in ways it hadn't before 2001, forcing defenses to play more honestly instead of liberally double-teaming Riley in the post.

"I think one of the things that Notre Dame didn't have [before 2001] was Ratay," Eagan said. "That was a big difference, because she was money from three. You didn't really have to worry about that with the Notre Dame team the year before. They really didn't have anybody that could beat you that way."

Ratay grew up in a basketball family. Her father, Greg,

played at Wichita State. Her sister Michele made All–Big Ten at Northwestern and later coached at Loyola (Illinois). Even her mother, Marilyn, played in high school and coached youth teams.

"My mom really helped me with my shooting form," Ratay said. "She's a miserable shooter, but she can really teach shooting."

Since arriving at Notre Dame, Ratay had also earned a reputation for letting her game do all her talking, literally. "Silent assassin" is the nickname that fit Ratay best.

"If you get more than three words out of her, you've done a good job," Ericka Haney told the *Sun-Times*.

"She's quiet vocally, but she's always heard on the court when she's playing. She's just a very unique person. I don't think you'll ever meet anyone like Alicia. She's just so funny in her own way. Once you get to know her, you'll just laugh at everything she does because she's so unique and so funny."

The term McGraw uses most to describe Ratay is "stoic." Her facial expressions rarely change during a game, regardless of whether she's made or missed the previous shot.

"I don't really talk much on the court," Ratay told the *Sun-Times*, in a rare interview during the 2001 season. "I'm a sophomore. I look to the seniors as the leaders and the people who are going to do the talking."

Taurasi tries to answer Ratay's bomb with her own three-pointer, but the freshman is not shooting the ball with nearly the same degree of accuracy as Ratay, her attempt hitting so hard off the back rim that the ball veers all the way back out to Bird, who is standing a good sixteen feet from the basket.

Having failed outside, the Huskies go inside, with Riley watching from the bench. But Cash, who has had Riley draped all over her nearly every time she's tried to take the ball strong to the basket, now chooses to shoot a fadeaway over the diminutive Ratay and misses. Schumacher, presently the tallest player on the floor, gathers the offensive rebound, but her putback attempt is short and the ball rolls out of bounds, possession to the Irish.

One more time, Notre Dame has the ball with a chance to take its first lead since 6–5, and for the first time in the second half, the Irish can take the lead with just a two-point basket. But Ivey, the steadying force of the Notre Dame offense, picks an inopportune time for a poor decision, pulling up for a rushed three-pointer early in the possession instead of working the Huskies for a good shot. Ivey, who is not nearly the long-range threat that Ratay is, back-rims the attempt, but the Irish get the ball back when Bird knocks the rebound out of bounds.

With 10:29 left, McGraw leaves Riley and her three fouls on the bench. Without a clear go-to player at the offensive end, and with Ratay inbounding the ball from under their own basket, disaster strikes the Irish again.

Ratay initially looks to get the ball to Siemon, leaning to her right to try and see past the gathered mass of post players in front of her. Two seconds into the five-second count, Ratay cannot find her first option, choosing instead to try and loft the ball to Ivey in the backcourt. But Bird, like John Havlicek did against Philadelphia thirty-six years earlier, reads Ratay's eyes and senses that her opponent's options are dwindling, which in turn allows her to easily knock the ball free and gather it for a UConn steal.

Another chance for Notre Dame to tie or take the lead goes by without so much as a shot at the basket, and UConn makes them pay dearly for the mistake, with Taurasi passing to Schumacher in the lane for a ten-footer and a 64–61 lead with 10:19 left.

The UConn basket—and, more significantly, the breakdown of her team's offense—prompts McGraw to finally summon Riley from the bench. But before Riley can check back in, the Irish must run another half-court set, and the rudderless ship continues to list.

Ratay tries taking Johnson off the dribble and pulls up for a twelve-footer from the wing—the kind of shot she rarely takes when Riley is on the floor—and the attempt hits the side of the rim and falls to Cash, who feeds the ball to Taurasi as the clock goes under ten minutes.

Taurasi goes again inside to Schumacher, but this time Amanda Barksdale, holding Riley's place in the paint, blocks the shot, and Siemon rebounds.

But with Riley still stranded at the scorer's table, the Notre Dame offense continues to stagnate. Again, it is Ratay handling the point duties, with Ivey working on the wings trying to execute a backdoor cut. But the UConn defense, feeling no urgency to double any of the Irish players, locks down the lanes and forces Ratay to pass outside to Siemon, who is barely able to handle Ratay's high pass.

As Siemon drives into the lane with the shot clock winding down to seven seconds, Ivey is finally able to successfully execute a backdoor cut, leaving a faked-out Bird in her wake. Ivey misses her first layup attempt but gets her own rebound and is fouled on her putback, missing the shot but earning a pair of free throws with 9:23 left.

Not only does Ivey get a chance to cut the UConn lead to one point, the stoppage of play allows Riley to check back into the game.

Ivey misses her first free throw as the substitution buzzer sounds and Riley takes her place along the free-throw line. Riley had dominated the first half, scoring fifteen points on 5-for-5 shooting. But in the second half, Riley is 1-for-4 with just two points.

"Why? The adjustment by Geno Auriemma," Burke says. "He starts the 6-5 Schumacher, so it's a different look. Even if she plays behind, the length of her inside is going to make it more difficult for Ruth. And Ruth has rushed things when she's touched it in the second half, because of Schumacher behind her."

"She's not used to seeing someone eye-to-eye with her," Roberts says.

Ivey makes the second free throw, and UConn's lead holds at 64–62. But even with Riley back in the game,

Schumacher continues to be a force, grabbing the offensive rebound off a Johnson miss and kicking back out to Taurasi, giving UConn a fresh thirty-second clock with 9:04 left. The ball works briefly back inside to Cash, when a scream pierces through the din at Gampel.

"Swin!" Taurasi shrieks. Inexplicably, the freshman sharpshooter has been left completely unguarded at the three-point line on the weak side of the court, prompting Taurasi to demand the ball from Cash, who quickly spots her open teammate and whips a pass right into her shooting position, not giving Haney any time to race over and bother the shot.

Taurasi has struggled from the three-point line in this game, but this attempt is so remarkably open, there's no chance it will miss. With 8:59 left, UConn's lead is back up to five, 67–62.

"You can't leave Taurasi to double," Burke says, a tinge of incredulity in her voice that Notre Dame could make such an obvious mistake at such a critical moment.

But with Riley back in the game, the Irish offense comes back to life. Notre Dame needs just ten seconds to get two of the points back, as Riley takes a pass in the post, then passes back out to Ratay, who hits a pull-up jumper from the foul line to make it 67–64 with 8:46 left.

For the first time in the half, both teams have their half-court games clicking at the same time. After Ratay's bucket, the Huskies work the ball around the perimeter with alacrity, the ball going through all five players' hands over the course of ten passes before finally, Bird gets Schumacher isolated on Riley, who is reluctant to foul, and Schumacher is able to score easily with a hook shot for a 69–64 UConn lead with 8:26 left.

"You can't beat a zone by just throwing the ball around the perimeter and taking jump shots," Auriemma said. "We weren't getting anything inside. Everything was on the perimeter. When we were patient enough to let someone in the lane touch it, pass-pass-pass, we would score."

UConn 69–64, 8:02 remaining

Schumacher's basket gives UConn five different players with at least ten points and gets the crowd roaring again. The sudden surge in noise seems to rattle the Irish, and they let the shot clock drift down to seven seconds without making any semblance of an open shot attempt, only to have the officials call yet another three-second violation.

Without realizing it, Joyce, under the watchful eye of referee Angie Lewis, drifted into the paint while Ratay was holding the ball on the perimeter, and Lewis calls her for it, giving the ball back to UConn.

Furthermore, during the sequence, the crowd had grown so loud that even though she is standing just a few feet away from Joyce and Ivey, McGraw could not get their attention as the play was breaking down, which lead to Joyce's three-second violation. And with the whistle, Taurasi urges the crowd to further increase the noise level, the Huskies sensing the chance for a knockout blow.

And Jones appears to apply one, following up her own missed jumper with an easy offensive rebound and layup, giving UConn a 71–64 lead with 7:34 left. But unbeknownst to the Huskies and their rabid fans, UConn will score just two more points over the next seven minutes, as the Irish will make one final, furious run to steal the tournament title.

After Jones's basket, Riley draws a foul on Cash with 7:23 left, prompting a TV time-out. And right out of the time-out, Johnson picks up her third foul, allowing Notre Dame to inbound a second time from under their basket.

But the third possession comes up empty, as Ivey attempts another backdoor cut, taking a pass from Riley but tripping over Taurasi's feet and hitting the underside of the rim with her desperation shot. The ball goes out of bounds to UConn with no foul called, an officiating trend that has frustrated both teams in the second half.

Now, with the clock ticking below seven minutes and with the chance to take their biggest lead of the game, the Huskies work the ball on the perimeter before Bird passes to Taurasi, cutting to the foul line right.

Taurasi sees Haney leaving Cash alone on the low block to come double, but Taurasi doesn't see Riley sliding across the lane to fill the void, and her quick pass to Cash is knocked away, sending Cash into the corner to retrieve it.

Cash is able to gather the loose ball and pass back out

to Bird at the top of the key with eight seconds on the shot clock. Bird then skips the ball over to Johnson on the left sideline with five. Johnson quick-passes back to the top of the key to Taurasi, who passes back to the left side for Bird, who releases a three-pointer over Siemon with three seconds left.

But the shot, which would have given UConn a seemingly insurmountable ten-point lead, back-rims, and Riley clears the rebound, passing to Ratay to start the Irish the other way with 6:40 remaining.

This time, Ivey tries driving to the basket the conventional way, taking the ball at the top of the key and going left. But Cash never gives Ivey a step and blocks the ball out of bounds with 6:30 left, staring Ivey down as the ball flies out of bounds.

But Notre Dame gets the last laugh. On the inbounds play, Ratay tries shooting over Schumacher from the low block, perhaps the most ill-advised attempt of the game. Predictably, Ratay's shot is long, but with Schumacher out of position, having missed the chance for a block, Riley is able to grab the offensive rebound and score.

Even better for the Irish, Johnson picks up her fourth foul in the process, and after Riley makes the free throw to complete the three-point play—cutting UConn's lead to 71–67—Auriemma is forced to make a curious substitution.

Now, with 6:21 left, Auriemma looks down the bench and calls the little-used freshman Maria Conlon into the game. Wanting to keep a three-guard alignment and looking to get rest for Cash, who has just checked out, Auriemma asks Conlon to hold Johnson's place for a minute or two.

And Conlon wastes no time getting herself into the box score. Holding the ball at the top of the key, Conlon spots Taurasi rushing toward her, moving through the lane from the baseline to the foul line and calling for the pass. Conlon delivers it, and without hesitation, Taurasi turns and fires a jumper over Riley, knocking down the shot for her team-leading fourteenth point and a 73–67 lead with 6:12 to play.

The Irish come right back with Riley, who gets position on Schumacher at her customary spot on the right block. But Riley is higher up the lane than normal, and though she successfully spins free of Schumacher to create daylight, she is left to take an eight-foot jumper rather than a layup, and her bank shot clangs hard off the rim and into the hands of Taurasi, who clears the defense and hands to Bird with 5:55 remaining.

Now the Huskies are in no hurry, and Bird dribbles alone just inside the half-court line, allowing the clock to start running down with her team holding a six-point lead. Bird and Conlon pass back and forth above the three-point line before Bird, on the left wing, passes to Taurasi at the top of the key.

Taurasi then passes to Conlon on her right. But Conlon does not pass the ball back. Instead, the freshman surprises every man, woman, and child in Gampel Pavilion by calmly spotting up and letting fly a three-pointer with 5:37 left.

If the shot goes, the kid from Derby, Connecticut, becomes an instant folk hero, giving UConn a nine-point lead. But there are no miracles just yet. Her shot is on line but just slightly long, and rims out.

But perhaps fortune is on Conlon's side tonight. Schumacher leaps over Riley for the offensive rebound but loses the ball as she returns to the floor, the ball squirting back out to the top of the key . . . right to Conlon, who beats Ivey to the ball and resets the offense.

This time, it's Taurasi, the freshman who is supposed to fire the three-pointers, who lets one fly a good five feet behind the line. Her shot, too, is on target, but it scoops out of the bowl and into the arms of Williams.

But before Williams can score the putback for an eight-point lead, she is grabbed from behind by Riley, as the whistle blows. A possession that began with the least likely player on the court trying a three-pointer ends with the game's most significant development since Ralph's injury. Ruth Riley, national player of the year, has four fouls with 5:24 remaining.

But Conlon isn't done, not by a long shot. In fact, she puts up another long shot on the ensuing inbounds, a three-pointer from the right corner. It's Conlon's second three-point attempt in a span of fifteen seconds.

"Conlon's not shy about shooting, for someone who doesn't get a lot of minutes," Roberts says.

"You certainly didn't think she was loose enough to start jacking 'em," Burke says with a laugh.

That Maria Conlon was even in the game to begin with was, of course, a function of injuries and foul trouble to several players ahead of her on the depth chart. In reality, on the night of March 6, 2001, very few observers of UConn basketball felt that Conlon should be on the team at all, let alone playing in the biggest game of the season.

The 5-foot-9 guard from Derby was the only scholarship player on the roster from the state of Connecticut. The only other Nutmegger on the team was Marci Czel, a walk-on from Guilford. The cynical view of Conlon was that she was a symbolic gesture—a token state player at a state university, placed on the team regardless of talent level.

And Conlon's freshman season leading up to the Big East final did little to dissuade the doubters. Arriving on campus out of shape, Conlon struggled to find minutes on the Greatest Team Ever Assembled, averaging just five per game over her first six games.

Then, in late December, a bout of mononucleosis knocked Conlon out for three weeks, including the first Notre Dame game in South Bend. It was not until the West Virginia game in February, after Abrosimova's season was declared over, that Conlon finally played more than ten minutes in a game. She made the most of her seventeen minutes against the lowly Mountaineers, scoring 16 points and hitting 4 of 6 three-pointers, then scored 9 more the next game against St. John's on 3-of-4 shooting from long range.

"Maria would be at the end of the bench, going, 'Put me in. Put me in. I know I can do it,'" assistant coach Tonya Cardoza told the *Courant* in 2003. "She wanted to be out there in the big games. She knew she could play."

That mental toughness, staying prepared to play and make an impact despite the difficult start to her career, impressed Auriemma enough to rely on her in this critical moment of the season.

"Half the battle of playing here and being successful at this level, you have to be a tough kid," Auriemma said. "I don't care how talented you are, you're not going to make it [if you're not]. And if you are tough, you can make up for whatever talent you lack. And you talk about Maria in that game, showing everybody she was a freshman. Maria Conlon as a junior and senior played seventy-seven out of eighty minutes in two national championship games and had one turnover. So sometimes when you're thrown into a game like that, and you see how they react, you can tell, she's got it."

But for the second time on this night, Conlon's three-point attempt is off the mark. However, just as they did with her first attempt, the Huskies control the offensive rebound, and Bird resets the offense, UConn still holding a 73–67 lead.

But this time, UConn's luck goes bad. After Bird and Conlon pass back and forth, Ivey attempts to get around Taurasi to harass Bird with the ball. Taurasi refuses to let Ivey get by her, locking up Ivey's arms like an offensive lineman in football protecting the quarterback.

Lewis watches the scrum and blows her whistle: illegal screen on Taurasi, her third foul. Notre Dame ball with 5:08 left.

UConn 73–67, 5:08 remaining

At this point, with Riley saddled with four fouls, McGraw takes her go-to player out of the game, planning to save her for the final minutes in hopes that the score will remain close enough for Riley to make a difference later on.

Ivey starts the Irish on that path, making both free throws after Taurasi's foul to cut UConn's lead to 73–69. At this point, Auriemma has come back with Johnson, ending Conlon's very busy seventy-three-second cameo.

UConn again eats some clock on its possession, working the ball on the outside for twenty seconds before Taurasi launches a jumper from the corner with 4:48 left. But Taurasi, who will finish 5-for-14 from the field, is long with the shot and Ratay controls for Notre Dame.

"We haven't been playing well as a team, but they're missing, finally," Ivey said. "We're getting stops and some big rebounds. It was hard, with them rebounding out of the zone. That was an issue. Even though they were hitting shots and making threes, we're still staying in what we do. Our staple was our 2-3 zone, and no matter what was happening, we had to stay in it. We didn't get away from our plan. It's amazing that you can stay in the zone for an entire game against a team that can shoot threes like that. It kills you to give them up."

After Johnson kicks an Ivey bounce pass out of bounds with 4:28 left, the shot clock resets to thirty seconds, and Cash and Jones replace Williams and Schumacher, while Riley continues to sit.

With neither of the 6-foot-5 players in the game, the lane opens up with all sorts of possibilities for guard play, and Ratay is the first to take advantage, driving from five feet behind the three-point line on the left wing all the way to the basket, shaking free from Bird at the last moment to score a layup with 4:23 remaining, bringing the Irish within a basket one more time, 73–71.

UConn has now not scored for two full minutes, and the scoreless streak continues as Cash once again cannot convert inside, forcing a shot against Barksdale and putting it on the glass too hard, the rebound going to Haney on the other side with 4:04 left.

"How about Ruth Riley goes out with foul number four, and they have responded," Burke says of the Irish.

For the eleventh time in the second half, Notre Dame has the ball with a chance to tie or take the lead. And finally, after all the squandered opportunities—0-for-7 from the field and three turnovers over the previous ten possessions—Notre Dame finds the mark.

Ivey and Siemon have looked to run the backdoor play on the Huskies throughout the second half, with limited success. But one more attempt finally achieves the desired result. When Ivey fakes to her right at the three-point line while Siemon holds the ball at the foul line, Johnson overcommits to Ivey's fake, allowing Ivey a clear path to the basket. Siemon then waits until the very last moment, lobbing a pass over Jones into Ivey's arms just as Taurasi slides over and knocks Ivey to the floor.

Again, the whistle blows. Again, the foul is on Taurasi, giving her four. And as if that wasn't enough trouble for the Huskies, the horn sounds and Riley trots back onto the court. Ivey then makes both free throws and for the first time in the second half, the score is tied, 73–73, with 3:51 left.

Ivey's second free throw ushers in the final television time-out, giving Auriemma and the Huskies time to figure out how to reverse the trend that has seen Notre Dame on a 9–2 run over the past 3:40, and now with the foul-prone Taurasi one false move from disqualification.

The first decision Auriemma makes is to leave his freshman on the floor. He has no choice. With Abrosimova and Ralph injured, Taurasi and Bird are the only two players left who can create their own offense, as well as offense for others. Auriemma must trust that Taurasi will be wise enough not to commit a foul with the game hanging in the balance.

Such trust was not rewarded in the Tennessee game on February 1 in Knoxville, when Ralph appeared to draw a charge against Kara Lawson in the final moments, only for the referees to swallow their whistles long enough for the play to continue, then ringing up a fifth foul on Taurasi. So infuriated by the sequence was Auriemma that he picked up a technical foul himself, effectively putting the game out of reach.

That second loss was the difference between the Huskies being ranked No. 1 in this game against the No. 2 Irish, instead of the other way around. This night, regardless of the outcome, both teams will be No. 1 seeds in the NCAA Tournament. But whichever team scores the most points over the final 3:51 is likely to take the top seed overall, meaning they'll have the easiest draw when the pairings are released five days later.

UConn's first possession after the time-out sends the ball back inside to Jones, who has not been the factor on offense in the second half that she was in the first, giving way to the resurgence of Schumacher. Now, Jones has a chance to make a big impact with 3:34 left, taking an entry pass eight feet from the basket and shooting over the smaller Ratay.

But Jones's shot bounces off the rim, and Haney clears the rebound to Ivey. Now it's Notre Dame's twelfth chance to take its first lead since 6–5. As expected, Ivey passes down low to Riley, guarded by Jones. And as expected, Riley turns to her right and puts up the shot from the middle of the lane. But unexpectedly, Jones rides Riley's shooting arm the entire sequence, causing Riley to shoot a rare air ball.

Siemon and Cash grab the miss simultaneously with 3:16 remaining, and Lewis signals for a jump ball. In the college game, tie-ups are decided not with a jump ball but by alternate possession, with a lit red arrow positioned at midcourt pointing in the direction of the team to be rewarded next. In this instance, the arrow points in Notre Dame's direction, allowing the Irish to retain possession.

With Notre Dame now inbounding from under its own basket, Auriemma quickly substitutes Schumacher for Jones, hoping to deny an easy lob pass to the 6-foot-5 Riley. And Schumacher does her job, forcing Riley up the lane, taking the lob away, and forcing Ivey to pass the ball to Haney on the left wing, guarded by Taurasi.

Realizing the opportunity presented her—Taurasi guarding her with four fouls—Haney goes right at the freshman, posting up Taurasi on the block, trying to draw the biggest whistle of the game.

But Taurasi is playing it smart and safe. As Haney backs her down, Taurasi puts both arms straight up in the air—unspoken code to the officials that she is making the effort not to foul. Besides, if Haney wants to try to score on a post-up, instead of Riley, UConn will gladly make that trade. Haney can't get Taurasi to bite and is left to try an awkward shot that never has a chance, cresting a good two feet short of the basket.

Schumacher easily clears the miss and hands to Bird, who slowly works the ball up court, dribbling in place near midcourt and not starting the offense until fifteen seconds remain on the shot clock, exactly three minutes and counting on the game clock.

The ball works its way around to Taurasi in front of the UConn bench. Taurasi then snaps an entry pass into Cash, with Riley looming behind her. After trying repeatedly to drive on Riley and coming away empty almost every time—and now with Ratay and Siemon forming a triple-team with the shot clock down to seven—Cash dribbles the ball out of the post into the left corner.

Trapped on the sideline and with the clock under five, Cash passes out to Taurasi, a good thirty-five feet from the basket. The shot clock at three, Taurasi heaves the ball at the basket, an impossible shot for most players, but almost routine for the fearless freshman. And Taurasi almost connects, the ball arcing directly online but just a shade long, hitting the back of the rim and moving into the arms of Haney, who has come to dominate the defensive board in the final five minutes.

Now, with 2:40 to play, the Irish try again to take the lead, after so many of their previous attempts to go ahead have ended without the ball so much as touching the rim.

This time, the ball does grab iron, but does not go in. Instead of setting up Riley on the low block, Ivey takes matters into her own hands, taking Bird off the dribble and driving the right side of the lane for a layup attempt.

Ivey's plan is to draw Schumacher off of Riley to contest the shot. Either way, Ivey figures, it's a win-win for

Notre Dame. If Ivey makes the shot, the Irish have the lead. If Ivey misses because Schumacher alters the shot, the Irish still take the lead, because Riley, left unguarded by Schumacher's switch-out, is alone for the easy put-back.

But as Riley backs into Schumacher for post position as Ivey starts her move to the basket, the Notre Dame center loses her balance and falls to the floor. Schumacher is now free to switch out and bother the shot, which Ivey puts high off the glass to avoid being blocked.

The ball glances off the backboard and bounces off the front side of the rim. But Riley is a split-second too late in righting herself, allowing Taurasi to slip inside and contest for the rebound.

Oblivious to their respective foul situations, Taurasi and Riley strain and grapple for the ball, only to have it come free and fall to the floor. Cash then grabs it and protects it with her elbows, shooing away Siemon and Haney to give the Huskies possession with 2:15 left, the score still deadlocked at 73–73.

"Boy, Niele Ivey did the job," Burke says. "She drew the help defender, so even if she missed, Ruth should have been there. But Ruth hit the deck! Otherwise, that's a Notre Dame layup."

Now, with Bird dribbling the ball at the top of the key and the game clock going under two minutes, the Gampel crowd collectively rises to its feet, ten thousand extra bench players exhorting their team to put the game away.

With thirteen seconds on the shot clock, Bird starts the play, passing to Johnson, who kicks back out to Taurasi at the top of the key, guarded by Ratay. Taurasi waits for Ivey to come over to double-team, then skips the ball back to Johnson, who feeds Bird in the left corner, staying ahead of the Notre Dame rotation and setting up the mismatch of Bird against the slower Siemon.

On cue, Bird races around Siemon into the lane, where she has an open twelve-foot pull-up waiting for her. But as Bird starts to square up, Ivey moves into her path, reaching in and knocking Bird to the floor, drawing a foul with 1:49 on the clock.

But though Bird continues with a shooting motion as she falls, both Mattingly and Lewis signal that the foul was before the shot, denying Bird two free throws.

His team not having run a successful half-court set for almost five minutes, Auriemma calls for a thirty-second time-out.

"With Svet out and Shea out, we only had two shooters, so the zone could come out and match up on the shooters and you can't spread the zone out enough, because your three-man is Tamika Williams, and she's not a scorer," Auriemma said. "We scored fifty-two in the first half because we had another ball-handler and scorer out there. Now, we're forced to go with two guards, unless I put KJ out there, and then we're really small. We just couldn't attack the zone the way we want to.

"Our defense was really good the second half, but you have to capitalize on opportunities. You can't come down and make two passes and get a jump shot. It was an odd game. That second half, you look at the last five minutes, there's not a lot to be proud of. Both teams were spent. We couldn't keep up that pace from the first half."

The play he calls is designed for Taurasi to drive the lane, either getting herself an open look for a layup, or drawing the defense and feeding Schumacher for an easy two. After taking a pass from Bird, Taurasi uses one dribble to get past Ivey, then another to launch herself from the three-point line into the paint with a jump-stop, landing with two feet at the free throw line, then propelling herself back into the air.

Now, Taurasi must either release the ball to the basket or pass to a teammate to avoid a traveling call. With Riley jumping out to block her path, Taurasi chooses the latter, dumping the ball down to Schumacher, who is open for a layup.

But Riley is able to get a hand on Taurasi's pass, knocking it to the floor and messing up the timing of the play. Schumacher is forced to adjust to pick up the loose ball, and that causes the gangly center to take too many steps. Lewis is right there to signal the travel, and Notre Dame has possession again with 1:40 left.

Score tied 73–73, 1:40 remaining

Taurasi was a gambler as a freshman, supremely confident her talent would bail her out when her technical skills, still raw and youthful, could not complete a task alone.

But the Gambler didn't always know when to fold 'em, leading her to foul out of four games earlier in the season. And twice in the first half of this game, her penchant for the behind-the-back blocked shot—a lazy, low-percentage defensive play after allowing her man to get past her—has now left Taurasi in serious foul trouble.

"I remember talking to her at the end of the year," Auriemma said. "I asked her, 'Do you know what our record was this year? We were 32-3. You know how many games we lost that you fouled out of? Three. You know how legends are born? The last three minutes of the game, they win the game. They don't sit on the bench and clap and say, "C'mon you guys!"' So I asked her, 'What do you want to be? You want to be a legend, or do you want to sit and watch someone else win the game?' She never fouled out again.

"She's very competitive that way, but I've had a few of those. Shea and Svet were the same way. If Shea lost the ball coming down on the break, what do you think she was going to do? A quick U-turn and hunt the guy down and tackle her. Down in Orlando [in 2000 against Penn State], what happens? Svet comes down and misses two layups with three minutes to go and we're up fourteen. She turns around and tackles the kid."

Now, Taurasi tries to make a smart play, but this final gamble backfires. With the bruising Siemon storming to the basket on a pick-and-roll from Riley, Taurasi sees an opportunity to make a big play, sliding into Siemon's path to draw an offensive foul. But Taurasi is a

shade late, her upper body still moving into the set position as Siemon slams into her, just as her father the linebacker did so often into a line of scrimmage.

It was close, very close. But not too close to call. De-
Mayo whistles for a blocking foul. It's Taurasi's fifth.
She's gone.

"Oh my god!" Taurasi exclaims while still prone on
the floor, her hands on her head in disbelief.

On the UConn bench, associate head coach Chris
Dailey and assistant coach Tonya Cardoza motion the
incredulous Taurasi back to the bench—the show must
go on—while Auriemma paces nearby, head down, one
hand on his forehead, dismayed that he no longer can
turn to his dynamic game-changer.

In the huddle during the automatic substitution time-
out, Taurasi, who scored fourteen points but made just
four of twelve three-pointers against the Irish 2-3 zone,
remains distressed, barely containing her emotions. She
is agitated as she listens to Auriemma's instructions from
the back edges of the huddle, instead of deep within it,
unable to accept that she will not be heading back onto
the floor to execute her coach's orders.

Once, then twice, Taurasi lets fly a monosyllabic burst
of profanity, then sulks to a seat on the bench. As she
passes Auriemma, his head is still down, but he reaches
out and gives Taurasi a quick, encouraging slap on the
backside. Hang in there, kid.

"I remember saying to myself, How about that SOB?"

Auriemma said. "The one time she tries to do the right thing and she gets screwed."

Eight years later, on a sunny, summer day in Phoenix, Taurasi watches a replay of the foul for the first time since it occurred. She watches a second time. Time has not changed her opinion . . . for the most part.

"I don't know," Taurasi says. "Both my feet are set. It's a little triangle play and you know it's coming, but I can't move until the pass is made. But look at my feet! I don't know. I don't know."

Taurasi had lost all her appeals with the officials, but she still found justice. Siemon, a 43 percent free-throw shooter, steps to the line with Notre Dame's best chance for its first lead since the first three minutes of the game. But Siemon back-rims her first attempt with a mocking thud as the crowd cheers with delight.

Siemon had made her previous eight attempts during the tournament. But now, with 1:15 left in a tie game, she comes undone. Apparently rattled by her miss, Siemon practices her follow-through before receiving the ball for the second shot, but it fails to reboot her system. Overcorrecting for the length of her first attempt, Siemon puts up a second shot that falls a good six inches short of the rim, barely grazing the net as it passes under the basket and into UConn's possession, score still tied at 73.

"She almost threw it out of her hands," Burke says. "She wanted no part of that basketball."

The crowd erupts again, chanting "Air ball!" as McGraw cajoles her players heading back to the other end, "It's all right, let's go!" McGraw knows they cannot lose focus now, even for just a moment, with the clock nearing one minute left and Sue Bird bringing the ball up court.

With Cash having replaced Taurasi, the Huskies have become longer and more agile in the paint, with another rebounder to join Kelly Schumacher and Asjha Jones inside while Bird and Kennitra Johnson work the outside.

But it's hardly the lineup that Auriemma wants on the floor in the final minute of a tie game in March. Eleven months ago, when he stood before the crowd at the state capitol and guaranteed a repeat, he didn't figure he'd be trying to do it without Abrosimova, Ralph, and Taurasi.

"I know for me, a few times, play is going on at the other end and I'm on the visitor's bench and I stand up and look down and I see Shea and Sveta sitting there, and I thought, 'There's 3,000 effin' points sitting there. We could use a couple right now.'

"And then, we're playing the last minute, and I'm sitting there going, There's three of the best players that will ever play at this school sitting here, two because they're hurt and can't play and one because she's just a dumbass who fouled out. So I've got three of maybe the best players ever to play the college game, and they're all sitting here while we're trying to win this god-damn game."

One player Auriemma needs to step up in the final minute is Cash, but she has turned in a poor performance so far, making 3-of-14 shots and grabbing just five rebounds in twenty-five minutes. But her two biggest contributions are yet to come, though both will go virtually unnoticed.

The clock down to fifty-seven seconds, Johnson ends a back-and-forth passing game with Bird on the perimeter and dribbles hard toward the goal from the right edge of the key, drawing Riley away from the basket and Haney up from the right baseline.

The path along the baseline cleared, Jones slides across from the right corner as the charging Johnson shovels the ball to her for a backdoor layup. But Riley is able to recover just in time to impede Jones's progress, forcing her to use the far side of the glass in order to avoid the block.

Jones tries spinning the ball onto the backboard, but her arm is extended too far to control the release. The ball ricochets hard off the glass, glancing off the front of the rim and out.

But while Riley was successful in altering the shot, her momentum leaves her unable to rebound it. Riley tries lunging back, and Ivey crashes hard. But Cash beats them both, getting a hand on the ball amid a thicket of arms, deflecting it over Ivey's head and into the boxed-out arms of Johnson, the shortest player on the floor at 5-foot-7.

"One play doesn't win a game," Auriemma said. "But if that doesn't happen, we're not in a situation for [the rest of the play] to happen. You can look at it and say, Generally, games don't come down to one play, but you look at it and say, Man, that was a huge play right there."

Johnson's right-place, right-time moment isn't over. The jostling for the rebound leaves Johnson's body facing out toward the perimeter as the ball lands in her hands. And at that moment, the only player on the perimeter is Bird.

Johnson fires the ball back out, leaving Bird all the time she needs to loft a wide-open three-point attempt. Only Ratay comes within five feet of Bird's follow-through, not nearly close enough to have any effect. The ball splashes down successfully. After just over three minutes of stalemate, the deadlock is broken. UConn leads 76–73.

"She has not played the greatest of games, Sue Bird," Burke says. "But stick it when you need it!"

"This is my favorite part," Bird said. "For KJ to get that rebound at all was intense, but as I'm shooting it, she already has her hands up, like, 'It's good.' I mean, how did KJ even get this rebound? It bounced out to her, but in the land of the giants.

"I'm out there watching and it's something we work on all the time: an offensive rebound and kickout for a three. When the post players get it, it rarely happens. But

I knew KJ wasn't going to go back up with it and there I was. We made eye contact and 'Boom.'"

The clock reads 47.9 seconds, but it is not correct. After rifling through the net, the ball was inadvertently kicked up court by Jones, causing the official scorekeeper to flinch and allowing 1.3 precious seconds to tick away. But after basketball's version of the booth review— DeMayo consulting a TV monitor at the scorer's table— the clock is reset to 49.2 seconds.

"Every second, every tenth of a second, so precious in a game like this," Roberts says.

While she waits for play to resume, Bird raises one leg and wipes the bottom of her sneaker with her hand. Then she repeats the process with the other. It mimics the iconic foul-line fidget practiced by that other basketball Bird, who also played the occasional game at the Civic Center and knew a thing or two about delivering in the clutch.

Sue's motivation is far from symbolic. The double-swipe gives her hands a fresh coat of sawdust and rosin, ensuring a better grip on the ball. But this time, with the championship at stake, it would fail her.

"At that point, I'm like, 'We're good, we're good,'" Bird said. "But I know there's a lot more to come."

UConn 76–73, 49.2 remaining

During the ninety-second delay, while DeMayo resets the game clock, both teams gather at their benches for an impromptu strategy session. Notre Dame uses the opportunity to design a play that will yield quick points, hoping to utilize the remaining time to get two possessions to UConn's one.

Because the shot-clock duration in the women's game is thirty seconds, as opposed to thirty-five in the men's game, Notre Dame can go for a quick two-point basket now, cut the deficit to one point, then play tough defense and regain possession with roughly ten seconds remaining to attempt a game-winning shot.

A quick possession would seem to call for one thing: a quick entry pass to Riley for a post-up move. And during the clock stoppage, Riley opens a coach's folder in the huddle and consults with McGraw on the most efficient way to exploit her advantage.

But the play McGraw calls is not designed to go there.

"It's a play we used to run as a last-second play for Alicia," Ivey said. "Alicia is supposed to run through [the lane] and that's the first option, getting it to Alicia for a three-pointer off a screen. It's either a three or a lob to Ruth in the post."

But Ratay cannot get open after Notre Dame inbounds the ball. With the clock down to forty seconds, Ivey goes to the second option, throwing the ball into Riley, who throws the classic right-shoulder fake at Schumacher.

After playing solid defense for the majority of the second half, Schumacher inexplicably bites at the fake, allowing Riley to spin back to her left and make an uncontested layup. UConn's lead is down to a single point at 76–75, and the entire sequence has taken just eleven seconds. Notre Dame immediately calls a thirty-second time-out with the game clock at 38 seconds.

As Schumacher retreats to the UConn bench, Auriemma is waiting for her. The UConn coach is incredulous that Notre Dame was able to score so quickly, and so easily.

"Are you [kidding] me?" Auriemma asks Schumacher with a sarcastic smile. Then the smile vanishes and Auriemma unloads both barrels into his player.

Riley now has twenty-two points, but after Auriemma's rant in the time-out huddle, Schumacher resolves not to let Riley get another uncontested shot.

With thirty-eight seconds remaining and a one-point lead, the Huskies will have to shoot the ball at least one more time, with the worst possible outcome being surrendering possession with eight seconds left, plenty of time for Notre Dame to call time-out and steal a victory.

With Taurasi gone, the only option for Auriemma is to give the ball to Bird and let her create. Knowing that the ball will be Bird's exclusively, McGraw switches out of the 2-3 zone for the first and only time in the game, letting Ivey loose on Bird to check her every move.

Now it is UConn that employs a clear-out tactic, allowing Bird to try and beat Ivey off the dribble. Wanting to use up as much of the shot clock as possible, Bird slowly works her way up court, taking nine seconds just to reach the half-court line.

But Bird, who has managed to play thirty-five minutes despite the back spasms, no longer has the burst in her legs to shake free and make a play. Once, then twice, Bird tries to get past Ivey along the left sideline, right in front of the UConn bench, but Ivey stays with her step for step, forcing Bird back to the top of the key to reset and try again.

Finally, with the shot clock down to ten seconds and the game clock at eighteen, Bird tries for a third time to run the sideline, dribbling all the way to the end line. But once again, Ivey shadows Bird all the way down, not allowing her an avenue to the basket.

Her path cut off, Bird turns to dribble her way back out. But as her body pivots to the left along the baseline, the ball is momentarily exposed in her right hand, just enough so that Ivey can get her right hand on it to try to spin it free.

"The design of the play was a pick-and-roll," Bird said. "I had to go back and forth a couple of times. Niele Ivey was a good defender, she was strong, and I couldn't get around her at all. And when I went to go back, that's when she hits it."

The swipe does not result in a steal, but for Notre Dame, it has the desired effect. The split-second backspin on the ball from behind, coupled with Bird's momentum moving forward, causes the ball to slip out of Bird's hand and roll out of bounds along the sideline with 16.3 seconds left.

Bird, believing that Ivey was the last to touch it, takes one step toward the rolling ball but does not attempt to save it. As the ball bounces into her teammates' legs on the bench, the whistle blows and Bird starts toward the spot where she will inbound the ball.

But Bird will not inbound the ball. Referee Angie Lewis, stationed in the corner of the court by the UConn bench, has a clear view of the play and emphatically points toward the Notre Dame basket, giving the Irish possession.

Bird is stunned. She is certain Ivey touched it last, and puts her arms out in a pleading motion before moving her hands to her head in disbelief. She turns to face Lewis to make her case, but Lewis is resolute.

"It went off of you," Lewis barks at Bird, ending the discussion before it can start.

Bird's hands remain on her head, a sarcastic smile breaking across her face. But two replays seem to show that Bird indeed touched the ball last before it squirted loose. Even worse for Bird's case, Auriemma says nary a word to the officials, a tacit admission that the call was correct.

"First of all, I know I have the 'I'm never wrong' attitude. It's part of my charm," Bird said. "You have to understand, in the heat of the moment when it happened, I knew she hit the ball out. Now, when I watch it [eight years later], I'm not stupid. But in the moment, I know she hit it out of bounds. I could have grabbed it. But I went, 'Okay, she hit it.' So when the ref said it was off me, I was like, 'What!?' I knew she hit it. The fact that it hit off me, I didn't really feel it.

"I remember thinking like, 'Aw [man], if we lose this game, I'm going to shoot myself.' I just wanted to make it right because that would be the play that people remember."

Suddenly, Notre Dame has possession, down by one point. The sequence could not have played out any better. Instead of having maybe seven or eight seconds to execute the winning play, the Irish have sixteen seconds in which to sink the Huskies again.

Emerging from the time-out, Notre Dame prepares for a carbon copy of their previous possession, with Ratay the first option, but again, the ball winds up going inside. Ivey takes the inbounds pass deep in the backcourt and rushes forward, motioning with her free hand for her teammates to clear the lane area, leaving Riley alone with Schumacher again, in order to apply the Shaq spin a final time.

With the clock down to eight seconds, Ivey makes the pass to Riley, who again lowers her right shoulder from eight feet away before spinning left to the basket. But Schumacher won't be fooled again. She ignores Riley's feint to the right and reacts to the move left. But for all her anticipation, Schumacher is still a half-second too slow, allowing Riley enough clear sky to get a shot attempt.

All Schumacher can do is lean her upper body into Riley to deny the shot, but the impact against Riley's left arm is too great to go unnoticed. Mattingly raises her arm and blows her whistle with 5.1 seconds left. Riley can win the game at the free-throw line.

While Riley prepares for her opportunity to put the Irish in the lead for the first time since the score was 6–5, Bird heads over to her bench to map out UConn's final possession. Bird asks if Auriemma wants to use a timeout after Riley's second shot, but Auriemma declines. He doesn't want to give Notre Dame a chance to set up its defense, which almost certainly would call for suffocating Bird's advance up the court.

"In any particular game, you have a certain philosophy," Auriemma said. "If the situation calls for it, sometimes you need a time-out. Sometimes you don't. So when is which? It depends. My feeling is, if I call timeout, Notre Dame says, 'This is how we're going to guard the inbounds, this is who we're going to trap, here's who we want taking the last shot.'

"So I'm thinking, 'Why do I want to give them the chance do that? Even if we screw the whole thing up, the worst that can happen is we're going to overtime.' So in that situation, I know who is going to touch it and who is going to shoot it. And there's nothing they can do about it. That's the thinking."

A year earlier, it was Abrosimova who got the ball with 4.4 seconds left against Tennessee. But the fleet-footed Russian is watching this sequence in street clothes, with Ralph and Taurasi also not available. Bird is the only player left on the court that Auriemma can trust to create a shot with just five seconds to work with.

Bird has already ended one half with a buzzer-beater. Can lightning strike twice, even in a snowstorm?

"Who's to say if Sveta had been available that night, who would have taken that shot?" Auriemma said. "Who's to say if Diana hadn't fouled out, who would have taken that shot? I think it just kind of came down to that. Not that I wouldn't have made the same decision anyway, but your decisions were almost made for you.

"All we did was do exactly what we had been doing every day in practice, after a made or missed free throw. That's why we didn't call a time-out. We didn't need a time-out. I looked over and Sue looked over at me and I said, 'Just run what we normally run.' I figure whatever she does, I'm good with it. I think Sue knew: This is up to me right now. This is where I want it to be, and there's no doubt in my mind I'm going to make this shot.

"Anybody who knows anything about basketball knows that. We all knew that. We all knew, beyond a shadow of a doubt, that if Dee or Sue got a shot at the end of the game, the ball is going in. And we were lucky to be one of the only teams in the country to have that in the backcourt. It's no mystery. If you have those kinds of players, you can make those things happen. If you don't, you're screwed."

UConn 76–75, 5.1 remaining

It remains one of the most famous buzzer-beaters in men's NCAA Tournament history.

On March 19, 1981, in the regional semifinals at the

Omni in Atlanta, Notre Dame takes a 50–49 lead over Brigham Young University on a pull-up jumper by Kelly Tripucka with eight seconds left. Brigham Young takes a time-out, then inbounds the ball under its own basket to its two-sport star, Danny Ainge.

With the Irish defense retreating to avoid a foul, Ainge weaves his way up court as the clock winds down, splitting three defenders near midcourt—among them future fellow NBA stars Tripucka and John Paxson—before driving right down the middle toward the basket.

With two seconds left, Ainge completes his remarkable rush, scooping a running layup just over the outstretched arm of another future NBA star, Orlando Woolridge, scoring the basket to give BYU a thrilling 51–50 victory.

Ainge, of course, would pass on a baseball career with the Toronto Blue Jays and go on to win two NBA titles in the 1980s as a guard for the Boston Celtics, then add a third title as the Celtics' GM in 2008. But in 1981, his coast-to-coast game-winner left Irish eyes crying.

Twenty years later, the Irish women found themselves in an eerily similar scenario.

After Schumacher's foul with 5.1 seconds left, Riley steps to the free-throw line, having made 6 of 8 attempts earlier in the game, poised to put Notre Dame ahead by one point.

But like Siemon only a minute earlier, Riley back-rims her first attempt. Tamika Williams, manning the spot on the lane closest to Riley, thrusts her fists into the air as the arena erupts once again. At worst, all the Irish can do now is tie the score at 76–76—unless Riley misses again and Notre Dame gets the rebound. That nightmare scenario comes to Williams's mind instantly, and she implores Schumacher, manning the spot on the foul line closest to the basket, to get the rebound.

But there is no rebound of the second shot. Riley calmly knocks down her second attempt, tying the score at 76–76. With the clock not starting until after her pass is made, Schumacher takes the ball out of the hoop and prepares to inbound. Bird is ready.

"I had a feeling Ruth was going to make the free throw," Bird said. "Before her second free throw, I told Swin, 'Give me the ball.' We've done this a lot in practice. I'm pretty confident in that situation, a lot of confidence. You just go. When you're tied, there's no pressure. The worst that can happen is overtime, so I was very calm. I got the ball and just went."

As Riley's game-tying free throw is going through the net, Bird rushes down from the three-point line toward the baseline, where Schumacher hands her the ball, starting the clock countdown from 5.1 seconds. The Irish still have a foul to waste, having committed only five in the half, but because the Irish do not have any time-outs remaining, McGraw is not able to communicate this potential strategy to her players in time.

As Bird takes the ball, four of the five Notre Dame defenders have begun retreating into the backcourt. The

Irish players are left to make their own decisions in dealing with this final UConn threat.

Ivey is the first to challenge Bird's progress, chasing
her down from the foul line as Bird takes the ball from
Schumacher.

But instead of waiting for Bird to come meet her with
the ball near midcourt, Ivey chases her prey from behind as Bird receives the pass. That allows Cash, who
has struggled the entire game, to make the most important play of the entire night, setting a barely notice-
able screen on Ivey that allows Bird to rush up the floor
unguarded.

One second into the final sequence, Notre Dame is
already doomed.

"Coming on the chase is always hard, because she has
the momentum and she always did a great job of getting
the ball and catching angles, which is what you're supposed to do as a point guard," Ivey said. "I just remember not keeping her in front of me from the beginning.
I called for help, but that was my man. I was like, Damn.
There was nothing I could do. I was just hoping someone would pick her up."

In less than two seconds, Bird has advanced the ball
from the baseline to half-court, Ivey a full two strides
behind her. With the clock ticking down to three seconds, Siemon is the next impediment, drifting into Bird's
intended path between the midcourt and three-point
lines.

Seeing Siemon moving to the right across her sight

line, Bird alters her course toward the middle. There, under the letter of the law, the play should have ended. A whistle should have blown, giving Notre Dame possession of the ball at midcourt with just over two seconds left.

Bird is running so fast, and her move to the middle is so sudden, her dribbling motion is thrown off ever-so-slightly, causing the ball to stick under her right armpit for a split-second.

But in those precious tenths of a second, with the ball off the floor, Bird's furious feet take one, then two, then an illegal third step, before she is finally able to get the dribble back alive.

Even by NBA standards, this is a major-league travel. But Mattingly, running alongside Bird the entire time, does not blow her whistle, and when the ball touches the floor again, Bird is at the Notre Dame three-point line, the clock down to 2.5 seconds.

Mattingly is not the only one who has not read Bird's movements correctly. Siemon, Notre Dame's last chance to prevent Bird from getting an open look at the basket, chooses instead to let Bird continue by her unimpeded, concerned more about fouling and giving Bird two chances to win the game from the free-throw line.

But by allowing Bird to race past her, she is still giving away a free-throw, however rushed, as the clock continues to run out. Bird passes to Siemon's left at the three-point line, switching her final dribble to her left hand to create a little more open space, the ball hitting the floor with 1.8 seconds left.

Now, Riley becomes the last line of defense. Bird picks up the dribble about twelve feet from the basket and stops on a dime, lifting for a fallaway jumper.

As Bird rises, Riley rushes up and reaches out with her right hand to block the shot.

"We knew Sue would attack us, like a good point guard does," Riley said. "My main objective was to keep her in front of me and not let her get by me to score and just challenge the shot without fouling her. We definitely didn't want her shooting free throws to beat us."

But Bird, who elevates with 1.2 seconds and counting, is able to hang in the air long enough to let Riley's lunging arm start its downward path. The sky clear, Bird releases the shot with 0.9 seconds on the clock, the ball barely avoiding Riley's fingertips on its way to the basket.

"I saw Ruth and I was like, 'Uh-oh,'" Bird said. "That was definitely the most I ever faded. I just wanted to get something up there. I knew I had to shoot it at that point. I threw it up with my right hand going, 'Please!'"

Because Bird has had to adjust in midair to Riley's wingspan, her shot produces considerably more loft than length. As the ball arcs, peaks, and falls back to earth, the crowd of 10,027 collectively sucks in its breath, and for that final half-second on the game clock, there is an eerie semisilence in Gampel Pavilion.

It is enough time for McGraw to realize what is about to happen.

"When the shot went up, from my vantage point, I thought Ruth was going to block it," McGraw said. "I saw Sue shooting it and I saw Ruth going up and then I thought, 'It's going in.' I just watched it go over Ruth and right in."

The ball finally comes down and clangs the front of the rim with a dull thud that echoes across the suddenly silent arena. At that same moment, the red light behind the backboard comes on and the buzzer goes off, marking the end of the game.

As the buzzer continues to sound, the ball gently nestles against the back of the rim, before dropping straight down through the net.

UConn 78, Notre Dame 76.

"Big time!" Burke yells.

Like that, the crowd erupts in a wild scream of joy. Bird, whose momentum had carried her from the foul line all the way to her team's bench, looks back over her shoulder at the basket, waits for the ball to fall through, then raises her arms triumphantly as Taurasi gathers her in a hug and hoists her into the air.

"I remember running right into Dee," Bird said. "She was right there. I don't know how it went in. I never wanted to hug her so bad. And then everyone tackled me and I was crying. When I turned that ball over [with 16.3 seconds left], I knew that if I didn't hit that game-winning shot, there were going to be problems in the UConn coaching offices.

"So, for my teammates, I owed it to them. For my

coaches, for myself, for everybody, especially for Shea and Svet, I really wanted to go for it. We played our hearts out for Shea."

The rest of the UConn bench mobs Bird, while Riley, who has come within a fingertip of forcing overtime, falls to the floor in despair.

"She put it up and I remember turning around and seeing it going in," Riley said. "After competing that hard, back and forth, to lose on a buzzer-beater that goes right over your fingertips, that's a tough one to take. But it's also one you learn from and move on from, and you play better the next time."

Ratay, who watched from under the net as the ball came through it, kicks the ball into the crowd by the UConn bench, nearly hitting Abrosimova on her crutches. The Russian does not see the ball coming, having covered her face, overwhelmed with joy and trying to figure out how to jump up and down safely. She is quickly met by Ralph, and the two injured stars share an emotional embrace.

"Having watched Sue in practice and knowing she was the go-to player who took over games and made big plays in practice when they needed to be made, it had that feel to it," Ralph said. "When the shot went up, I never felt we were going to lose that game, so I felt it was going to go in. And the celebration was a blur."

But technically, the game isn't quite over. While the Huskies celebrate and the Irish ruminate, the officials debate. In the rush of the moment, it wasn't immediately clear—to the refs, anyway—that the shot had been released in time, and they are now huddled by the scorer's table, wanting to see a replay to confirm the authenticity of the ending.

Seeing this, some of the Irish players by the Notre Dame bench began signaling "no good" with their arms, trying to talk the officials into it. But McGraw does not join the lobbying effort. If anything, McGraw seems confused by the conference. Wasn't it obvious the shot was good?

It was. While the officials gather on one sideline, reporters and fans jockey for position behind Burke and Roberts at their TV table, clamoring to see the replay being broadcast worldwide.

And there it is. In slow-motion, Bird dribbles into the lane, pulls up with 1.2 seconds left, and releases the shot at 0.9. Even before the officials can signal the basket good, the roar of the crowd by the ESPN table confirms it: UConn has won the Big East Tournament title.

With that, the celebration begins anew. Bird grabs Taurasi around the neck for a second time and shakes her like a rag doll. Jones then rushes in to embrace the two guards in both arms. Near the sideline, a tearful Ralph is embraced by Williams. They hold the hug for several long seconds, while the stage is set literally at midcourt for the tournament awards ceremony.

Although she has just won the tournament tile with her coast-to-coast shot, Bird is not even named to the All-Tournament team. Riley, Siemon, and Ratay are picked from Notre Dame. For UConn, it's Jones, Ralph, and the tournament MVP, Diana Taurasi.

Once the awards are handed out, and Ralph poses with the other four seniors while holding the championship trophy aloft, the teams finally retreat to their locker rooms. Ironically, it is the UConn locker room that is subdued, while the Irish are upbeat.

"That was actually the first and only time in my coaching career that I went into a locker room after a loss and said, 'That was a great game,'" McGraw said. "I remember thinking, Why am I not devastated? I remember people saying, 'It's okay if you lose a game. It gets you ready for the tournament. Now maybe you'll be more hungry.' All these things run through your head afterwards. But in the moment, it's the disappointment of losing a game that way.

"But at the same time, what a game. It was a fun game to watch, a fun game to play. Yeah, we probably made some mistakes and could have changed things. But I remember the locker room—and I'm sure the team was shocked, because I had never had done that—I just said, 'It was a great game.'

"There was nothing more we could do. We played hard, we played well. They played well. It was great to be a part of that. I said, 'Hey, we're pretty good. We're going to be good in the NCAA Tournament. Here are two teams that are one and two in the country. That's what you expected.' I thought going in, it was going to be a huge test for us. We battled them at every turn. I was proud of the team. You want to win, but we did everything that we could do."

Still, the players are downbeat. An opportunity to win the program's first-ever conference tournament title has barely eluded them. Four times they have come this far. Four times Connecticut has blocked their path.

"We had a lot of opportunities," Ivey said. "We missed free throws, [we shot] air balls, we gave them a lot of second-chance points, the offensive rebound that gave them the three. Their pressure got us out of what we wanted to do. Their defense really frustrated us. We learned a lot from that game, but it hurt. We'd never won the tournament. We've wanted to win the conference. That's what I wanted to do."

Over on the UConn side, the emotions generated by Bird's remarkable shot dissolve as the team confronts a new reality. For the second time in five weeks, a senior leader has succumbed to a season-ending injury. This time, their heart and soul has been taken from them.

"By the time we got to the locker room, we were done," Auriemma said. "It was gone. I don't think anybody had any incentive to jump up and down and spray champagne, like you see in a pro locker room after a big win. I think it was more like, How much does that suck about Shea? What an amazing game, but how much does that suck about Shea? So you could never really allow yourself to fully enjoy it, because there was a big chunk of your team in the trainers' room."

Dr. Joyce emerges from the trainers' room and gives

the media the anticipated but nonetheless grim diagnosis.

"It was clear the ligaments in the knee are loose, in particular, the anterior cruciate ligament," Joyce said. "Of course, we need to confirm that with an MRI, which we will be doing in the very near future. The very strong clinical impression at this point in time was that she tore the anterior cruciate ligament in her left knee. And that would mean, of course, that the season's over for her."

Eventually, the principals arrive for their postgame press conference. Notre Dame goes first. McGraw laments not being able to communicate to her players the opportunity they had to disrupt the final sequence—the Irish had a free foul at their disposal—and credits the raucous crowd for preventing her from getting her message through to her team on court.

"I thought for the first thirty-nine minutes and fifty-nine seconds it was an excellent basketball game," McGraw says. "I thought Ruth blocked it. I thought she got a piece of the ball and it was going to be an air ball. Sue Bird should have been the MVP for the shots she hit.

"I'm extremely hopeful there will be a trilogy in this series."

Next up are Bird and Auriemma. Bird is normally the cool and collected one on the team, the Joe Montana to Ralph's Brett Favre. But now, having seen Ralph's career end right before her eyes, Bird cannot contain her emotions.

"This is tough to talk about," Bird says. "But I think

we all really did come together tonight. Marci Czel [at halftime] pulled us all in, it's all about right here."

At the word "here," Bird taps herself on the chest and begins to cry.

"It's all about our heart. We've got to win this for Shea. Not just for Shea, but ourselves. I thought about how she has given so much to me, so much to this program. I just want to give something back to her."

The night before, Auriemma was playful when he took the podium, having watched C. Vivian Stringer's assault on the media from the side of the room. Now, he sits at the table and is barely audible, the shock of Ralph's injury still acute.

"Some people have to constantly prove their greatness, and this team, for whatever reason, has had to continually prove that they have great character," Auriemma says. "How many of these shots are they supposed to take? How many of these hits is one group of kids supposed to endure?

"It's not easy being in our situation. It's not easy being us. It's not. We played this game today without Shea and Svetlana, and everybody would still have expected us to win. That's just the way it is. The weight sometimes becomes a little too heavy. When you have to carry it for six months, it becomes a burden. You have to learn how to carry it and enjoy carrying it, but I don't know how many people enjoy carrying it every single day. What's fun about now is you don't have to carry it that much longer. Just about six games."

Table 3. Box Score, Final, Big East Women's Tournament Final, 2001

Official Basketball Box Score–GAME TOTALS–FINAL STATISTICS
CONNECTICUT vs NOTRE DAME
3/6/01 7:30 p.m. at Harry A. Gampel Pavilion, Storrs, CT

VISITORS: CONNECTICUT 28-2, 15-1

## Player Name	TOT-FG FG-FGA	3-PT FG-FGA	FT-FTA	REBOUNDS OF	DE	TOT	PF	TP	A	TO	BLK	S	MIN
15 Jones, Asjha....... f	6-15	0-0	1-2	3	3	6	3	13	0	0	0	0	22
32 Cash, Swin.......... f	3-14	0-0	1-1	1	5	6	1	7	1	2	1	0	27
03 Taurasi, Diana...... g	5-14	4-12	0-0	0	2	2	5	14	3	1	0	0	29
10 Bird, Sue.......... g	6-12	3-5	0-0	2	2	4	1	15	3	5	0	2	35
33 Ralph, Shea........ g	4-5	1-1	2-2	1	1	2	1	11	6	0	0	3	14
05 Conlon, Maria.......	0-2	0-2	0-0	0	0	0	0	0	1	0	0	0	1
11 Schumacher, Kelly...	4-7	0-0	2-2	4	2	6	2	10	0	1	0	1	18
23 Johnson, Kennitra...	1-6	1-5	0-0	3	0	3	4	3	5	0	0	1	34
34 Williams, Tamika....	2-4	0-0	1-5	1	3	4	2	5	2	1	0	0	20
TEAM...................				4	2	6							
Totals................	31-79	9-25	7-12	19	20	39	19	78	21	10	1	7	200

TOTAL FG%	1st Half: 21-40	52.5%	2nd Half: 10-39	25.6%	Game: 39.2%	DEADB
3-Pt. FG%	1st Half: 6-12	50.0%	2nd Half: 3-13	23.1%	Game: 36.0%	REBS
F Throw %	1st Half: 4-8	50.0%	2nd Half: 3-4	75.0%	Game: 58.3%	2

HOME TEAM: NOTRE DAME 28-2, 15-1

## Player Name	TOT-FG FG-FGA	3-PT FG-FGA	FT-FTA	REBOUNDS OF	DE	TOT	PF	TP	A	TO	BLK	S	MIN
03 Haney, Ericka....... f	2-5	0-0	0-2	1	7	8	1	4	2	0	1	0	26
50 Siemon, Kelley...... f	7-13	0-0	2-4	1	7	8	1	16	3	3	0	2	38
00 Riley, Ruth......... c	8-13	0-0	7-10	3	6	9	4	23	2	5	3	0	33
22 Ratay, Alicia....... g	5-8	3-3	1-2	0	2	2	3	14	3	2	0	1	30
33 Ivey, Niele........ g	3-10	0-2	5-6	1	4	5	1	11	9	4	0	0	40
04 Severe, Le'Tania....	0-0	0-0	0-0	0	1	1	0	0	0	1	0	0	2
05 Joyce, Jeneka.......	3-6	2-5	0-0	1	2	3	1	8	0	1	0	0	24
31 Barksdale, Amanda...	0-0	0-0	0-0	0	0	0	0	0	0	1	0	0	7
TEAM...................				3	3	6							
Totals................	28-55	5-10	15-24	10	32	42	11	76	19	17	4	3	200

TOTAL FG%	1st Half: 17-28	60.7%	2nd Half: 11-27	40.7%	Game: 50.9%	DEADB
3-Pt. FG%	1st Half: 4-7	57.1%	2nd Half: 1-3	33.3%	Game: 50.0%	REBS
F Throw %	1st Half: 8-13	61.5%	2nd Half: 7-11	63.6%	Game: 62.5%	6

Officials: Dennis DeMayo, Lisa Mattingly, Angie Lewis
Technical fouls: CONNECTICUT—None. NOTRE DAME—None.
Attendance: 10027

Score by Periods	1st	2nd	Total
CONNECTICUT...................	52	26	78
NOTRE DAME...................	46	30	76

Points in the paint—UCONN 42, ND 42.　　Points off turnovers—UCONN 20, ND 9.
2nd chance points—UCONN 21, ND 13.　　Fast break points—UCONN 11, ND 7.
Bench points—UCONN 18, ND 8.　　Score tied—4 times. Lead changes—6 times.

4

Overtime

One more time, UConn entered the NCAA Tournament at an extreme disadvantage. In 1997 they had lost Shea Ralph for the first time in the opening round of the tournament. In 1998 Nykesha Sales injured herself in a game against Notre Dame late in the regular season and was lost.

Although UConn's roster, even when depleted, still featured healthy players most programs would kill for, the Huskies could not overcome these losses, bowing out in the regional final each season.

In 2001 the Huskies were dealt a double-barreled blow. For a month, they had been figuring out how to play without the sleek scorer Svetlana Abrosimova. Ralph, in particular, had picked up the fallen mantle and helped guide the Huskies to the Big East Tournament final.

Now, for the second time in five years, Ralph found

herself unable to play. The Huskies would have to redis-
cover their identity for a second time, with less than two
weeks before the start of NCAA Tournament play.

"It was a unique situation trying to balance all that,"
Bird said. "To lose Svet, you're trying to figure it out, and
you have to do [everything] all over again. And then you
lose another player, and you have to figure it out all over
again. It was draining at times that season."

Turning the negative into a positive was Auriemma's
challenge during the lengthy break between the end of
the Big East Tournament and the start of the NCAA Tournament. Stripped of their senior leadership, the remaining UConn players had to be convinced that they could
overcome what to virtually any other team would be the
fatal subtraction of two All-Americans.

"The big thing that we have to do over the next ten
days is make them understand that nobody expected
us to be as good as we were after we lost Svet, and we
were," Auriemma told the media on Selection Sunday.
"And now the expectation level is going to be that they
are certainly going to have to take a step back now that
we don't have Shea. Again, here is another opportunity
to accomplish something that is going to be even more
meaningful than if none of this stuff happened throughout the season."

The players had already been steeling themselves for
the challenge, but the junior class of Bird, Cash, Jones,
and Williams now had to assume roles they hadn't expected to fill until their senior season in 2002.

"Swin Cash said something after the game like, 'This is just like a preview for next year,'" Bird said. "As sad as it is, it's true. I want to do this for [Ralph and Abrosimova]. They deserve to go out with a national championship. I think we all will step up."

The "next year" for the Class of 2002 would be the greatest by a starting lineup in the history of the women's game. With Diana Taurasi playing the role of Fifth Beatle, the senior quartet of Bird, Cash, Jones, and Williams led the Huskies to their second undefeated season in UConn history, matching the 1998 Lady Vols as the only teams to go 39-0 (the 2009 and 2010 Huskies would be the third and fourth, and first back-to-back).

So dominant were the four seniors that they were all selected within the top six picks of the 2002 WNBA draft, an accomplishment that will probably never be duplicated, by women, men, or extraterrestrials.

But when they were still juniors, the foursome—particularly the three frontcourt players—were not quite ready for prime time. Still in the role of understudies to Abrosimova and Ralph, the junior forwards struggled to find consistency in their games. Often, one or two of the trio would play well, but rarely did all three click at the same time.

"This team was an uneasy fit for a little while, because they were trying to grow into larger roles, but at the same time you still had Svet and Shea, so it was hard for them to figure out who was supposed to do what," Eagan said.

"The only one who didn't have those issues was Sue, because she had the ball and was better than the person that was guarding her."

Cash, Jones, and Williams—along with Bird and Keirsten Walters—made up the best freshman class Auriemma had ever assembled, signing with UConn in the fall of 1997. Williams, from Dayton, Ohio, was the national high school player of the year. Cash, from McKeesport, Pennsylvania, just outside Pittsburgh, was ranked third. Jones, from Piscataway, New Jersey, was ranked sixth, but many felt she was the best of the bunch.

All three were 6-foot-2, all were versatile. And all three were African American. The last, by itself, made the class unique in UConn history. Never before had Auriemma brought so many high-profile African American players to his team at the same time, something totally new to the overwhelmingly white UConn fan base.

But the trio broke down any racial barriers they encountered as easily as they did defenses. By the end of their sophomore season in 2000, Cash was a starter and Jones and Williams were the top post players off the bench. Cash made third team All-Big East, Williams was the Big East Tournament MVP, and Jones was named to the Final Four All-Tournament team.

Not until the on-campus championship rally after the victory over Tennessee would the issue of the players' race finally bubble to the surface. The emcee of the event, Scott Gray, who handled radio play-by-play for WTIC-AM, the largest station in Connecticut, introduced the three forwards together, as so often happened because of their identical position, height, and class.

But he did so by referring to the players as "the Gold Dust Triplets," making a reference to Red Sox rookie outfielders Jim Rice and Fred Lynn, who were affectionately dubbed "Gold Dust Twins" in 1975. What Scott, and the vast majority of his listeners, didn't know was that the term "Gold Dust Twins" actually had its origins in an early twentieth-century ad campaign that featured racially insensitive caricatures of two black children.

When one elderly listener in Hartford made that connection, a call was placed to UConn's Bias Response Committee, and the unintentional slight became a brief media firestorm, culminating with Gray privately apologizing to the three juniors and Auriemma.

The incident was quickly forgotten, and focus on the three returned strictly, and appropriately, to their basketball. Although the inconsistency in their individual levels of play had continued throughout their junior season, there were signs that they could carry the load with two key players missing.

In the Big East Tournament semifinal against Rutgers, with Abrosimova and Bird out of the lineup, Cash, Jones, and Williams combined for 40 points and 15 rebounds in a 94–66 rout. For the tournament, Cash averaged 13.7 points, Jones 10.3, and Williams 8.3.

"No more nights off," Cash declared on the eve of the NCAA Tournament. "Our junior class has to grow up fast. This is what we came here for and we have to prove to everybody why we came here and get this team to where it is meant to be. We came here for a purpose and now we have to be ready for the challenge. We're down two people and we know we have to stay focused and ready to go. Everybody's looking forward to starting."

The difference from one year to the next in Storrs and South Bend could not have been more different. In 2000, while the supremely confident Huskies prepared for a six-game championship run, the Irish were reeling, and on the verge of a Sweet Sixteen collapse.

In 2001, even with the sting of their loss to the Huskies in the Big East final still fresh, the Irish entered the NCAA Tournament with confidence, while UConn continued the search for its identity,

"We were in great shape," McGraw said. "We didn't have to go back to the drawing board and do a lot of work for the NCAA Tournament. I liked where we were. I worried if that was the right approach to take, but that's how I felt."

If anything, the last-second loss to UConn at Gampel Pavilion actually reinforced Notre Dame's belief that they were ready to challenge for the national championship. A few minor adjustments here and there, a few more possessions resulting in baskets instead of turnovers, and Sue Bird's basket at the buzzer would have been meaningless.

"Just being down the entire game and not playing well,

being in a hostile situation, we took a lot away from it," Ivey said. "We knew we were beatable, because we had lost to Rutgers, but time is getting short now and we don't want to come out flat and not be sharp and be done in the Tournament. No one remembers what we did in October and November. They're going to remember us in March. That's the most important thing."

Like the Huskies, Notre Dame opened the 2001 NCAA Tournament with a pair of home games, the last games Riley, Ivey, and Siemon would ever play at the Joyce Center, though not even close to being the last two games of their college careers.

Installed as the No. 1 seed in the Midwest Region, Notre Dame faced No. 16 Alcorn State, a 21-10 team from the Southwest Athletic Conference, in the first round. The game, as expected, was no contest, and Notre Dame advanced with a 98–49 victory.

The second-round game against Michigan was another cakewalk. In their final home game, Riley scored 21, Siemon 16, and Ivey had 8 points and 8 assists.

"They've done so much for this program and so much for me," McGraw said afterward. "They have set all kinds of records this year. For the four years they've been here, they have all been such a joy to be around."

The victory sent the Irish to Denver for the Midwest regional, where they faced Utah in the Sweet Sixteen game. At this point a year ago, everything had come crashing down for Notre Dame against Texas Tech, but in 2001, just hours before their contest against the Utes,

the players received news that would make all the difference for them this time around.

In Birmingham, Alabama, Tennessee, the No. 1 seed
in the Mideast Regional, had been taken out by No. 4
Xavier, easily the biggest upset of the tournament so far.
Not long after, No. 1 Duke was chopped down by prolific
scorer Jackie Stiles and Southwest Missouri State.

If Notre Dame needed a reality check in the high al-
titude of the Pepsi Center, this was it.

"Someone from the NCAA came in and told us, 'Xavier
just knocked off Tennessee,'" McGraw said. "And Kelley
Siemon said, 'That's not happening to us.'"

It didn't happen, but the team still faced a scare. With
12:04 remaining, the fifth-seeded Utes trailed just 40–
38. But led by Riley, who scored a game-high 24 points,
the Irish responded with a 23–8 run to seize control in
a 69–54 victory.

That set up a somewhat-uncomfortable regional final
for McGraw. On the other side was Vanderbilt, coached
by McGraw's mentor from her Philadelphia days—the
man who had called Notre Dame to recommend her for
her present job—Jim Foster.

"After the game you're just not very happy," McGraw
said before the game. "You're not happy if you lose, and
if you beat somebody you like, you're not very happy."

But for one night, anyway, McGraw was very happy.
The game was billed as a showdown between Riley and
Vanderbilt's All-American center Chantelle Anderson,
but in the second half, after the teams had played to a

40–40 tie twenty minutes in, it was all Riley. With Notre Dame clinging to a 50–47 lead with just over twelve minutes left, the national player of the year scored 18 of Notre Dame's final 22 points—part of a season-high 32 overall—and Notre Dame advanced to its second Final Four in five seasons with a 72–64 victory.

"We're ready to move on," McGraw said. "The first thing our players said when we got back to the locker room was 'Two more games.' I think they're happy, but not as happy as me. We're ready to get down to business."

Before UConn could even take the court at Gampel Pavilion for the first-round game against Long Island University, the team had to deal with yet another obstacle— at least one they perceived as such.

The announcement of the NCAA Tournament pairings on March 11 had left the Huskies equal parts annoyed and confused. Although the team entered the Big East Tournament final as the No. 2 team in the nation and had beat No. 1 Notre Dame to capture the tournament title, the Selection Committee demoted the Huskies to a seeding of third overall, behind Notre Dame and No. 1 overall Tennessee, which lost early in the SEC Tournament.

Thus, although UConn was the top seed in the East, they would have to face Notre Dame as early as the Final Four semifinals, then potentially face Tennessee in a title-game rematch.

"I said last year I thought the committee did a better job than anytime I could remember," Auriemma told the media. "I said it was the best bracket I'd ever seen. Well, this year it's one of the worst."

What angered Auriemma most was the tortured—and seemingly duplicitous—logic that Selection Committee chairwoman Maryalyce Jeremiah offered to explain the rankings.

Most assumed that UConn had been penalized because of Shea Ralph's injury. Both Notre Dame and UConn had been victimized by this in the past: UConn was dropped to No. 2 in 1998 after the injury to Nykesha Sales, and Notre Dame was bumped all the way down to No. 5 in 1999 after Ivey went down.

But in a conference call with reporters after the seeds were announced, Jeremiah insisted that Ralph's injury had played no role in the decision-making process.

UConn was not the overall No. 1, Jeremiah said, because they had not won the Big East regular-season championship. According to her, Notre Dame was ahead of the Huskies because they had won the regular-season championship.

When a *Hartford Courant* reporter informed Jeremiah that, in fact, UConn and Notre Dame were co-regular-season champions (although Notre Dame won the lone regular-season matchup), she was unable to respond.

"We're happy to be in," Auriemma stated, his voice lathered in Philly sarcasm. "There are a lot of teams who didn't even get in. I'm not going to complain. Forget it. I'm going to take my team and we are going to go in and we're going to play. That's it. I'm not going to say anything else. You all can write what you think."

In the first two rounds at Gampel, the seeding controversy had little effect. UConn overwhelmed LIU 101–29 in the opening game, then buried Colorado State in the second round with a 45–18 second half for an 89–44 victory.

Cash posted double-doubles in each of the two games; her reward would be a regional homecoming. The Huskies were headed next to her home city of Pittsburgh to face North Carolina State in the Sweet Sixteen.

Cash continued her strong play with another double-double in the regional semifinal at Mellon Arena, but two games away from the Final Four, the big story was Diana Taurasi. Finally given the keys to the car, the freshman phenom delivered against the Wolfpack, hitting six three-pointers for a total of twenty-four points, matching her season high.

"By [the Big East final], they were starting to figure it out," Eagan said. "This is how we're going to play. This is where everybody fits and this is how we're going to do it. And then Shea goes down and they have to figure it out all over again. Their answer was, We're going to hold the ball and shoot it.

"They committed a fair amount of turnovers, because they played so fast and so creatively. And once Shea went down, they didn't do that. They brought the ball up court, and Diana shot it, and somebody got a rebound, and that's how they won."

The junior forwards continued their combined solid performances in the regional final against Louisiana Tech, but it was Taurasi again who made the headlines with 17 points, 10 rebounds, and 4 assists in a 67–48 victory, setting up a round 3 meeting with Notre Dame in St. Louis.

"We don't believe we should lose," Taurasi said. "I know I'm not satisfied to get to the Final Four."

St. Louis, Missouri, March 30, 2001

Niele Ivey stepped off the team plane at Lambert Airport to a hero's welcome, having led Cor Jesu Academy in St. Louis to its first Missouri state title in 1995.

The day after Notre Dame earned a spot in the Final Four at the Savvis Center, Cor Jesu retired Ivey's jersey number (33). Now, the faculty and students of Cor Jesu had gathered at the terminal to support Ivey's quest to win a national title in her home city.

UConn–Notre Dame III was, in most observers' minds, the de facto national championship game. While the opening act, Purdue–Southwest Missouri State, featured a pair of singular stars—Katie Douglas for Purdue and the NCAA's all-time leading scorer Jackie Stiles of SMS—the completion of the epic UConn–Notre Dame trilogy drew the majority of attention from the gathered national media.

As Muhammad Ali biographer and Pulitzer Prize winner David Remnick once said of Ali–Frazier III—the "Thrilla in Manila"—this third meeting between UConn and Notre Dame wasn't just a fight for a spot in the final, it was a fight between two heavyweights to establish which of them was the best.

"I think people are looking at the seeds and saying, 'Here are the two number one seeds playing each other in the semifinal; would it not be great if that was the Final?'" McGraw said at the press conference the day before the semifinals. "Our game, because we have played them before, I think everybody knows that level of play in that game, and they are thinking they would like to see that sort of game in a final. That's not to say [a great game] won't happen regardless of who wins the other [semifinal]. But I think people are just going off that game in the Big East Tournament, and their expectations are high for a great game."

Among the storylines the media followed that weekend was a second look at Auriemma's (in)famous guarantee. Had his April boast become a March curse? Auriemma responded in characteristic fashion.

"All bets are off," he quipped. "We have Coach of the Year [at Notre Dame], Defensive Player of the Year, Student of the Year, Best Shooter of the Century, Most Improved Player, so all bets are off. We just want to not get blown out."

Another hot topic was the Philly friendship between Auriemma and McGraw, both disciples of Jim Foster. In 1980 McGraw had succeeded Auriemma as an assistant under Foster at St. Joseph's. Early in their head coaching tenures at Notre Dame and UConn, McGraw looked to join forces. In 1987 she gauged his interest in taking the assistant job at Notre Dame vacated by Bill Fennelly, her zone-master, who had left to coach Iowa State.

"What? Are you nuts?" Auriemma told McGraw. "I know this [UConn head coaching position] ain't the greatest job in the world, but it ain't that bad."

Auriemma regaled the media with Muffet tales, claiming that the newfound rivalry between them had actually raged for years off the court.

"Oh, yeah," Auriemma insisted. "You should see us play golf. She gets so mad if she can't hit the ball by me. And then she goes, 'Man, I killed it. I'm twenty yards past you.' I go, 'Muff, the tee you're playing from is sixty yards in front of mine.' She doesn't care. If she makes a double-bogey and you make eight, she's thrilled. At least she beat you.

"I do think she has softened a little over the years. In the early days, I think she took basketball so seriously and put so much of herself into it, it was hard for her to enjoy it. She's got one of the best jobs in America. The fact you couldn't beat UConn isn't the end of the world. I think that [January 15] win took the piano off her back and made her enjoy the whole process. That's what you got to do. But I'm telling you, next time she plays from the blue tees, it's like, 'Muffet, are you a woman or are you a golfer?'"

To beat Notre Dame for the second time in a month,

UConn would need another big performance from their star freshman, who, seemingly impervious to pressure, had already taken regional MVP honors with her 20.5 two-game scoring average.

"This is cool. It's like the circus," Taurasi said after UConn's practice, which was open to the public. "I've never really been exposed to all of this. I came last year, but I was looking at it from the outside point of view. It's definitely better to be here.

"It's just basketball. I've been playing it all my life. Why start getting nervous now?"

In the first semifinal, Purdue's defense shut down Stiles, and the Boilermakers advanced to the championship game with an 81–64 victory. Now came the main event.

UConn won the opening tap and Taurasi launched the first shot of the evening, taking a wide-open three at the top of the key from just inside NBA range. Such shots were money in Pittsburgh, but this one clanged off the front of the rim.

Then it was Bird's turn. Five months earlier, she'd scored the final five points to beat Notre Dame. Now, she banged home the first three of the semifinal, followed by a three-point play by Schumacher, who had earned the start with Ralph on the sidelines.

In the inverse of the start of the Big East final, UConn established a 6–0 lead, and the score was 28–22 with 6:35 left in the half when Riley picked up her second foul. Ivey already had two fouls, and she would pick up her third with 2:32 left. UConn was not immune to foul trouble, either. Both Taurasi and Kennitra Johnson picked up three in the half, as the officials combined to call twenty-two first-half fouls. Taurasi's problems weren't limited to foul trouble. At halftime, she was 0-for-7 from the field, having missed five three-point attempts.

The loss of manpower that resulted from the foul trouble affected the Irish more adversely. With Riley out of the game, the Huskies went on a 19–9 run to take their largest lead of the game at 47–31 with 2:02 remaining. The hero of the run was, of all people, Maria Conlon, the freshman who had made such an impression in the Big East final when she'd fearlessly hoisted a pair of threes that missed.

Tonight, Conlon buried her first three-point attempt to put UConn up 42–31. Moments later, after a Bird steal, Conlon snuck behind the Notre Dame defense, took a perfect lead pass from Bird, and scored a fast-break layup while drawing a foul, the three-point play giving Conlon six points and making the lead sixteen.

UConn had a chance to extend the lead to seventeen points in the final moments of the half. With her team leading 49–34, Cash was fouled with twenty-four seconds left. She missed both free throws, however, and at the other end of the floor, Ratay, free at the top of the key with the clock under ten seconds, knocked down a three-pointer to cut the deficit to twelve at the half.

This shot did not generate the same buzzer-beating histrionics that Bird's halftime bomb had at Gampel, but its effect on the game would be even more profound.

"I was really pissed that Ratay made that three at the end of the half," Auriemma said. "If she doesn't make the three, they don't have any momentum. They've got nothing. We've got it all going our way. And we miss the two free throws and they make the three and now it's twelve instead of seventeen and I went in at halftime and I was pissed, and I let them know I was pissed. And I think it probably wasn't the right approach to take with them at that time."

McGraw wasn't any less angry with her team. The Ratay basket was but a flicker of hope, something for McGraw to use as she lit up her team in the locker room.

"I remember when that shot went in, it was like, 'Thank God something went right,'" McGraw said. "There was no momentum jolt. We were in a downward spiral. Niele and Ruth were out for quite a bit.

"My thoughts at halftime were, We have the wrong people shooting the ball. We're not doing the things that got us to this point. Everyone is jumping out of their role and trying to win the game for us and we're five separate people trying to play a game.

"But I think the work was done before I got in there. They talked about it a little bit. Alicia, who didn't say three words the entire year, said something, and then the guys took over. They were like, 'We're not ending our season today.' I could have come in and said, 'Hey, let's go,' and it would have been the same result. They were ready. And then the tide began to turn."

For a moment after the intermission, it appeared that Ratay's shot would have little effect on the score. Having ended both halves of the Big East final with clutch shots, Bird opened both halves of the national semifinal with three-pointers, the latter of which, seven seconds into the second half, restored UConn's fifteen-point advantage.

But Ratay countered with another three of her own two minutes in, and the lead was down to 54–44. At the other end, Taurasi continued to try and shoot her way out of it, but like John Starks in Game 7 of the 1994 NBA Finals, she would find that her shots continued to bounce out. Two missed three-pointers in the first 2:10 of the half made her 0-for-7 from three, 0-for-9 overall.

Then, the rest of the Huskies went cold too. Cash made a layup with 17:47 left to put UConn back up by twelve, but after that, the Huskies managed just one field goal over the next 6:30, allowing Notre Dame to roar all the way back and take its first lead in nearly sixty-five minutes of game action. Ratay, of course, buried the three-pointer that put the Irish up 61–59, with 12:40 left to play.

"Asjha, Tamika, Swin, and Sue didn't play particularly well and Dee tried to do it all herself," Auriemma said. "So there just wasn't enough. It finally came down to those guys, and it seemed like the more we missed, the more they felt like, 'Uh-oh, it's on us now,' and I don't know if they were ready for that.

"I think if the game was tied at halftime, we had a better chance to win. I think getting up and then the lead is slowly dwindling, and it's like [choking sound], and the screw is slowly turning and you could see it happening right in front of your eyes."

During this stretch, UConn managed only 1-for-11 from the field and turned the ball over five times. By the time Taurasi gathered a rebound and started the Huskies up the court with 11:37 remaining, she was 0-for-11 from the field, 0-for-9 from three. Such was the effect of the 2-3 zone at its absolute nastiest.

"We couldn't score inside as well, we're limited to jump shots, and they're not going in," Auriemma said. "I talked to [Notre Dame assistant] Kevin McGuff about this one time. I said 'Kevin, we're up fifteen against you guys. Did it ever dawn on you to get out of that dumb zone?' He goes, 'We sat on the bench and said, 'One more possession, if they make one more shot, we're out of it.' And you didn't. So we stayed in it.'

"So that's the play you make as a coach. We're staying in this. How long? Until we have no choice. And to their credit, they were committed to it. I say this about the Syracuse men all the time: if you don't beat them in the first or second round, you're in trouble. Because as the tournament wears on, and the pressure to keep making shots grows, you get to the Final Four and you have

to keep making jump shots. Every shot that doesn't go
in is like, 'Doh!' And that's what got to Dee."

McGraw attributed Taurasi's struggles to a higher
power.

"I always thought she had Catholic guilt," McGraw
said. "She never seemed to play well against us."

Taurasi finally managed to score with 11:12 left, con-
verting a conventional three-point play to regain the lead
for UConn at 63–61. Williams scored forty seconds later
to establish a 65–63 advantage.

Then Ratay finished the job she'd started. Her jumper
with 10:10 left created the game's final tie, and then,
after Ivey made two free throws, Ratay buried her third
three-pointer of the half (her fourth since the final seconds of the first half). Having established a lead of 70–
65, Notre Dame went on a 14–0 run, and the rout was
on. After extending the lead to 77–65 with 5:47 left,
Notre Dame would maintain a double-digit advantage
for the rest of the way.

But the 5:47 mark did bring a shock to Notre Dame's
system. On the play that produced the final points of
the run, Ivey and Taurasi both dove for a loose ball. Having gotten more body than ball, Taurasi picked up her
fourth foul. Once back on her feet, she walked away, obviously disgusted at the latest development in her national [semifinal] nightmare.

Ivey did not get up. Although no one saw exactly
what happened, an injury has clearly occurred, and it

had caused her to grab at her left leg. First Shea, now Niele?

"My heart was in my throat. I had knots in my stomach," McGraw said. "I was sort of paralyzed on the sideline, wanting to run out to comfort her, but not wanting to, hoping she would get up and play."

To the great relief of the coach and the vast Niele Ivey fan club in Section 105, it was not the knee. Ivey had sprained her left ankle. Although she was not exactly feeling wonderful, this was hardly the disaster everyone, including Ivey herself, had feared.

"I remember when I first did it, I thought it was my knee," Ivey said. "Then I knew it was my ankle, but I was crying. I was frustrated. I thought, This better not be the end. This can't happen."

Ericka Haney came in to take the free throws for Ivey, but Ivey soon returned to the game, making two free throws late to help seal the 90–75 victory.

Auriemma's Guarantee was officially dead.

"I don't think we can put into words, you know, how you feel when something that you really, really want, and come so close to getting, and you don't get it," he said after the game. "I think anybody who has ever been in that situation probably understands, but, you know, I don't think we can play any better than we played in the first half. I don't think I've ever seen our team be as focused and ready to play as we were in that whole first half.

"And then it all kind of fell apart for us in the second half. I thought Notre Dame just made so many big shots, and made a couple big stops. And when we could not get anything to drop, I think it just took the wind right out of us, and we never really recovered. It's a shame, because, you know, you hope it doesn't happen, but it happened. To Notre Dame's credit, they made every big shot they had to make, and they deserve to win, they are a great team. The best team we've played all year; no question about it."

In the final moments of the game, after Taurasi had fouled out of a game for the final time that season, having finished 1-for-15 from the field, 0-for-11 on threes, Auriemma bent down in front of her on the bench. The giggly kid with no conscience and an ego so big it seemed to need its own zip code was awash in tears, barely consolable because she couldn't help her teammates win.

Auriemma tried anyway. "It's not your fault," he told her. "We wouldn't have gotten this far without you."

At the other end, the celebration got underway.

"We knew UConn was going to make runs at us and make incredible plays, but we are the type of team that is going to accept those and come back with some even better plays," Ivey said after the game. "We just decided to come together and do it—we had twenty more minutes regardless of what the score was. I think our leadership and chemistry came together again. That's been helping us the whole year. We are not going to fight or give up. It's our only opportunity right now, so we are going to take advantage of every second out there."

St. Louis, April 1, 2001

Ruth Riley has always loved the movie *Hoosiers*. In the film, as Hickory High advances round-by-round toward its destiny, a different hero emerges in each game. It is little Ollie, who never intended to actually play—and wasn't expected to, either—who recovers from two embarrassing free-throw misses to make the game-winner in the sectional final. And in the state title game, it's the shooting star, Jimmy Chitwood, who dominates and makes the championship-winning shot.

The 2001 NCAA Tournament championship game would be an all-Hoosiers final between South Bend and West Lafayette, but the game would be hard-pressed to match the intensity of the UConn–Notre Dame clash.

"A lot of people said [the UConn semifinal] should have been the final, and it should have been, because we were spent, in every way," McGraw said. "We were tired. We were mentally drained. And then Niele sprained her ankle during the shootaround. What else is going to go wrong?"

The game reflected the ragged condition of the Irish. Nearly four minutes into the game, Purdue had amassed a lead of just 4–2, but then the Boilermakers went on a 15–5 run over the next five minutes, hitting five consecutive three-point plays—four from long distance (two by Katie Douglas)—to take a 19–7 lead.

Riley responded with nine points in an 11–2 run that cut the gap to 21–18. The differential would waver only slightly during the rest of the half, and at intermission, the score favored Purdue, 32–26.

Riley kept Notre Dame alive, scoring fourteen of her team's twenty-six points.

"You're excited, because it's the national championship game, and you hope your adrenaline will kick in, but that was the ugliest game I've ever seen," McGraw said. "It was horrible. I watched it once afterwards and was like, Oh my god, I hope nobody watched this. They must think women's basketball is awful. It was terrible. I think we were winning for 1 minute, 26 seconds. We were down the whole game. Then Alicia hits the three to tie it and we got back in the game."

Ratay's three-pointer tied the score at 62–62 with 4:09 left. Shereka Wright made one of two free throws for Purdue with 2:37 left, and then Ivey scored the final basket of her career, taking a feed from Ratay for a layup and a 64–63 lead.

With the clock under two minutes, Notre Dame retained possession. Hoping for an easy basket, they looked to get Riley, who had twenty-four points on 8-for-12 shooting—but just 8 of 12 from the free-throw line—an easy basket on a pick-and-roll with Siemon. The play began perfectly, with Siemon rushing to receive the ball at the free-throw line, while Riley made a perfect spin move to elude center Camille Cooper and get her right hand open to receive Siemon's pass on the way to an easy layup.

But Siemon, sensing a late weak-side double-team by guard Kelly Komara, double-clutched on the pass, then compounded the mistake by telegraphing her pass to Ivey on the wing, allowing Douglas to swoop in and steal it. Even worse for Siemon, Douglas absorbed her hit from behind and made the layup for a three-point play, putting Purdue ahead 66–64 with 1:22 remaining.

The game now belonged to Riley. She became Jimmy. She became Ollie. She became a champion in Indiana.

Notre Dame brought the ball up and called the same play that had earned Riley a basket and a pair of free throws in the final forty-nine seconds of the Big East Tournament final. The ball went to Ratay above the three-point line at the top of the key, but she was not open and lobbed the ball into Riley, who, having yet again sealed off Cooper on her way down the lane, was able to throw in a hook shot to tie the score at 66–66.

With thirty-three seconds left, Wright missed a layup and Riley cleared her thirteenth rebound. Taking a thirty-second time-out, McGraw called the same play that had failed to work moments earlier: Siemon flashing to the foul line, taking a pass from Ivey, and hitting the cutting Riley at the goal.

Ivey worked the clock down to ten seconds—seven on the shot clock—and passed to Siemon, who was forced to throw a very high lob into Riley, over the onrushing Hurns. Passing into a converging triple-team, in this case one formed by Cooper, Wright, and Douglas, is usually considered very dangerous, but Siemon's lob not only traveled like a rainbow but ended with a pot of gold.

Using all of her 6-foot-5 frame, Riley lunged for the

ball with her right hand after it passed over her head. Douglas, who had completed the triple-team with a perfectly-timed rush at Riley's blindside, appeared to be in position to make another steal, but Riley's awkward, twisting leap forced Douglas to duck underneath in a desperate attempt not to create contact.

That allowed Riley to tip the ball to herself unimpeded, square up, and shoot from five feet.

"Ruth has amazing hands and great timing, and there were three people in there, but that was the game plan to go right into Ruth," Siemon said after the game. "So regardless of the people around her, I was just going to throw that ball up. She made an amazing catch and it was . . . it was perfect."

The last line of defense, Wright fouled Riley in the act of shooting. One more time, Riley went to the line with a chance to win it herself.

"Ruth wanted another chance," McGraw said. "She wanted to be in that situation again. And it was so similar. It was like, 'Wow, we were just in that situation.' And I think that's why we won. I can't imagine the pressure, but Ruth wasn't feeling it. What a great mental game she had."

At Gampel, with 5.1 seconds left, Riley had missed her first free throw. But like Ollie in *Hoosiers*, Riley made the one that really counted. With 5.8 seconds on the clock, her first free throw deadened on the front rim—shades of Bird's teardrop—then fell through the net.

The second shot caught front iron as well, but then it

hit softly off the backboard and rolled in, giving Notre Dame a lead of 68–66. In the biggest game of her life, Riley amassed 28 points, 13 rebounds, and 7 blocked shots.

"As crazy as this might sound, I wasn't really nervous," Riley said after the game." I was in the same situation with Connecticut and did not pull through. I practiced since then, and today I was pretty confident in my shot, and I just got a lucky bounce and was able to pull through."

Decidedly unlike UConn's Auriemma in the Big East final, Purdue coach Kristy Curry called not only one, but two time-outs during Riley's visit to the free-throw line. The first, a thirty-second time-out, was called before the first shot. A full time-out preceded the second free throw.

This time, Notre Dame was ready when possession changed hands. Ever since Bird's coast-to-coast winner in the Big East game, Notre Dame had devoted time in every practice to preventing a repeat. The time-outs gave the Irish time to plan their approach.

"We felt like we won the game because of the Big East championship game," McGraw said. "It was almost the exact scenario: Ruth is on the line, there's 5.8 seconds left, and she's got two shots to win. This time she makes them both. And we had gone back, after Sue made the shot, and practiced it: Okay, we're on the line, five seconds to go, here's how we're going to pick them up."

But even the best-laid plans . . .

Taking the inbounds pass below her own foul line, Komara started up the court. Two dribbles later, with Ivey backing up to keep Komara in front of her, Komara noticed Cooper sprinting over midcourt totally unguarded, Riley having focused instead on the advance of Douglas, the most likely shooter.

Komara launched a pass to Cooper but in doing so matched Riley in the category of imperceptible errors. The pass to Cooper fell short, forcing the 6-foot-4 center to halt her stride and reach back for the ball as the clock ticked under three seconds.

Wanting to continue advancing with the ball, then suddenly seeing Douglas rushing toward her at the top of the key, Cooper took an obvious third step without having begun to dribble. But just as with Bird's midcourt rush—in fact, this is far more egregious—the referees did not call the travel.

Now, once again, Notre Dame watched as the best clutch shooter on the other team, in this case, Katie Douglas, headed for a shot at the basket as the clock dropped to two seconds. Even worse for Notre Dame, Riley was not in position even to alter the shot, much less block it. Douglas launched a shot from a foot inside the three-point line.

"Here we go again," Ivey said. "I was like, 'They can't get 2-for-2 on us.' It was the same thing again. They threw it long, I'm chasing, Kelley is trying to stop her, and she shot it in front of Ruth. They even had a blatant travel. And it did look good. Either luck was with us, or we're tied. I'm like, 'Lord, please, let her miss.' There were a bunch of prayers."

The ball hit the front rim, but lacking the trajectory of Bird's shot, it clanged hard off the iron and bounced harmlessly off the backboard.

The buzzer sounded. Notre Dame had won the national championship. Ivey led the charge to the Notre Dame bench, arms raised over her head.

"It was like that whole commercial thing," Ivey said. "How would I react? I just ran and jumped in Coach [Kevin] McGuff's arms. It was jubilation. It put my whole career in perspective, my time at Notre Dame. All the blood, sweat, and tears of what I went through. There were many times I doubted myself as a player. Doubted myself, as far as what I came here to do. I knew I helped build Notre Dame. We're a good program and I know that I had something to do with that.

"My goal was to go someplace and make an impact and leave my mark. I wanted to do it by going out on top. And to take it back home, where my support system was from, my family, Mr. Glasscock, you couldn't script it any better. It was amazing. I still think today, How was I able to do that?"

The team arrived back on campus in South Bend late that Sunday night, but the campus was still very much alive. The celebration certainly woke up the echoes.

"It was such a release," Riley said. "As a player, you're so focused on what you need to do to win and compete and you never let up until the buzzer sounds. For that fi-

nally to happen, you realize what's just happened and that
we won. It was a relief that she didn't make the shot and
unbelievable joy about what we'd just accomplished.

"And that was a four-year process. I felt so blessed. Not
many athletes have a chance to win a championship, but
to have that kind of senior year and to go out on top,
that was something really special, especially for that core
group. We had worked so hard to get to that, and now
we were leaving our legacy behind with a championship,
it was something really amazing to experience."

The team entered campus by bus, heading up Notre
Dame Avenue, flanked by a crowd of three thousand.

"It was surreal," McGraw said. "I still look back on it
and go, Wow, we really did it. I don't think I appreciated
it as much when it happened. You think, you get to go
through the whole summer without thinking about losing the last game.

"I think Niele, with the knee injury, I always think of
that. God had a plan. Every time I see Ruth, I see her as
a champion. I just feel like, Here's this girl from Macy,
Indiana, the whole season was like destiny. I always felt
like, Something's just working for us right now. Something would happen to the other team, but not our team.
And at some point you just believe it's going to happen.
And it happens, and you think, Wow."

ESPN thought "Wow" as well.

Notre Dame's victory in the national championship
was a triumph for the program, but it was their defeat in
the Big East Tournament final—and the dramatic fash-

ion in which they lost it—that had a bigger effect on the future of women's basketball as a whole.

As with so much of big-time college athletics, success and failure are often gauged not by wins and losses but by viewer shares and ratings. And Bird's buzzer-beater had been a bonanza in that sense.

The Big East final earned a .96 TV rating, making it the highest-rated women's game ever broadcast on ESPN2. The viewing audience of 730,914 made it the third-most watched non-NCAA Tournament women's game in ESPN's twenty-two-year history. It was the most for a women's game outside the UConn–Tennessee rivalry.

The March 11 "Instant Classic" rebroadcast was a symbolic gesture by ESPN to the NCAA that it was serious about showcasing women's basketball. Then ESPN proved it with their wallets, agreeing to an eleven-year, $200 million contract four months later.

By 2003, the Final Four had moved from the Friday–Sunday format to Sunday–Tuesday, in order to take the championship game out of the long shadow of the men's final.

"I think it gives us a home that has a true identity," Auriemma said of the new ESPN contract that July while in Washington DC preparing Taurasi and the rest of the U.S. Junior National Team for the World Championships. "Now it can become the home of women's basketball. This is going to be the next big step that the game needed to take. I think it will be a great boost to the growth of the game."

Epilogue

Muffet McGraw had finally beaten UConn on the basketball court in 2001, not once, but twice. And along with it, she had captured the first national championship in Notre Dame basketball history. Now, armed with the shiny trophy, McGraw could take the battle against UConn to the only area more significant than the court: recruiting.

McGraw had already scored a coup over UConn the previous year, when center Teresa Borton chose Norte Dame, becoming first in line to replace Ruth Riley, who had been drafted fifth overall by the Miami Sol in the WNBA draft.

With Niele Ivey also leaving, McGraw was in the market for a point guard. And in early September, that search sent her east, to the Boston area, to make a home visit with one of UConn's top targets, Nicole Wolff.

The daughter of Boston University men's basketball coach Dennis Wolff, Nicole had been a 2,000-point scorer for Milton Academy in Walpole, Massachusetts, and was ranked in the top ten of most national recruiting surveys.

As was so often the case for coaches during the September home-visit period, McGraw's trip to Boston would be brief. No sooner had she arrived for the weekend visit with the Wolff family than McGraw would be headed out to California on Tuesday morning, the 11th.

"I have to go to California and I call my travel agent and say, 'I have to get to LA,'" McGraw said. "He said, 'There are two flights: American and United. Which one do you want?' I think I said United."

The travel agent punched it up. McGraw was booked on the first available United flight out of Logan Airport, scheduled for takeoff at 8:00 a.m. Flight number 175.

But soon after McGraw's travel plans had been confirmed, her young assistant coach, Kevin McGuff, made a recruiting pitch of his own. McGuff had made his travel arrangements for the same Tuesday morning out of Providence, Rhode Island. No sense traveling separately, he argued. Come with me out of Providence.

"And I said, 'Well, then I can't go direct,'" McGraw said. "'I have to fly out of Boston.' And then he said, 'I'm not driving you to Boston to get on a plane. Fly out of Providence.'"

The two coaches went back and forth, debating the pros and cons. Finally, McGraw relented. Providence won.

"He was pretty stubborn," McGraw said. "Had it been another assistant, I would have gotten on the plane."

McGraw and McGuff were on their aircraft at Providence's T. F. Green Airport, waiting to take off, when suddenly the announcement came over the cabin PA system. Two planes had crashed into the World Trade Center in New York. No more flights were being allowed to leave.

Stunned by the news, McGraw and McGuff headed back into the airport terminal. By chance, they ran into Notre Dame men's coach Mike Brey, also making a recruiting trip. Together, they learned the identity of the two flights, both out of Boston, heading for Los Angeles: American flight number 11, and United flight number 175.

"I knew because of where it was going. I was pretty shook up," McGraw said. "I just didn't want to talk about it. It felt funny. The three of us drove home. And I was a little shaky. I was transfixed by it. I had to watch hours and hours of it, and then I put it behind me.

"I had a hole in one in there, too, that year. You know how people say good things come in threes. They say, you won the championship, you had a hole in one, and you didn't get on the plane. It was a good year for me."

St. Louis, April 7, 2009

Sports history is littered with tales of teams that needed to overcome a nemesis in order to finally secure a championship. The 1980s "Bad Boy" Pistons needed to get past the Celtics. The 2006 Colts needed to get past the Patriots. And the 2004 Red Sox needed to get past the Yankees to put an end to eighty-six years of frustration.

The latter two needed epic comebacks—one in a game, one in a series, before they could hoist the trophy. So, too, did Notre Dame require a historic turnaround to put the Huskies behind them and reach the NCAA title game against Purdue.

"They grew up a little bit and they all matured," UConn coach Geno Auriemma said. "What happened the year before showed them, Hey you're not there yet. I think that happened to us against North Carolina in 1994. We're up nine against North Carolina [in the regional final] and they have Marion Jones and Charlotte Smith and Sylvia Crawley and Tonya Sampson, I mean they're unbelievable. We've got two freshmen, and Kara [Wolters] and Carla [Berube] and Jen [Rizzotti] and Jamelle [Elliott] are sophomores, and Rebecca [Lobo] is a junior and we're like, To hell with Carolina, who do they think they are? We're up nine in the second half and they just took the game away from us.

"And I looked around and thought, You know, we're just not mature enough yet to handle this. And we came back the next year and went 35-0. So I think teams and players have to go through a certain stage where they look at themselves in the mirror and go, You know what? We just weren't mature enough to handle that. Not because we're not good enough physically, because I think we are. And then you come back the next year and put the physical and the emotional thing together. And I think that's where Notre Dame was in 2001. They had paid their dues, they had suffered appropriately, like you have to suffer, and then they got the rewards the following year."

The Huskies would go on to experience much the same thing following their loss to Notre Dame in the Final Four. Devastated by the fifteen-point loss after leading by seventeen in the first half, the four returning juniors—Sue Bird, Swin Cash, Tamika Williams, and Asjha Jones—resolved never to feel the sting of defeat again. And they didn't, joining forces with a maturing sophomore Diana Taurasi to go 39-0 in 2001–2, defeating Oklahoma in the title game in San Antonio.

All four seniors would go in the top six of the 2002 WNBA Draft, with Bird going number one overall to Seattle, cementing their place as the greatest starting five in the history of the sport. Taurasi stayed behind and led UConn to two more titles, in 2003 and 2004, making the Huskies only the second team—along with their old pals from Knoxville—to win three straight national championships.

Bird, Taurasi, Cash, and Riley would be reunited in 2004, as members of the U.S. women's Olympic team, taking the gold medal in Athens, Greece. Already, the alums of the 2001 Big East final were enjoying strong professional careers, often as teammates.

Ivey and Schumacher became the first to join forces, drafted by the Indiana Fever in 2001. Cash and Riley went from low-post rivals to teammates with the Detroit Shock, winning WNBA titles in 2003 and 2006 under head coach Bill Laimbeer. Riley would later be traded to San Antonio, where she lost to the Shock in the 2008 Finals.

Bird would win a championship in 2004 with the Seattle Storm, before winning gold that same summer. By decade's end, Taurasi sat atop the sport, winning titles with the Phoenix Mercury in 2007 and 2009, capturing the first league MVP award won by any former UConn player in 2009.

Notre Dame would bring in an All-American caliber player, Jacqueline Batteast, to replace Riley in 2002, but with Ivey and Kelley Siemon also gone, the Irish were never able to duplicate the success of 2001. Not until the end of the decade would Notre Dame challenge UConn for Big East supremacy, rising to No. 3 in the polls by the midpoint of the 2009–10 season.

The year before, with the Final Four returning to St. Louis, the Huskies had been the ones to go there in search of destiny. After three straight seasons of failing to reach the Final Four, UConn would go there for a ninth time under Auriemma, losing to Stanford in the semifinals.

But in 2009, in St. Louis, a player possessing even more talent than Taurasi, Maya Moore, led the Huskies to another 39-0 record. This time, against another conference rival, Louisville, there would be no collapse. With Shea Ralph back on the UConn sidelines as an assistant coach, the Huskies rolled to a 76–54 victory for UConn's—and Auriemma's—sixth national championship.

With the sour taste of St. Louis at last purged from his system, Auriemma gained an even deeper appreciation for what he witnessed the evening of March 6, 2001, when Bird won the Greatest Women's Game Ever Played.

"It's somewhat unusual, with the hype that goes into two great teams facing each other, it's rare where it lives up to hype of both teams playing great," Auriemma said. "You get that in the Super Bowl a lot. One team does play up to their ability and you say, Damn, that's why they're here, and the other team has its first clunker of the year, and that happens a lot.

"In this situation, both teams played about as well as they could play. Even now when I see the end of it, I see the raw emotion that we generally don't have. We're always like, 'Yeah, act like we've done it before, man. We kick everybody's ass. Why do we need to celebrate like that? Let's just acknowledge that and say, That's cool.'

"But that night, whoo, it was raw, man. It just exploded out of everybody, coaches, players, fans, everybody. It was like, I don't want to leave. I want to stay in this building and just keep this and drape this all over me. I don't want to leave, because if I leave, it means I'm walking away from it."